OBSCURE INVITATIONS

OBSCURE INVITATIONS

■ THE PERSISTENCE OF THE AUTHOR

IN TWENTIETH-CENTURY

AMERICAN LITERATURE ■

BENJAMIN WIDISS

STANFORD UNIVERSITY PRESS ■ STANFORD, CALIFORNIA

Stanford University Press
Stanford, California

©2011 by the Board of Trustees of the Leland Stanford Junior University. All rights reserved.

No part of this book may be reproduced or transmitted in any form or by any means, electronic or mechanical, including photocopying and recording, or in any information storage or retrieval system without the prior written permission of Stanford University Press.

Library of Congress Cataloging-in-Publication Data
Widiss, Benjamin Leigh, author.
 Obscure invitations : the persistence of the author in twentieth-century American literature / Benjamin Widiss.
    pages cm
 Includes bibliographical references and index.
 ISBN 978-0-8047-7322-5 (cloth : alk. paper)—ISBN 978-0-8047-7323-2 (pbk. : alk. paper)
 1. American literature—20th century—History and criticism. 2. Authorship in literature. 3. Authorship—History—20th century. 4. Authors and readers—History—20th century. I. Title.
 PS228.A88W53 2011
 810.9'005—dc22

2011004861

■ FOR LOUISA AND ABEL, AND NOW SARAH ■

CONTENTS

	Acknowledgments	ix
	Introduction	1
1	Fit and Surfeit *As I Lay Dying* (seesawing)	31
2	You Know Me, Alice *The Autobiography of Alice B. Toklas* (driving)	53
3	See Monkey, Do Monkey *Lolita* (aping)	76
4	The Gospel According to Dave *A Heartbreaking Work of Staggering Genius* (imbibing)	109
5	The Death of Kevin Spacey *Seven* and *The Usual Suspects* (envisioning)	134
	Epilogue	161
	Notes	177
	Works Cited	193
	Index	203

ACKNOWLEDGMENTS

One of the greatest pleasures of bringing this book to completion is the chance to thank the many who helped it and me along the way. It is no overstatement to say that without them the book would not exist. Foremost among these is Dorothy Hale, who has been central to my intellectual and professional development from my sophomore year of college to the present moment. No one has taught me more about how to write, and I suspect no one save the members of my own family (and perhaps a favorite author or two) has taught me more about how to think. Her singular blend of unfailing personal generosity and unstinting critical insight is crucial to these pages, and inspires me far beyond them. The specific genesis of this book lay in a seminar on William Faulkner led with incomparable verve and rigor by Carolyn Porter; while the book has gone on to embrace many other figures, it remains grounded in that experience and in her responses to my work. Eric Naiman not only taught me much about Vladimir Nabokov, but offered stringent and incisive critiques of many other elements of my thinking as well. The project has further benefited from discussions with Charles Altieri, Ann Banfield, John Bishop, Catherine Gallagher, Celeste Langan, and George Starr, and from tenacious early readings by Erika Clowes, Gillian Epstein, Luciana Herman, Heather Levien, Kim Magowan, Diane Matlock, Mayumi Takada, and, most especially, Joseph Jeon and Florence Dore, who have continued to give enormously of their time and sagacity—and, far from least, their good humor—through every stage of its advance.

I am powerfully indebted to many colleagues and students at Princeton who have propelled and sharpened this work through timely conversations, engaged readings, acute questions and suggestions, and general cheer. I would particularly like to thank Oliver Arnold, David Ball, Matt Bieber, Daphne Brooks, Christopher Bush, Anne Cheng, Lawrence Danson, Maria DiBattista, Jeff Dolven, Diana Fuss, Sophie Gee, William Gleason, Claudia Johnson, Ann

Jurecic, Soo La Kim, Ulrich Knoepflmacher, Meredith Martin, Lee Mitchell, Deborah Nord, Jeff Nunokawa, Heather O'Donnell, Sarah Rivett, Gayle Salamon, Elaine Showalter, Nigel Smith, Anne Sobel, Susan Stewart, Kerry Walk, Tim Watson, Tamsen Wolff, Susan Wolfson, and Michael Wood. And with them Christine Faltum, Pat Guglielmi, Kevin Mensch, Karen Mink, Marcia Rosh, and Nancy Shillingford, who together keep both the department and me moving forward. Mark Maslan and a second, anonymous reader for Stanford University Press offered capacious, keen, and entirely constructive responses to the manuscript; it is enriched by their input. My editor, Emily-Jane Cohen, assisted by Sarah Crane Newman and a truly stunning production team—eagle-eyed, tireless, and dizzyingly fleet—has shepherded the project to its final form most fluently.

And then there are those relationships that leave the institutional wholly behind. I am endlessly grateful for the support, friendship, and high spirits, all along the way, of Loretta Chen, Jonathan Davis, Stephanie Green, Brian Lee, Matthew Pincus, Ted Robertson, Jackie Starr, Alex Thompson, Abigail Trillin, Charles Tung, Paula Vielmetti, Alex Winter, and especially Jim Hinch and Ramu Nagappan, with whom I have shared classes, houses, peregrinations near and far, and the most wide-ranging of reflections. And in the final going: Christopher Chyba and Deborah Pearlstein, Debbie Finkelstein and Mike Silverberg, Tom Hagedorn and Julie Landweber, and Wey-Wey Kwok and Blue Montakhab. Louise Chegwidden and Jaclyn Boone made the work physically possible, and in the best moments joined the mighty, mighty KALX in setting me to dancing.

My parents, Alan and Ellen Widiss, first taught me to cherish authorial invitations, albeit invitations construed in somewhat less abstruse terms. Their influence colors this writing obliquely but profoundly, and their belief subtends it at a yet deeper level. My extraordinary sisters, Deborah Widiss and Rebecca Widiss, have ever provided counsel, creativity, and conviviality of the very highest order. Doug Goldstein, indefatigable comrade-in-arms, has joined their ranks, too. The last phase of this book's long gestation brought first Louisa Ruffine and then Abel Widiss into my life. In ways far too numerous to recount, or even count, they have offered the most joyous of distractions from the work and the most selfless encouragement to return to it. My words can neither recognize nor thank them enough.

OBSCURE INVITATIONS

INTRODUCTION

Why obscure an invitation?

It seems, for a moment, like a contradiction in terms—the open hand half-withdrawn, the beckoning path perversely shrouded, the appeal hobbled and slowed before it is even properly advanced. This dissonance can be resolved by imagining pragmatic grounds: decorum, or established protocols, or even self-protection. Such considerations will enter, obliquely and intermittently, in the chapters that follow, but I am primarily concerned with two alternative motivations—less immediate, less urgent, one might go so far as to say more willful. The first is a spirit of play, in which obscurity serves to augment the more recondite pleasures, for both inviter and invitee, inhering in a veiled interaction. The second is a process of tutelage, each step in the discernment and pursuit of an invitation changing the seeker in small but finally significant ways. These two rationales are far from mutually exclusive, and they have in common their welcome of the delay obscurity confers, freely distending the interval in which an invitation wholly emerges, or profiting by the lengthy expanse (of time, of text) in which it might fully unfold. Both will factor, in varying combinations and degrees, in each of the works I discuss herein, each embracing the longueurs and divagations of the narrative form to stage a dialogue equally as sustained as it is surreptitious.

The texts are, in many other respects, a relatively heterogeneous grouping: two novels, two memoirs, and two feature films; dating from 1930 to 2000;

ranging from high modernism to a foray into post-postmodernism, from the projection of an airy elitism to that of an earthy populism, and from the thoroughly canonized to the all-but-untouched-by-academic-critique. They are drawn together here by the particularly artful, and broadly consistent, ways in which they both manage and figure the practice of authorship in twentieth-century America. In so doing, they complicate received wisdom regarding the constitution of and distinctions between literary movements and moments, and shepherd us to a fuller understanding of the stakes and strategies of writing throughout the century. The obscure invitation that each text issues is to a self-conscious apprehension of, and perhaps by extension a form of communion with, its author. At its most basic this is no more than a simple structural homology between reader and author, at its most extreme a full-on annexation of Eucharistic ritual. The emotional valence of this convergence is highly malleable; it may constitute a threat to the reader or a reassurance, a promise or a plea, at the limit a mere observation of proximity otherwise unremarked. That is to say, the call to like an author, or to be like an author, is susceptible to considerable tonal variation; the relationship does not rise free of the text, but instead partakes of all the emotional vagaries of any accomplished artwork.

In all cases, the demands made on the reader are less than straightforward (even the most direct-seeming of appeals masking considerable indirection, or indeed misdirection). The key to describing them adequately lies in parsing the varieties of attention we bring to artistic texts, noting the significance in this light of the interplay—so crucial to twentieth-century aesthetics—between the representation of a story-world and consciousness of that representation itself. Modern and postmodern texts have in common their propensity to solicit our participation at two levels: via our experience of characters, which in turn yields emotional investment in plot situations and their resolutions, and via our tracking of rhetorical and conceptual games that highlight our relationships with authors, which may exist at any number of tangents to the more obvious or traditional bonds tying us to characters.[1] Fully attending to a text in this binary fashion places the reader at a lively crossroads, measuring authorial figurations in tandem with those of character and plot, and at the same time understanding that the binary is itself something of a heuristic fiction. That is, that attention to aesthetic experiment and linguistic play—and thus identification of, sometimes with, the author—not only coexists with but subtends investment in mimesis and affective identifications with characters, and vice versa. Narrative progress and rhetorical digress function conjointly: narrative establishes the stakes of play, while play distinguishes the layers of narrative and often enlarges their number.

Connecting this dynamic with the author, however, has been an uneasy move (at best) in academia for some decades. Beginning with W. K. Wimsatt and Monroe Beardsley's nomination of "the intentional fallacy" in 1946, continuing through Roland Barthes' and Michel Foucault's assaults on the figure of the author in the late 1960s, the reign of deconstruction over the next two decades, and on to the present day, we have been rigorous in our disavowal—frequently our suppression—of any interpretive move that purports to glean an authorial agenda from a close reading of primary text. But as with any zealously voiced protocol—especially one frequently enforced in a spirit of staunch rectitude—a penumbra has long fallen in excess of the actual taboo, leaving us blind to much that goes on within texts themselves, irrespective of any actual appeal to external authority. Of course, the most cursory examination of the arts pages of our newspapers, the profiles in glossy magazines, the discussions abounding online and on the radio and on the road (whether or not graced by the author's presence) indicates that we have never stopped caring about authors as intentional beings, and that we all—lay readers and academics alike, more or less responsibly, exuberantly, fantastically—generate our accounts of them partly based on what we find in their works. This has required of those of us in the business a degree of doublethink, given not only the proscriptions regarding intentionality but also the modernist dicta from which they issued, positing the most successful literature in no small degree as that which is least impinged upon by the biographical persona of its author. With the enormous rise of self-depiction (thinly veiled or otherwise) in postmodernist literature, we have arrived at a literary history that defines the twentieth century as stretched between two opposed constellations of expectation: at its start, the modernist mandate of impersonality, elusiveness, and allusiveness; by its end, celebrity culture's appeals for writing revelatory of authorial personality and biography, writing that signals its accessibility and that cultivates within its readers a sense of intimacy.

I argue, instead, that both horizons of expectation are in play throughout, and that the project of navigating between these opposed demands makes for much of the richness of twentieth-century literature. That neither the ostensible authorial evacuations that we read as the signature of the early part of the century nor the roiling self-portraiture of its close are as straightforward as they seem, and that they are at base quite similar strategies. Both approaches sensitize readers to the vexed status of the author and engineer related responses—inquisitiveness, investigation, investment—in the reader. Neither technique is transparent, of course; both progress by way of repetitions and revisions, gestures and allusions, elaborations and elisions that I group under the heading of obscure invitations—invitations to the reader not just to seek out the author from whom they spring, but to imagine him or her in a particular fashion and to attend to that imagination as a constitutive element of the reading process. Both approaches reveal, then, that the hermeneutic strategies we have been taught by modernism, and taught as well that they serve to elucidate texts that at the very least strive to be hermetically sealed, instead derive essential energy from the specter of the author standing behind and beyond—whether as aid, arbiter, or prize for the process of interpretation. That this author has been placed intrinsically off-limits by poststructuralist theory and is (I agree) never wholly accessible should not blind us to the fact that she or he is very much in play notionally in texts from every point in the century.

This is not to say that I see a surface-level shift in approaches to self-portraiture as the only way to delineate between representational strategies early and late in the century. Particularly salient for my discussion, too, will be a rising and increasingly explicit self-consciousness regarding the materiality of the text conjoined to the modes of its circulation. And, even more importantly, in the last third of the century a conversance and thoroughly imbricated relationship not just with the history of literature but also with academic literary criticism— most importantly with the notion of the death of the author. An animating conceit of the book as a whole is that, across multiple media, genres, literary movements, and temporal divides, each of the texts I treat here thematizes—in fact enacts, in one way or another—authorial distance, absence, or death, but uniformly with an end of reaffirming authorial presence, and with it a highly particularized and pointed relationship with the reader. In elucidating these less-than-fatal authorial deaths, I begin with dramatic evacuations of authorial voice and responsibility in William Faulkner's *As I Lay Dying* (1930) and Gertrude Stein's *The Autobiography of Alice B. Toklas* (1933), both works that obliquely advertise concerns regarding authorial signature in their very titles. Each book would seem to answer to the demand for an authorless or de-authored text, but each reinstates the author in spectacular and far-reaching fashion in its final sentence. I turn then to Vladimir Nabokov's inverse strategy of clotting the fictional space with authorial stand-ins and shadows in *Lolita* (1955), which I argue (given the novel's moral quandaries) makes locating a solid, extratextual Nabokov of paramount importance—but also impossible.

While Nabokovian shell games remain the order of the day in a great deal of work over the subsequent decades, my interest in the final chapters is in late-century texts that extend their reflections into a consideration of surrounding cultural formations, and with them the material substrate of textual circulation itself. The project of staging authorial death becomes more pointedly literal here, too, as we move from texts predating Barthes' writing, but amenable to being read according to his postulates, to those created a generation after "The Death of the Author," and palpably in dialogue with it. Dave Eggers' memoir *A Heartbreaking Work of Staggering Genius* (2000), David Fincher's film *Seven*, and Bryan Singer's film *The Usual Suspects* (both films 1995, and both starring Kevin Spacey as an especially pernicious author-figure) all yoke an abiding concern regarding the very media of textual production to a reexamination of Barthes' ideas, affording a fuller imagination of the itineraries of reception and interpretation. Each of these last three texts embraces the undeniable pithiness and melodrama of Barthes' memorable formulation in the service of an ironic script for actual narrative events in which the author is effectively killed off and then resuscitated, which is to say repeatedly demonstrating that resuscitation was not necessary in the first place. Thus, we find a continual rehearsal of Barthes' claims, but never an affirmation of them. These performances help us recognize illustrations of much the same point within the earlier works, whether couched in the modernist language of ostentatious self-effacement or via Nabokov's kaleidoscopic self-portraiture, thus fostering a fresh understanding of authorship throughout the twentieth century.

Indeed, for a long time, I called this project "The Dearth of the Author." The central claim, which continues to inform the current work, was that Roland Barthes' tremendously influential account of complete authorial self-effacement as the sine qua non of modern textual production—while rhetorically prodigious, conceptually dazzling, and endlessly provocative—was (and remains) largely inaccurate. Barthes wrote a polemic for a late-'60s critical and artistic avant-garde, and his prose points toward the barricades. Where he might have spoken of the stylistic liberties increasingly afforded by the twentieth century's many experimental forms, Barthes conjures not an opportunity but an inexorable "necessity to substitute language itself for the subject hitherto supposed to be its owner" ("Death" 50). He trumpets this development as one that "utterly transforms the modern text" (52), calling the result both "counter-theological" and "properly revolutionary" (54). Indeed, part of the continuing interest of a document that is, at one level, the product of a cultural moment well behind us is its predictive value for any number of anti-institutional literary-critical regimes of the succeeding decades. The brevity and stylistic exuberance of Barthes' essay count heavily for its enduring appeal, but so too does the fact that it so ably distills the animus not just of much deconstructive criticism but also of the various politically inflected approaches that held sway in deconstruction's wake, for all that their attention was no longer focused on the linguistic free-play at the heart of Barthes' endeavor.

Barthes' extreme formulations—"the author absents himself from [the text] at every level" (52), "every text is written eternally *here* and *now*" (52, emphasis Barthes'), "the claim to 'decipher' a text becomes entirely futile" (53), "writing constantly posits meaning, but always in order to evaporate it" (54)—accurately describe a mere handful of limit texts.[2] Barthes clearly evokes a sense of possibility, sometimes even an impulse, contributory to a great deal of the last century's artistic production, but as a blanket description his contentions overshoot the mark. Only the most radically chance-driven works, it seems to me, prove so eager to shed all authorial design; only in describing the content of such works do we fully relinquish euphemisms for, or interpretive circumlocutions taking us back to intimations of, intentionality. Far more often an apparent or incomplete authorial evacuation masks a deeper strategy of self-inscription—a studied self-occlusion that provokes in the reader not liberation or even indifference but rather a desire to find precisely that which initially eludes detection. Thus my revision of "death" to "dearth": that the ostentatious absence of the authorial hand actually drives us to locate its traces. And, in corollary: that the more hidden the author, the more fixated the reader becomes on finding him or her; and the more fixated the reader, the more subject to being choreographed in that search by the author—precisely the opposite result from the new freedom and self-determination Barthes triumphantly proclaims.

It is in this light that I want to tarry briefly with Michel Foucault's work in "What Is an Author?" (1969), the essay most often treated in tandem with Barthes'. While my primary engagement—for reasons of style, imagery, and influence, and of my own critical predilections—is with Barthes, Foucault's more systemic and dynamic account of what he calls the "author-function" (148) is illuminating here. Foucault paints the death of the author not as a singular occurrence but as, "since Mallarmé, . . . a constantly recurring event" (145)—which immediately raises the question of finality. Indeed, he offers an extremely astute analysis of the ways in which both individual readers and society as a whole continually reconstruct conceptions of authorship in the face of the historical and formal developments he arrays in hopes of supplanting them. A rehearsal of all these recuperative habits and impulses is unnecessary; the point is simply that Foucault's attempt to demystify them in favor of a "historical analysis of discourse" (158) runs up against precisely the entrenched behaviors that authors draw on as they seem to enact their own disappearance, "assum[ing] the role of the dead man in the game of writing" (143). It is a game, in a sense much more insistent and pervasive than Foucault allows, such that when (echoing Barthes) he predicates his analysis on the claim that "writing has freed itself from the dimension of expression" in favor of "an interplay of signs arranged less according to its signified content than according to the very nature of the signifier" (142), he is merely playing into the hand of the "dead man." Foucault's robust historical analysis of the epistemic shift that produced the modern sense of authorship here gives way to his ideological preference for a subsequent shift. He eagerly anticipates a new critical stance that would take up the kinds of questions he proposes in the late stages of his essay, for example, "How, under what conditions and in what forms can something like a subject appear in the order of discourse? What place can it occupy in each type of discourse, what functions can it assume, and by obeying what rules?" (158). Foucault presents these queries as "a matter of depriving the subject . . . of its role as originator, and of analyzing the subject as a variable and complex function of discourse" (158), but the second protocol does not necessarily entail the first. Foucault's commitment to an ineluctable textual primacy producing the author as no more than a discursive effect blinds him to the way a canny "originator" might mobilize the discursive thicket stretched between herself and her readers, precisely by grasping its rules and engaging its functions to inscribe it with an occluded but ultimately accessible self-representation or self-expression. The "variability" and "complexity" of this subject would then be revealed as products of readerly assiduousness, more sustained and engaged readings generating fuller realizations of the self-accounting written into the discourse. Steadfast opposition to any invocation of authorial intention thus becomes self-defeating, an obstacle to a full appreciation of a text's workings.

Seán Burke, in his magisterial dissection of the anti-authorial commitments of poststructuralist criticism, *The Death and Return of the Author* (1992), reads this as our current impasse: the acceptance of "authorial disappearance . . . almost as an article of faith" in contemporary criticism (16), a "primary claim in itself" (15), rather than the "essentially provisional" strategy it once was for Russian Formalism and New Criticism as they defined themselves against earlier biographical modes of reading (13). He warns that criticism must now make "reparations [and] revisions, or continue to neglect the question of the author at the cost of remaining regional, selective, inadequate to the literary object" (48–49). Burke sees his own work as "prolegomena" to this end, a "negation of the negation" that—focused on close readings of theory and philosophy—does not itself arrive at articulating "the positivity of [authorial] presence" in literary works (xix), but he points the way quite cannily. He observes that, as in the Foucault I have just quoted, "[a]nti-authorialism has always found itself in complicity with anti-representational poetics" (40), that even Barthes is perfectly hospitable to "the authors of texts which make no claim to a representational 'truth'—Mallarmé, Sollers, Bataille, Robbe-Grillet, and so on" (43). Burke argues that Barthes' basic hostility is to reading text as conforming in simple and unequivocal ways with the external world, that the resistance to authorial intention arises only from the construal of the author as "the possessor of meaning," who makes language "obeisant to an extratextual reality" rather than allowing it an "unlimited variety of interpretations" (41). Burke then argues that the death of the author thus becomes wholly unnecessary for Barthes in the context of writerly texts. But if the creators of such texts thus earn Barthes' approbation, at a level commensurate with his castigation of a bluntly positivist understanding of literary endeavor, we are left still with a considerable intermediary space in which representational strictures loosen and pure mimesis gives way—but only partially—to aesthetic play. The organizing intelligence here is palpable but fugitive, its actions consequential but far from straightforward; such an intelligence does not condemn the exegete to mere tracery of extratextual objects temporally anterior and logically prior to the writing, nor does it free her entirely.

It is a particularly pleasing irony that Barthes has reemerged as one of the most useful and energizing theorists for me to draw on in order to theorize that middle space, precisely by virtue of the zeal with which he limns the zones at its borders. Barthes' increasing embrace of the idiosyncratic in the last decade of his life almost allowed him to overcome the programmatic claims for which he is most famous.[3] *The Pleasure of the Text* (1973) offers sustained ruminations on the distinctions and the slippages between the radical kinds of writing championed in "The Death of the Author" and those more traditionally representational eighteenth-, nineteenth-, and even twentieth-century works that also were the subject of his exquisite delectation. Counterpoising the two as texts of bliss and texts of pleasure—along the binary split that had, in previous instantiations, been that between scriptor and author, the writerly and the readerly, text and work, writer and author, and writer and writing[4]—Barthes considers, intermittently, the possibilities for playing across that line rather than staunchly defending it as he does in "The Death of the Author."[5] If *The Pleasure of the Text* still differentiates powerfully between modern texts and older forms, going so far as to renege on the liminal status Barthes had previously accorded to authors like Mallarmé and Proust—"The Death of the Author" places them ambiguously in a teleological "prehistory of modernity" (51), while *The Pleasure of the Text* cordons them into the realm of culturally sanctioned pleasure, as opposed to the unpredictable, ecstatic space of bliss (21, 31, 40)—he at least now condones readings predicated on each textual mode. Further, he articulates these two "systems of reading" (12) with clarity and verve, and allows as well that he himself practices both: reading for pleasure, which "goes straight to the articulations of the anecdote, it considers the extent of the text, ignores the play of language"; and reading for bliss, a reading that "skips nothing; it weighs, it sticks to the text, it reads, so to speak, with application and transport, grasps at every point in the text the asyndeton which cuts the various languages—and not the anecdote" (12). Reading for "pleasure," in this schema, accords with investment in what I am calling the mimetic, storyworld concerns of a text, while reading for "bliss" is attending to linguistic play and aesthetic experimentation. The crucial difference between our systematizations is Barthes' insistence on the radical distinction between these two regimes, and on his own extreme atypicality as an individual invested in both.

Barthes suggests that this catholicity of tastes and reading practices makes him an "anachronic subject," at home neither in his own literary moment nor in the past, for such an individual "simultaneously and contradictorily participates in the profound hedonism of all culture (which permeates him quietly under cover of an *art de vivre* shared by the old books) and in the destruction of that culture" (14). The grandiosity of these claims fuels Barthes' insistence on their mutual exclusivity, but they beg relatively obvious questions: Why couldn't one read for anecdote but be sidetracked by linguistic play, or read for aesthetic delectation yet be carried along by plot? Indeed, why couldn't a book be constructed such that it not only envisioned these dynamics but aimed for them, and in such a way as to make them mutually reinforcing—the distraction and derailment only apparent? My argument is that this is precisely the turn that a broad swathe of the culture took over the course of the twentieth century, in works that we might otherwise describe as varying widely in their registers and aims. It does not seem surprising to me that Barthes, a singularly sensitive and independent reader, and one who increasingly dedicated himself to avoiding any single ideological or interpretive matrix, would apprehend and articulate these two modes so persuasively. Among his few sustained critical commitments is precisely that which bedevils him here: the continuing devotion to analytical binaries, as exemplified by those above and, enduringly, in the radical distinction between authors and readers. His steadfast refusal to sanction any notion of authorial conscription directing the reading process grounds one of the most fascinating sections of the work, in which Barthes describes texts as fetishes in order to moderate his stance on authorship without utterly compromising it.

Barthes admits that even though, per his own earlier claims, "[a]s institution, the author is dead ... no longer exercis[ing] over his work the formidable paternity whose account literary history, teaching, and public opinion had the responsibility of establishing and renewing; ... in the text, in a way, *I desire* the author: I need his figure (which is neither his representation nor his projection), as he needs mine" (27, emphasis here, and throughout this paragraph, Barthes'). This author is construed as a mere function of Barthes' own reading praxis, an imaginative construction "lost in the midst of a text (not *behind* it)," just as the text is endowed with its fetishistic force by virtue of Barthes' individual history and psychology. But this is an animate fetish, endowed with the drives that Barthes refuses to countenance the possibility of attributing to the author apprehensible within the text. "[T]*his fetish desires me*," he maintains, the reciprocity emerging by way of what Barthes calls "a whole disposition of invisible screens, selective baffles: vocabulary, references, readability, etc." that together engender a situation in which, he feels, "[t]he text chooses me" (27). The sense is that the text has Barthes' internal library—and his specific preferences therein—in mind, that it calls to him and ensures that he hears that call by way of an appeal predicated on his personality. But the fact that Barthes introduces this notion as fetishistic puts it under the sign of the hallucinatory—not, as he says, the author's projection into the text but entirely his own. He anatomizes the sources of his dual reading modes in similar fashion quite late in the book, glossing them as the product of a singular, and markedly personal, formation: "it is at the conclusion of a very complex process of biographical, historical, sociological, neurotic elements (education, social class, childhood configuration, etc.) that I control the contradictory interplay of (cultural) pleasure and (non-cultural) bliss" (62). I am arguing that what Barthes staunchly defends as his profound singularity, fruit of the myriad particulars of his positioning at an entirely specific cultural and historical juncture, is in fact characteristic of that juncture in much broader terms. So intensely is he focused on his personal delectation, Barthes fails to recognize that his dual enthusiasms ultimately define his century as well as himself—that myriad texts of otherwise widely disparate description not only allow but aim for precisely this doubleness of investment, in mimetic representation as well as aesthetic play, and for its synthesis in the reading process.

I take up Barthes at such length, and return to his critical apparatus in spite of disagreeing strongly with some of his premises, because he articulates the strategies and stakes of his reading process so tremendously eloquently, and with such a clear sense of emotional investment matching—indeed motivating—his interpretive acumen. What Barthes offers, in comparison not only with current critical modes but also with more strictly defined reader-response theorists of his day (some of whom I'll discuss shortly), is a markedly vibrant and visceral sense of the affective experience of his engagement with text. The attention Barthes accords to the aesthetic dimensions not just of the texts he treats but also of the project of reading, of the psychological dynamism of interaction between reader and text, yields an extremely compelling account vitiated only by its unrelenting refusal to countenance any appeal to the author. This refusal manifests itself not only in the personal fetishizing of individual texts that Barthes freely owns up to here, but also in his critical fetishization of the concept of the text as a bulwark against the biographical criticism he was so intent on burying. Barthes objects in "The Death of the Author" that "criticism still largely consists in saying that Baudelaire's oeuvre is the failure of the man Baudelaire, Van Gogh's is his madness, Tchaikovsky's his vice" (50). This complaint is well founded, but it reduces authors to their shortcomings rather than envisioning the possibility of exploring their successes, and it imagines that any author-based criticism must be grounded in extratextual events and behaviors.

My approach, however, is not primarily to explore authors as historical individuals, to plumb the lives they have lived outside of the texts on which I focus. I will make some reference to external biographical details, and I will on occasion quote the statements authors make in other venues. But I am far less interested in establishing anything concrete about these authors as actual personages than I am in describing the authors who emerge as spectral presences from our readings of their works. This is a literary model of identity, one that toys with reference to the real but that is finally produced and constrained by the literary itself. Maria DiBattista calls these specters "figments," arguing that while "the person who writes never appears to us except as a figment of our imagination" (5), it does not follow that we make her up: "Quite the opposite. It is Woolf [in the case of DiBattista's study] who makes things up, who *makes* herself up—that is what it means, at a very fundamental level, to have an imagination and to use it in your writing" (6, emphasis DiBattista's). DiBattista distills from the vast body of Woolf's writing five "portraits," emphasizing different facets of Woolf's personality. She draws explicitly on a Barthesian notion of multiplicity in doing so, taking exception to his contention in *Sade, Fourier, Loyola* that the author so lacks the unifying force of personhood as to present no more than a "mere plural of 'charms'" or a "discontinuous chant of amiabilities" (7–8),[6] but affirming a vision of an authorial career as an "ability to imagine herself not as a single person, but as many persons" (8). These are selves both private and public, sometimes cohabiting peacefully, sometimes not (36), visible piecemeal across the broad expanse of diaries, letters, essays, and novels, and arranged here as a form of "critical biography" (9).[7] Such a composite portrait emerges from DiBattista's thirty years of reading and reflecting on Woolf—"a writer," she says, "I know as well as I know anyone or anything" (35).

My interest, on the other hand, is in the way we are solicited and taught to know writers within individual works, the way a writer "makes herself up" for us within the space of a single text. I want "making oneself up" to mean not just "imagining oneself" in a certain fashion or fashions over a lifetime, but also "constituting oneself" and "presenting oneself" (in the sense of applying "makeup") within the delimited space of a given work, mobilizing all the resources that serve to render that work coherent in support of a similarly coherent—if, as I have suggested, elusive—self-representation. The notion of a self constructed within the confines of the literary work recalls modernist and New Critical conceptions of textual personae that bar any conclusive apprehension of the author, and with them a very different construal of the work as a discrete entity. While I do affirm the author's ultimate inaccessibility, I do so without thereby ratifying assumptions traditionally attendant: for example, that all masks serve only to disfigure or hide, that all texts should be treated as resolutely closed systems. What earlier criticism has slighted or ignored is the degree to which texts' intervenient authorial figurations are chips in compositional modes that repeatedly appear to promise precisely the elucidation they cannot be trusted to deliver. Against New Criticism's unwavering methodological commitment to conceiving of works as hermetically sealed, and equally against the modernist notion of impersonality, I propose that texts are filled with masks that self-consciously and advisedly borrow their contours from the faces behind them.

My concern at all times is to read each text as thoroughly as possible with the language it provides, then, attending to the ways in which that language speaks simultaneously to the mimetic world depicted within the text and to the author as well. I append to each of my chapter titles a single gerund—seesawing, driving, aping, imbibing, envisioning—that encapsulates these multiple vectors, a term generated by the work in question that characterizes its particularities at the level of both language and theme, and that measures the crossover points between the two. Each describes as well the operations recipients are encouraged to reproduce outside the text in response, and thus comes to stand for a distinct mode of reading under the larger umbrella of my method. These characterizations are not meant to be exhaustive, or even wholly mutually exclusive, but they do measure the importance of a reading practice that allows itself to be directed by the text.

Advancing an analysis of both text and reception through terminology readily provided by each individual work accords with a growing interest in moving beyond the "symptomatic reading" strategies so pervasive in the last generation of academic criticism. Eve Kosofsky Sedgwick's conception of "reparative reading" in *Touching Feeling: Affect, Pedagogy, Performativity* (2003) and Sharon Marcus's of "just reading" in *Between Women: Friendship, Desire, and Marriage in Victorian England* (2007) exemplify this drive away from what each characterizes as a Jamesonian imperative to exhume repressed political content of which the literary is a mere epiphenomenal symptom. For Fredric

Jameson, an interest in the "microscopic experience of words in a text" as such—or, worse, as pointedly distinct from the political—"maims our existence as individual subjects and paralyzes our thinking about time and change," and, a fortiori, our potential as agents for change (20). Thus the clarion exhortation to "Always historicize!"(9) that initiates *The Political Unconscious* (1983), opening into an insistence that interpretation is and should be "an essentially allegorical act" (10) dedicated to exhuming political content "repressed and buried" beneath the text's surface "poetic" concerns and effects (20). Jameson's commitment to "the unmasking of cultural artifacts as socially symbolic acts" (20) is both foundational for and emblematic of a panoply of structurally homologous interpretive practices that have emerged in subsequent decades, each dedicated to unearthing one or another of their objects' unrealized or "desperately" repressed "logical and ideological centers" (49). His mandate has become virtually a given of literary criticism, such that twenty years on, Sedgwick finds the "extraordinary stress on the efficacy of . . . exposure" (138)—an exposure routinely imagined in terms of its salutary political fallout—"by now nearly synonymous with criticism itself" (124). A similar diagnosis motivates Marcus's opposition between the pervasive practice of "symptomatic reading" for the ideological "absent cause that gives the text its form" (74) and her own "just reading" of precisely what "Jameson . . . dismisses as 'the inert givens and materials of a particular text' "—"what texts present on their surface but critics have failed to notice" (75).

Both Marcus and Sedgwick acknowledge the importance of symptomatic reading strategies, but both recognize the limitations of a discipline that approaches texts only in this fashion. Sedgwick's essay constitutes an exhortation in its own right, toward the elaboration by future critics of myriad "local theories and nonce taxonomies" predicated on the mechanics of individual texts—theories and taxonomies whose attributes and accomplishments are, perforce, not articulable by her, but that she considers salutary for precisely this reason (145). Marcus, on the other hand, does perform extensive "just readings," attending at length to immediate, referential content (forms of female relationship in Victorian society) placed before her by the novels she considers. She conceives of the textual surface as "complex and ample," rather than as "diminished by, or reduced to, what it has had to repress" (75), and indeed culls from it evidence for a substantially revised understanding of Victorian mores. In the chapters that follow, I am construing a notion of textual surface not simply as referentially ample with respect to the cultural matrix out of which it emerges, but as gesturing simultaneously toward the storyworld it describes (as in Marcus's practice), the author generating that description, and the reading thus solicited. This is perhaps not "just reading" in the simplest sense Marcus envisions, but it is nevertheless a manner of working with textual givens, of recognizing that they are not mere "inert" symptoms, and thus of parsing the complexities of the textual apparatus as presented to us rather than searching for its "unconscious." The result is a series of nonce taxonomies that jointly theorize something more than their own localities—that in the aggregate will, I hope, offer a degree of traction in analyzing works beyond those I take up, and in rethinking certain of our claims about twentieth-century literature and culture.

Beyond the thread of the author, as a preoccupation of individual texts and of the century's artistic output taken more broadly, these claims coalesce in three main critical arenas. The first is the legacy of reader-response theory, into which I am happy to think of this book as a late entry. It enters, though, as both an extension and a corrective, the former because reader-response largely lost its currency just as postmodernism's hectoring might have made it most apposite; the latter because response theorists' accounts of modernism, too, seem to me largely to make of the author too quiescent a being. This is true irrespective of the predominating interpretive lenses adopted by individual critics. For example, Wolfgang Iser's major focus as he moves through the centuries in *The Implied Reader: Patterns of Communication in Prose Fiction from Bunyan to Beckett* (1974) is on literature's potential to trouble social determinations of individual behavior, but he imagines that modernism leaves the reader to his own devices rather than prodding him in a certain direction, and imagines too that the endpoint of a developing system of interrogations of the surrounding world is phenomenological reflection rather than behavioral change. Thus, the eighteenth-century reader is "cast by the author in a specific role" and "guided . . . toward a conception of human nature and of reality," and in the nineteenth century, while the reader must at least appear to "discover the fact that society had imposed a part on him" on his own, the "object" remains that he arrive at what he merely takes to be an independent critique of this role (xiii), spurred on by "a variety of cunning stratagems [sic] to nudge the reader unknowingly into making the 'right' discoveries" (xiv). In the twentieth century, for Iser, the author loses this directive quality, leaving the reader simply to explore his "own faculties of perception . . . establishing for himself the connections between perception and thought" (xiv). Modernist rhetorical innovations then are only a means to highlight the discrepancies between any attempt at description and the actual world around us: Joyce's "historical panoply of individual and period styles" in *Ulysses* exposes "the characteristic quality of style—namely, that it imposes form on an essentially formless reality" (193), and the "constant and elusive fragmentation" of Benjy's monologue in Faulkner's *The Sound and the Fury* reflects "acts of perception" that "lack coordination" and leave the phenomena sparking them to "constantly disintegrate" (139). Style, in these formulations, is a capacious and synthetic term, a blanket quality that achieves its force in the aggregate precisely by virtue of the incoherence it fosters at the more local levels both of realist detail and of aesthetic effects. Because Iser is so committed to charting the "realization accomplished by the reader" who sutures the text together (274), he leaves largely unexplored the role of the author in facilitating and shaping that realization.

Jane P. Tompkins, in the essay with which she closes her anthology *Reader-Response Criticism* (1980), reaches similar conclusions by way of economic analysis. For her, the "self-containment" of the modernist artwork is the logical result of literature's becoming a series of freely circulating artifacts sold to anonymous readers, beginning in the late eighteenth century (210–14). She argues that the essential attribute of twentieth-century literature is that its demands—however convoluted—are solely interpretive, that "we equate language not with action but with signification" (203). Because it is "not a gesture in a social situation . . . [t]he first requirement of a work of art in the twentieth century is that it should *do* nothing" (210, Tompkins' emphasis), in contradistinction to the political purchase aesthetic work might have aspired to in the Classical period (204) or—more importantly for my purposes—the patronage of specific members of a coterie audience sought by and through Renaissance poetry (207–10). The Renaissance poet knows those to whom and for whom he writes, and the resulting literature is fundamentally both personal and transactional, in these respects the polar opposite of the hermetic modernist art object as it has traditionally been conceived. By way of illustration, Tompkins cites a lengthy catalogue of Ben Jonson's occasional verse "celebrating the birthdays, christenings, marriages, and sundry accomplishments of the royal family and the nobility" as a way to sustain his livelihood and "a means of accomplishing specific social tasks" (208).

The thematic implications of the poet's (and the poetry's) situation are patent here, and Iser and Tompkins are right to see them as fundamentally altered in the twentieth century. But the fantasy of an audience at hand to be courted and swayed endures and informs literary undertakings well beyond the historical moment in which it is justified by immediate and personal financial relations. Indeed, Garrett Stewart's study of direct address in the nineteenth-century novel, *Dear Reader: The Conscripted Audience in Nineteenth-Century British Fiction* (1996), grounds itself in Dante's savvy grasp centuries earlier that "in the vernacular literature of a new print culture, reader address amounts to a trope of tropes. The previous, presumptive ground of all rhetoric, a present audience under exhortation, becomes that metatextual horizon of a modern literary culture that Dante ... chooses to make explicit" (35). Stewart's monograph then elaborates on reader address as "the rhetorical trace of rhetoricity per se, the troping of all tropology as the solicitation of attention by direct utterance" (35). The question I am pursuing, translated into Stewart's language, is how to trace rhetoricity in the absence of its most obvious signposts, how to read the troping of a pervasive textual praxis of solicitation when it is not represented as explicit importuning, or even as direct utterance at all. Here, although Stewart significantly postdates the heyday of response criticism, and forcefully distances himself from it precisely in terms of the volatility and variability of textual encounters he will take up (10), his estimation of modernism closely resembles Iser's and Tompkins'. "[T]he open invitation to response," Stewart writes, "is wiped clean from the burnished surface of a modernist text that stresses inscape over outreach, as well as from a vision of community too besieged for the gesture of familiarity and affiliation sketched by address," yielding a work that is "closed, self-contained, introvert" (33), "sheathed against penetration by the leisured reader" (41).

But Stewart's conclusion outpaces his observations. The disappearance of "open" invitations and conventional "gestures" need not produce a text wholly sealed within itself. The language he uses to describe nineteenth-century narrative techniques—"the premium placed [by direct address] on both manifested mimetic presence and attentive readerly presence, on willing submission to a made world but also on direct solicitation from a narrative voice" (5), the insistence that "form has a transitive as well as a static sense, designating the formative as well as the shaped" (20)—speaks beautifully to the dynamics I find at play in twentieth-century writing. I want to claim for the next century, too, the specific quality of play informing his interest in the ways in which "a text might encode—might teasingly encipher—its own reading" (11). For

Stewart, all of this serves "narrative interest itself" (5) rather than the pursuit of the author standing behind the text. Not only do I think Stewart's formulations are apposite to discerning the author within what all these critics correctly describe as a textual environment far more conducive than is nineteenth-century fiction to self-consciousness and thus to active reflection on the manner in which texts are made, but I also see his language as providing the beginning of a response to the limitations Wayne Booth draws on the tenor of author-reader interactions in *The Rhetoric of Fiction* (1961).

Booth, whom Frank Kermode once termed "the rejected father" of response criticism,[8] is much more willing than the figures I have just discussed to view the modernist author as intervening wholesale in the reception of the text, indeed as designing the text to engender a specific reading. But it is a reading predicated on the simplest form of accord with the author. Thus, Booth envisions the "wink and nudge" given the reader by the author, who is "observing as from a rear seat the humorous or disgraceful or ridiculous or vicious driving behavior of the narrator seated in front" (300), issuing in a shared "mature moral judgment" (307)—for example of Jason Compson's behavior in *The Sound and the Fury*. Booth reads the rewards of this joint evaluative work as far outstripping the pleasures to be had in "providing the source of an allusion or by deciphering a pun" (307): "*Finnegans Wake* has often been attacked as merely a long crossword puzzle," he notes, "but so far as I know it has never been defended as such" (302). He does not explore the possibility that puzzles, allusions, and puns might prove to be the very stuff of which broad thematic substance is made. Booth's more abstract vocabulary is revealing here; he speaks frequently of "collaboration" (302–8) and at the limit of "communion" (304), which in his usage means the reader's thoroughgoing assimilation to the author's stances, as in perhaps the most-quoted lines from the book: "The author creates, in short, an image of himself and another image of his reader; he makes his reader, as he makes his second self, and the most successful reading is one in which the created selves, author and reader, can find complete agreement" (138). The game-playing implicit in the crossword-puzzle metaphor and the practice of deciphering—which I would assimilate to the volatility that Stewart reads as crucially missing from response criticism, and to the "teasing" textual strategies that lead him to insist on it—points in another direction, to a relationship that may savor of the adversarial, of hidden ulterior motives, even of inequalities. Precisely because the author is not just the originator of textual experience but also in many respects the stake, a mere aligning of opinion does not describe the complexity of his or her interactions with the reader.

Implicit, too, in metaphors of the text as a puzzle or a tease is an elaboration, as well as a revision, of one of reader-response theory's most prominent and enduring formulations: Stanley Fish's postulation in *Is There a Text in This Class?* (1980) of interpretive communities delimited by their members' adherence to common sense–making protocols. Fish's account holds in the sense that I can advance my readings and convince others of their validity only if we already share certain standards regarding what signifies—or, more accurately, is capable of signifying—in a text. But when he argues that these communal interpretive strategies "exist prior to the act of reading and therefore determine the shape of what is read" (171), that "directions for making" meanings "will only *be* directions to those who already have the interpretive strategies in the first place" (173, emphasis Fish's), he elides the question of just how the strategies do in fact evolve—how communities are formed and how they change over time—and, perforce, what role individual texts and by extension individual authors might have in the process. Fish recognizes that an interpretive community's "stability is always temporary," that "communities grow larger and decline, and individuals move from one to another" (171–72), but this is "instability" measured simply by population, as if there were but a fixed number of immutable interpretive regimes merely jockeying for adherents. He notes that our construction of, for example, the pastoral is not "indisputable, objective" fact (168), and implicitly therefore that our approaches to it may change "('no one reads that way anymore')" (172), but he does not stipulate a mechanism, only a wholesale switch in affiliations. In highlighting the way an obscure invitation can unfold at length within a single text through—and only through—particularly attentive reading, I am affirming Fish's insistence on the temporal dimension of interpretation but carrying it beyond the sequential apprehension of words in a line of poetry to far more complex and protracted nonlinear navigations and revised understandings. In noting the capacity for a text to cultivate in this fashion a single reader's ability to discern the significance of textual elements that previously appeared mute, I am also indicating a root cause for development within larger communities—and, indeed, hoping to incite just such a change. Each text's campaign to fashion its readers to its own specifications, irrespective of their origins, speaks back as well to the belabored articulation of interpretive communities and critical positionalities in the decades after Fish's writing, and to our continuing investment in sociological constructions of readership. Identity, for these texts, is a function of reception rather than a precursor to it.

This notion of a diffuse but still eminently robust form of exhortation considerably alters the stakes of Stewart's account of the decline of direct address, and in so doing turns us to a second group of critics. Stewart observes that direct address is "[p]rogrammatically outlawed by modernism" (33), but his book, the last published of the five I have just discussed, appeared two years before Lawrence Rainey's *Institutions of Modernism: Literary Elites and Public Culture* (1998) spearheaded a sea change in our understanding of the relationship between modernist dicta and the behavior of actual modernists. Stewart of course describes an objectively verifiable formal shift within texts themselves, but the force of Rainey's work—and that of several other critics writing in his wake, including Catherine Turner's *Marketing Modernism Between the Two World Wars* (2003) and Aaron Jaffe's *Modernism and the Culture of Celebrity* (2005)—is to so profoundly alter our understanding of modernists' real-world activity as to necessitate thorough reevaluation of the significances granted to modernist form. This work reveals the modernists' brave and haughty stance of serene indifference to the worldly fate of texts secure in their status as great art—a corollary or contributor to what I have quoted Stewart calling "a vision of community too besieged for the gesture of familiarity and affiliation sketched by address" (33)—as, to a large degree, mere posturing. This radical revision of long-standing received wisdom is effected by an exploration not of primary literary texts but instead of myriad contemporaneous documents: "lecture programs, travel-guides, bibliographies, biographies, mass distributed periodicals, publishers' ledgers, newspapers, little magazines, family histories, memoirs, exhibition catalogues, letters, reviews, and criticism" (Jaffe 6, of Rainey's corpus); "modernist limited editions, small magazines, little reviews, introductions, editing, anthologies, and other cultural furnishings" (Jaffe 8); publishers' records, publicity flyers, industry newsletters, bookstore circulars, mass-market magazine and newspaper advertisements, and oral histories (Turner). Together, these documents reveal modernist authors as sedulous for recognition and willing to undertake a great deal of extraliterary labor in order to achieve it—a dynamic I see refracted in the writing itself, sometimes as straightforward, earnest appeal for understanding, sometimes in more ambivalent terms. Rainey attests to an array of activities "involving theatricality, spectacle, publicity, and novel modes of cultural marketing and media manipulation" (4) undertaken by modernist authors themselves to facilitate their integration into an "economic circuit of patronage, collecting, speculation, and investment" (3), making them, in Jaffe's words, "aspirants to the status of capital" (14). While Rainey attends to the showier aspects of this self-fashioning, Jaffe concentrates on the quieter industry of "reviewing, introducing, editing, and anthologizing," through other "collaborative work," all of which he collects under the notion of authorial signature—"imprimatur"—as "durable promotional vehicle" (3). For her part, Turner emphasizes not the authors' activity but that of the publishing houses promoting modernist books to a skeptical general public—the bulk of her attention is given to advertisements—but she too adverts to "growing evidence that modern authors played a role in making their own artistic works into commodities," and proposes an understanding of modernism as an "integrative mode" that blends opposition to mass culture with an ongoing "fascination" and intermittent collaboration with its demands (6–7).

But what I want to emphasize is that while all three of these monographs radically revise our understanding of the goals of the writing they address, they pay very little attention to that writing itself. This is an admission all three critics make readily, part and parcel of what they deem a salutary shift in focus at the time of publication. Rainey suggests in passing the sort of thematic exegesis that might emerge as corollary to his undertaking, highlighting the importance of Stephen's and Bloom's "tireless search for patrons and patronage" in *Ulysses*, as well as the etymological tie between "patron" and *pater*— "dead or missing" fathers being central both to Joyce's novel and to *The Waste Land* (7). Such asides notwithstanding, his work here stands steadfastly opposed to textual analysis. He offers a trenchant critique of traditional scholarship's penchant to "define modernisms through a unilateral focus on formal devices or ideological constellations," yielding "arguments derived solely from the reading of literary texts or artworks, a procedure that evinces excessive faith in our capacity to specify the essence and social significance of isolated formal devices and to correlate them with complex ideological and social formations" (4). This is a fair criticism, particularly of the kind of criticism predominating in the 1980s and '90s, work that often does imagine itself as illuminating the broadest of societal configurations by dint of close reading. But Rainey's corrective response is equally one-sided. He dedicates himself to an elucidation of modernism as a "social reality" through close study of the "intervenient institutions" connecting readers, works, and social structures (4), but he allows this study to all but eclipse attention to textual particulars.

At intervals, the judiciousness that characterizes most of his writing drops away, and he makes ringing statements such as "the effect of modernism was not so much to encourage reading as to render it superfluous" (56) and "[t]he best reading of a work may, on some occasions, be one that does not read it at all" (106). In the second case, the conditional at least mitigates the superlative, and Rainey admits that the assertion of a "principle" thus defined would be "misleading" (106)—and indeed it is quite possible to read the book in less pugilistic terms, as a complement to then-extant critical modes rather than an attempt to replace them. Nevertheless, the effective force of Rainey's intervention is to draw a stark line between the inside and the outside of literary works, a line that largely defines Jaffe's and Turner's approaches as well. In dialing my attention down from broad "social formations" and the economic analytic so conducive to such study, I am able to build from the work these and other critics have done situating modernist texts externally by way of author behavior to say more about the texts themselves—to reexamine the behaviors they inscribe and encourage, and to rethink the accustomed dividing lines between textual space and the larger world.

Turner's account differs from the other two, however, in its emphasis on the processes by which the forbidding artifacts of modernism, with their most formidable reputations, were domesticated for purchase and perusal by a mass audience through advertisements presenting the literature as "difficult but not unapproachable, different but not unrecognizable" (9).[9] These dynamics of recognition and approach provide a bridge to the last critical arena I want to consider here, a loose grouping of theorists exploring the relationships between American mass culture and literary art. Perhaps because the linkages between the two are today so manifest—Joe Moran, in *Star Authors: Literary Celebrity in America* (2000), finds the explicit treatment of celebrity "a constant preoccupation . . . in both fictional and non-fictional forms" in the speech and writing of those authors in its throes (10)—most academic treatments initiate their explorations near the turn of the twentieth century, typically discerning at that historical juncture a vexed resistance to this interpenetration of mass and high culture. Thus, not just Moran but also Loren Glass in *Authors Inc.: Literary Celebrity in the Modern United States, 1880–1980* (2004), Mark McGurl in *The Novel Art: Elevations of American Fiction after Henry James* (2001), and Janice Radway in *A Feeling for Books: The Book-of-the-Month Club, Literary Taste, and Middle-Class Desire* (1997) all position themselves, more or less explicitly, in the wake of Andreas Huyssen's notion of the Great Divide between the modern and the postmodern and Pierre Bourdieu's of cultural distinction. They advert to the complexities that any account of literary modernism as resistance to mass culture runs into on the ground of the American novel, which "seemed toward the turn of the century to have no tradition of elevated discursive status of its own," and was thus deprived of the opportunity to join "other modernist genres and art forms" in an easy "continuation and intensification of a centuries-long partnership in the discourse of aesthetics and social elitism" (McGurl 4). But, these critics argue, novelists made strenuous efforts to construct just such an apparatus of distinction through their work.

Glass pushes a strong notion of psychosexual demarcation showily brandished in autobiographical texts—authorial performances of "a virile masculinity bordering on caricature" standing against an increasingly feminized mass culture (18)—that accords only very loosely with the more subtle effects and appeals I trace. The principal convergence is the simple fact that he, too, reads authorial concerns about reception into the construction of primary texts and literary persona; the principal divergence is his insistence on the stark oppositions born of a strategy of authorial self-differentiation, a strategy he sees as soldiering on until the advent of multinational publishing conglomerates, second-wave feminism, and postmodernism make such performances untenable. More conducive to my readings is McGurl's conception of significantly more fluid dynamics of distancing and melding between readers, characters, and authors. McGurl proposes that the novel's ambiguous cultural status in the late nineteenth century yields an attempt "to reinvent itself as fine art" (5), and he introduces this attempt as one of differentiation, manifested through the presence of and fascination with, in each of the novels he reads, a "dialectical foil"—the "naïve, stupid, low, primitive, childish, [or] uneducated" (9). Thus, for example, "Faulkner's intense narrative identification with the simple mind of the idiot [Benjy Compson] produces perhaps the most technically sophisticated, notoriously difficult, and prestigiously 'Joycean' stretch of prose in American literature" (111). But the delineation thus achieved is itself no simple thing, predicated as it is on a profound imaginative bonding with Benjy, such that distinguishing the author or the accomplished reader of the section from the less adept masses is a move also pregnant with the possibility of educating the masses in exactly this manner of intellection (112–13). McGurl calls modernist texts "antipedagogical" (111) and observes that Faulkner "occults the presence of a pedagogical narrator" who might offer assistance in navigating Benjy's section of the novel (132), but McGurl also describes "the strong reader" of the monologue as one who "patiently (and usually with help) reconstructing the chronology and sense of the section, performs an intellectual operation precisely opposed to the confusions, if not to the thinking, of Benjy himself," and who thus emerges as "[s]imultaneously smart and stupid" (133). Similarly complex intellectual and emotional dynamics attend the reader of even so dissimilar a book as Loos's *Gentlemen Prefer Blondes*, wherein the narrator "Lorelei's 'unreliability,' arising not from duplicity but stupidity, may be intended to place author and reader in a position of intellectual superiority to the story's narrator," but "this 'pathos of distance' hovers remarkably close to a stream of discourse that continues to solicit the reader's identification and sympathy" (107).

McGurl's charge that readers parse Benjy's section "usually with help" arises from a conviction that modernist fiction can be understood only in school (112), part of a larger observation of the historical irony that a movement that "initially tended to despise" the university has been so thoroughly incorporated into it (113). But I want to divorce the pedagogical impulse from the institutional housing, to suggest that even novels like Faulkner's function in a fashion akin to far more approachable work like Loos's, that both teach us how to read in and on their own particular terms, and that those terms entail precisely this variance of affection and identification. McGurl's elaboration of the ways in which we are assimilated at some times to character viewpoints and at others to authorial ones accords with what I am calling, respectively, mimetic and aesthetic investments. Where his work is summary and tends toward the synthetic, mine dilates at length on the dynamics, and developments, of individual works. And where his preserves the pole of distinction by its focus on the uneducated foil to the sophistication of author, novel, and reader, mine explores the possibilities afforded by the blurring of these positions. This places the works I discuss halfway into territory Radway claims for the middlebrow, in pointed contradistinction to the long-reigning construction of modernism that in fact helped give birth to it.

Radway's history of the Book-of-the-Month Club describes lead judge Henry Canby, for example, as "distressed by the extreme distance between writer and reader that a highly idiosyncratic and demanding language like Joyce's created," and relates his interpretation of "the hermeticism of such language as the product of an attitude of arrogance and dismissal, a move prompted by disdain for the ordinary and the commonplace and by a disrespect for the audience" (291–92). The club, which debuted in 1926, swiftly consolidated its position as an arbiter and expediter of emergent American middlebrow culture in the middle decades of the century by repudiating this stance.[10] Radway not only notes that modernist works were "conspicuously absent" in the aggregate list of monthly main selections, although they frequently appeared as alternate choices (279), and that middlebrow culture "developed partly as a reaction to the arrival of various forms of literary modernism, which both critiqued and exploded the conventions on which claims to realistic representation were based" (364), she sees as well in the club's embrace of realism a commitment to literature that suggests "a fundamental continuity and congruity between an author, a book, its evoked presences, and its readers" (282). This fourfold homology no doubt outpaces, and is emotionally more straightforward than, the slippages between authors, readers, and characters that I trace in the following chapters. Both books and the "evoked presences" within them become mutable chips in the play I chart between author and reader, and the latter two figures are also much less than static. One indicator of these layered complexities is the way middlebrow culture itself figures in the texts I treat: Stein appeals to it throughout the *Autobiography*, but Nabokov parodies it in Lolita's tastes; its genre conventions are harnessed in the Kevin Spacey films and, more diffusely, in Eggers' memoir. Middlebrow is, in Radway's construction of it, less arch than any of these works, less knowing and certainly less formally self-conscious, but it shares key impulses with them. But tracing these continuities, at least implicitly, is an important project, not least because middlebrow so often serves critics as an other to high literary art.[11] Rather than trying to parse the modernist or postmodernist brow's descent, or to place its final elevation, I would argue that what the century witnesses most importantly is a continual furrowing of that brow, which registers neither capitulation nor resentment so much as a strategy of engagement, accompanied as it routinely is by an education in how to dig oneself in and out of those furrows.

William Faulkner and Gertrude Stein, for example, writing a mere three years apart, offer diametrically opposed but finally deeply consonant ruminations on relinquishing the authorial I. Each effects a theatrical self-effacement and surrendering of narrative agency— Faulkner through maximal modernist stylization and formal innovation in *As I Lay Dying*, Stein by apparently backsliding into the anodyne voice and diction of *The Autobiography of Alice B. Toklas*—that I read as no more than theater, in that both ultimately underscore authorial control rather than cede it. In Chapter One, I argue against the critical consensus that Faulkner's fracturing of *As I Lay Dying* into the disparate voices and psychologies of his characters—famously giving the narrative over entirely to their many disparate monologues—in the final analysis wholly immerses the reader in the atomized world described. While the reader certainly experiences the novel's disjunctions and the resulting pathos, her ultimate relation to it mirrors that of the author—whose absence is neither total nor final. The reading process, like that of the writing before it, integrates the whole, in part via an awareness of novel-spanning rhetorical and metaphorical consonances that afford an entirely different relation to narrated event than that experienced by the characters. Thus, while most critics see the novel as ratifying Addie Bundren's claim that "words dont ever fit even what they are trying to say at" (171), I contend that it is actually predicated not on linguistic failure but rather on surfeit, that the novel's essential claim is precisely the difference between experience inside it and outside. *As I Lay Dying* provides a counterpoint to the works that follow, however, in that the character of the author himself remains obscure. Faulkner's self-proclaimed "tour-de-force" is clear-eyed in its bid for posterity, but he exercises no charismatic appeal to the reader in pursuit of that goal. Instead, he posits a purely structural identification between reader and author, one he does not sweeten in affective terms.

Gertrude Stein does the opposite. She treats herself in the third-person, abandons her highly identifiable voice in order to write in that of her longtime partner, Alice Toklas, and cedes her almost stolid narrative mode to Toklas's more flighty and freewheeling associative leaps. But when Stein reveals her authorship in the final sentence, the effect is considerably more personal than in Faulkner's case; she trades on the appeal she has made through Toklas's chatty persona to construct an avenue into the daunting remainder of her own literary corpus. Finding the hidden and ostensibly forbidding author here means also finding that one already likes her, cementing the book's repudiation of the caricatured Stein—pretentious, gnomic, inane—long pilloried and parodied in the American press. But if the book's explicit closing revelation is that it is not just predominantly about Stein but also by her, I argue in Chapter Two that its deeper agenda returns Toklas to the fore by measuring linguistically and syntactically the progress of her education in avant-garde aesthetics. As Toklas's itinerary converges with Stein's, so too does the reader's, schooled as Toklas is in a new aesthetic and likewise driven onward by teleologies both formal and temporal, the endpoint of which—in both cases—is Stein herself. Toklas thus becomes the ideal intermediary between Stein and the reader by standing in for both, hyperbolically auguring the reader's own transition from a project of identification of Stein as celebrity to one of identification with her as artist, and further—by way of a pun on "know" in the book's last sentence—from comprehension to intimacy.

In Chapters Three, Four, and Five, apparent relinquishing is replaced by studied deployment of authorial persona multiplied, displaced, sometimes fractured. Indeed, the overlap and variance from one text to the next with regard to what we perceive as an author come to the fore in these discussions. In Chapter Three I argue that the task conferred on the reader by *Lolita* is less finding the author per se (traces and avatars abound in the text) than finding a version of the author she feels comfortable believing. The chapter is grounded in Nabokov's short essay "On a Book Entitled *Lolita*," which first appeared (in a bid to secure American publication) a year after the novel it now routinely appends. Nabokov blurs the boundaries of the novel, fuzzing the line between production and reception, by rendering material found only here central to the project of interpreting the work as a whole. But these exegetical keys are offset by the fashion in which the novel offers itself as a lens through which to view the afterword, constructing even the earnest Nabokov found here as another character, one meant to be read—over his own protestations—through Humbert Humbert rather than against him. Indeed, while Nabokov offers a defense of his book in both aesthetic and ethical terms, he employs numerous images and metaphors all too readily deconstructed by reference to Humbert's own. Thus I argue that Nabokov not only foresees but foreordains the formal defenses as well as the moral condemnations of the work, that he counts on both to fully realize its potential. The energy of Stein's book is dedicated to encouraging the reader's recognition of parallels between author, narrator, and reader; here the same parallels constitute *Lolita*'s greatest threat: only by successfully distinguishing between Nabokov and Humbert, and allying him- or herself with the former, can the reader feel safe in enjoying the book. I argue that the novel is devoted to making this task imperative, and equally to making it impossible.

Dave Eggers' memoir, *A Heartbreaking Work of Staggering Genius*, consolidates much that precedes it: a Stein-like appeal for popular approbation written (intermittently) in avowedly Nabokovian prose, it features as a leitmotif a reiteration of the dilemma at the heart of *As I Lay Dying*—in this case Eggers' mother's death and his attempt to dispose of her remains and memorialize her properly. Eggers betrays only a limited recognition of these inheritances from my other texts, but not for any lack of immersion in twentieth-century writing. In fact, the reviewers' standard line was that the work is all but derailed by its literary self-consciousness, that the extended self-referential game-playing of the fifty small-print pages at the outset and the continuing formal experiments in the remainder of the text consistently detract from an otherwise forceful performance. I argue in Chapter Four, instead, that the book's ultimate success is in fact predicated on precisely this self-consciousness, which extends as far as an extremely canny—finally transformative—perspective on the postmodern conventions that Eggers famously imports into the work of memoir. The book begins mired in awareness of its own apparently insuperable distance from the reader it so zealously courts, fixated on its mediated and commodified form, only in order to refine a radically new stance from these givens. Eggers ultimately exhorts the reader to crucify him, and then proposes the book to the reader as a Eucharist-like transmuted form of Eggers' own body, making good on his brother's earlier observation that in Eggers' set celebrity and divinity are more or less equated. While this elaboration of the vapidity of contemporary culture, like the ontological play subtending it, may be read as confirming Eggers' status as an ideal postmodern subject, it also speaks to a yearning for an alternative. Various critics have noted a sporadic embrace of premodern ontologies within certain strains of postmodern writing; Eggers' innovation is to render this desire in performative terms, to collate it with a hunger for the author, and to enroll his reader as a collaborator in meeting it.

My turn to film in Chapter Five highlights, again, the degree to which contemporary artworks (and not merely books) are not simply legible by way of literary theory, but indeed are a form of literary theory. I take up *Seven* and *The Usual Suspects* as a self-conscious continuation of the debates I've traced in the preceding pages (and thus an ideal site for my own renewed explicit engagement with Barthes)—but one that trades handsomely on the opportunities afforded by carrying this reflection to the narrative and visual space of film.

The language at the end of *AHWOSG* conscripts the reader into effecting Eggers' metaphorical crucifixion and then his resurrection in an instant, coincident with simply reading the last sentence of the work. But the sequence remains notional, of necessity unnarrated, because the death can be enacted and registered only by the cessation of Eggers' writing. This "death" yokes the book's author to his self-representation within the text more firmly than in any of the previous examples, but the very collation requires that the death itself constitute a representational limit. *Seven* and *The Usual Suspects* sidestep this limit by divorcing the matter of their own authorship from the construction of the authorial stand-ins they introduce within their narratives. Each focuses on a character who is a magisterial, but metaphorical, authorial figure: a sublimely malevolent criminal mastermind who unfailingly snares all those around him in his designs, who enrolls the police pursuing him as interpreters and exegetes, and who eludes them completely through his own death (literal or figurative) at the close of the film.

By situating the "author" firmly within their diegeses, the films are able to rehearse the dynamics of the reader's experience of the death of the author within their narratives themselves. Unlike Barthes, who cagily elides any claim as to exactly when or even whether the author has died, these films imagine the moment as one we can, on the strength of the best detective work, identify and witness. This dramatization offers a different mode of literary critique, one that makes it possible not only to theorize but also to narrate—to theorize by narrating—the aftermath of the death of the author. The argument, in both cases, accords with the one I make throughout *Obscure Invitations*: that apparent authorial death (overstated as it almost invariably is), rather than liberating the reader, only tangles him further in the author's plots. Envisioning this development becomes a literal and self-conscious undertaking; each film turns finally on concretely assimilating the audience-member's point of view to that of the author. Both films propose the project of envisioning as the only way to track the author, but both suggest that such an undertaking courts thoroughgoing cooptation by the author. Ultimately, however, both yoke their deepest reflections to the advent of digital technologies of storage, transmission, playback, and response that render cinematic images virtually as navigable as prose, and thus to a final transmutation of the status of the visual text. *Seven*—in keeping with its modernist imaginary—proposes the resulting ascension of the reader as the most ingenious and malign element of the author's plan, but *The Usual Suspects* finishes with a post-postmodern flourish, affectively rehabilitating the author even as the reader stands poised to complement or perhaps to supplant him—suggesting that what theory got wrong about literature in the middle of the twentieth century may yet prove a crucial, if still only partial, insight regarding a much broader swathe of culture in the twenty-first.

1

FIT AND SURFEIT
As I Lay Dying
(seesawing)

"'Meet Mrs Bundren,' he says."

Anse Bundren's introduction, "kind of hangdog and proud too" (Faulkner 261), of his new wife to his astonished children, less than twenty-four hours after they have finally managed to inter Addie Bundren, Anse's first wife and the children's mother, strikes many readers as an outrage. The brief, five-word declaration closes the novel in a stunned silence, borne on currents of shock and disbelief. These responses stem from two related sources. To any reader of the novel, as to the children themselves, "Mrs Bundren" means Addie. In nominating a new Mrs. Bundren so precipitously on the heels of the old, Anse flouts not only the social decorum of mourning rituals and the emotional well-being of his offspring, but also conventions of linguistic usage, wrenching the appellation from its accustomed denotation without warning or fanfare.[1]

For all that it shocks, however, Anse's dramatization of the potential mismatch between a word's immediate context and the greater range of signification that might conceivably accrue to it merely represents a final surfacing at the level of plot, and in a form inescapably flagged for the reader's attention, of the novel's deeper schema. Here, the doublings and confusions of mimetic vocabulary yield an increasingly robust and pointed aesthetic play.

An earlier version of this chapter appeared in *Novel: A Forum on Fiction*, 2007 Fall; 41 (1): 99–120. Copyright © Novel Corp., 2007.

Faulkner liked to boast of having written the manuscript "in six weeks, without changing a word," in later years adding that he "set out deliberately to write a tour-de-force." "Before I ever put pen to paper and set down the first words," he maintained, "I knew what the last word would be."[2] While the veracity of the first of these claims has been marginally attenuated by subsequent critical excavation,[3] the latter grows only more convincing if we read it as speaking not just to the last words' emotional force, but also to the broader highly specific and thoroughly premeditated lexical strategy they might imply.

Anse acts with an authorial hauteur, not just in the deictic panache with which he introduces the new Mrs. Bundren, but also in the careful design that suddenly seems evident in his apparent floundering. Anse, a sublimely lazy man who undertakes no labor he can impose on someone else, effects a "tour-de-force" of his own, a literal "turn" from his rural home to the county seat for the first time in more than a decade (42). He, too, may well have known the last word of this journey from the start.[4] His sad-sack demeanor and stumblebum parenting give over to an audacious assertion of paternal authority that, in its frank and determined harnessing of linguistic indeterminacy, positions the novel's unexpected ending as a lesson in how best to read the book as a whole. On the final page, no one can avoid thinking "Addie" when Anse says "Mrs Bundren" and means, quite obviously, someone other than Addie. But *As I Lay Dying*, throughout, as if building to and from this dénouement, consistently rewards the reader who remembers a word's meaning from one context and imparts it to another even when the latter appears self-evidently sufficient.

Until the book's abrupt conclusion, however, nothing directly provokes the reader into such maneuvers, even if one might retrospectively register a series of invitations proffered by the frequent repetition of particular words, the echoing use of a cycling set of metaphors, the occasional stutter of a single word into multiple significations in an individual monologue. But for all that Faulkner criticism has long set itself the goal of evaluating Addie's acerbic contention that "words dont ever fit even what they are trying to say at" (171), and has been deeply sensitive to the swirling network of metaphors constituting the text,[5] it has generally followed the implicit drift of Addie's pronouncement (and its pugnacious closing preposition) to focus on what appear to be words' intended objects.[6] Readings have centered, therefore, on the degree of language's adequacy as representation of external or internal monologues: on its attempts to articulate self-knowledge or the position of the self in the midst of a social sphere, to convey the weight of death, loss, motherhood, poverty, and so on.[7]

Criticism of *As I Lay Dying*, then, has organized itself around referentiality, while I will explore what I might call "cross-referentiality," and which I would nominate as the most underappreciated mode of aesthetic play in the novel. That is, I will concentrate on what words do not immediately appear to be trying to say, what lies outside their obvious mimetic purview, but what they are nonetheless also saying. Formally, the instances I examine are close kin of puns, but for the difference in their etiology. Puns trade on swiftly apprehensible overdeterminacy of meaning deriving from their immediate surroundings or from words or phrases readily at hand in the lexicon. I am concerned, instead, with words that seem to be wholly defined and delimited by their local contexts, arriving at further signification only through a process of willful and initially counterintuitive distortion on the reader's part, a distortion I argue the novel slowly nudges the reader toward. By looking at words' meanings imported into new contexts across swathes of text both great and small, I argue that the opposite of "not fitting" is not necessarily "fitting" in a strictly delimited sense, that it may instead be resonating and echoing in ways that Addie does not even pause to consider. This phonic reverberation yields a new interpretive framework in which mimetic referentiality is coupled with and complicated by a sporadic cross-referential appeal to words retrofitted to new ends. At stake is not a deconstructive, endlessly free play of the signifier, but rather a more limited degree of play harnessed to the specific objectives not only of adding new layers to our understanding of particular moments in the narrative but also of stressing aesthetic qualities of the text that are pointedly not reducible to the representation of either particular moments or solitary psychologies.

Attention to this facet of *As I Lay Dying* demands reading not just against the characters' explicit referential goals, but also against the text's most obvious divisions—against the chapters as discrete units and against the isolation of individual consciousnesses that the chapter breaks reflect—in order to illuminate larger coherences born of the characters' multiple voices, but utterly unassimilable to those voices and unavailable to the characters themselves. The novel presents itself as totally interior to the characters—devoid of framing devices, scrupulously mimetic (if in its own maddeningly idiosyncratic fashion), steadfastly refusing narratorial suturing of its motley parts—and yet it has always struck readers by the manner in which it transcends that interiority: its dark humor at the characters' expense, the strange consonances of disparate characters' deeply internal metaphysical ruminations, the repetitiveness or complementariness of imagery distributed through the text.

In adding to the catalogue of indices of this fundamental irony, further yoking the monologues and stressing the ways in which the language of the novel exceeds that of its myriad individual speakers, I aim to highlight what emerges over time as a series of salient differences between readers' and the characters' experiences of the novel's events. Much of the strongest criticism of *As I Lay Dying* has pursued—implicitly or explicitly—a goal more or less diametrically opposite, reading for what Eric Sundquist, in one of the most incisive and lasting readings of the novel, calls the "analogous form" of the characters' travails and our attempts to navigate Faulkner's text.[8] Sundquist argues that the novel is governed for both character and reader by fragmentation, its motherless characters mirrored by the discontinuous, "orphaned" monologues that foster in its readers a sense of disarray and desolation (39), "the vacuum created by [Faulkner's] own authorial absence . . . bound up with the vacuum created by Addie's death" (32). Sundquist's reading of the novel's challenges is highly compelling; the profound gaps and jumps—temporal, perceptual, affective, stylistic—that are the price of our progress through the work indeed radically underscore the lack of an obvious guide to help us along, and they manifest the threat of what a novel without a controlling intelligence might feel like. But the sense of loss thus engendered—whether of a mothering hand or of an authorial one—is only part of the experience provided by the book as a whole, underselling precisely the wholeness of the final experience. For all that we remain keenly attuned to, and even share in, the characters' frustrations throughout, the novel also encourages responses at odds with them. To the end, the characters remain isolated from one another; readers, however, come not only to recognize the patterns and proclivities of individual narrators, but also to find themselves increasingly adroit at jockeying between them, registering and reveling in the myriad connections lurking within the monologues' distinct rhetorics. The specific brief of the pages to follow is to show how Faulkner facilitates and accentuates this developing acumen at the level of the individual word, encouraging a reading process that at last reaps from the vocabulary of loss a syntax of plenitude. This plenitude, predicated on a syntax that is the novel's rather than any single character's, constitutes an alternative emotional register, an invitation to indulge in aesthetic satisfactions denied to the characters—and thus an invitation that leaves us seesawing between an empathetic identification with the characters' plight and an intellectual-cum-emotional pleasure that we share with the author, whose putative absence is, in fact, repudiated in this very fashion.

Reading for plenitude, for what the novel says with cross-referential winks and nods and feints tonally at odds with its referential subject matter, means reading not just with Addie, for linguistic fit, but also beyond her, for linguistic surfeit. *As I Lay Dying* provides a heuristic for the work I do throughout this book thanks to the starkness with which it makes this opposition visible, the fashion in which its formal design facilitates our grasp of dual understandings of the text: the referential, identificatory experience we share with the characters, and the cross-referential, linguistic experience we share with the author. *As I Lay Dying* is anomalous, though, in that Faulkner makes so little effort to invest the authorial side of this equation with any pointedly personal flavor. He provides a simple structural model, alone, that will be elaborated upon by the various charismatic appeals I trace in the following chapters. My focus here, then, is on making clear the operations of this divided system itself. This should not distract, however, from my overarching insistence on the dialectical relation between referential and cross-referential modes of response. While I spend considerable time detailing the latter (in contradistinction to the prevailing critical focus on the former), my largest point is that rather than diverging entirely, the two are ultimately very much in dialogue with each other. Faulkner does not simply hold the aesthetic in opposition to a more constrained sense of the mimetic, but rather each informs and ultimately re-forms the other, making the novel not merely a step forward on the long trajectory from mimetic realism into modernist and postmodernist aesthetics of textual play, but also a highly self-conscious, productively oscillatory performance of and commentary on that transition.

Parsing and placing that intervention require mapping the nudges toward cross-referentiality that pepper the novel, initially by attending to the many linguistic details that first begin to suggest to the reader the import of the book's extensive verbal reiterations. A particularly resonant group centers on the verb "to lie," immediately brought into relief by the conspicuous ambiguity of its usage in the title: potentially either grammatically correct past tense or colloquial present. The unresolvable tension between present and past tense not only gestures, as numerous critics have noted, toward the stupefying challenge faced by the characters in relinquishing an intimate to the grave, but also flags the range of other associations the novel draws for the reader between instances of "laying" and "lying."

Vardaman's infamous youthful misapprehension, "My mother is a fish" (84), for example, is the fruit not just of the psychological mechanisms of a child dealing with death, but also of Faulkner's several descriptions of the fish "laying" or "a-laying" in the dust (31, 56, 70), as Addie "lies" or "lays" in bed, will lie in the coffin and in the earth, and so on (5, 8, 15, 18, 23, etc.). The posthumous decomposition of Addie's body likewise stands ironically foreshadowed when Doctor Peabody, finding his hopes of dining on the fish frustrated, overconfidently assures Dewey Dell that "it'll save, I reckon" (60). But in the hardscrabble world the novel describes, once the time is put out of joint by Addie's death, little is saved and nothing keeps; Peabody does not get to eat the fish at a later point, and Addie's body rots. While the fish lies motionless in the dust (31), and Addie lies "still in bed" (32), Anse worries—correctly—that she'll die before the corn is "laid-by" (33), and the fragile stasis of the novel's opening chapters (Addie poised at the brink of death, the weather "fixing up to rain" [18]) is disrupted by Tull's observation that "clouds like that don't lie" (32), meaning both that they don't deceive and that they won't sit still (and that, therefore, a hard rain will fall). Later, much of the angst of Addie's affair with Reverend Whitfield—and the conflict between sex as an expression of desire and sex as domestic procreative duty—is captured in the rueful twinge of Addie's "[t]hen I would lay with Anse again—I did not lie to him: I just refused" (175), and Whitfield's own self-recounting which immediately follows: "'Rise,' He said, 'repair to that home in which you have put a living lie'" (177). The book's biting comic side, meanwhile, is already revealed when the ominous close of Darl's first monologue—"Addie Bundren could not want a better one, a better box to lie in" (5)—is speedily offset by the opening of Cora's—"We depend a lot on our chickens. They are good layers" (6).[9]

In this last example, the bathetic displacement of steely, taciturn Addie by prattling Cora's chickens offers not only a quick wash of humor, but also a degree of insight into the interpretive purchase that may be gained by interrogating such verbal juxtapositions. The reader is invited to compare not only Addie dying and the chickens giving birth, but also the "boxes" associated with each: Addie's coffin and the hens' coop. While Darl has assured us of the quality of the former, Cora complains that the latter is not always sufficient proof against possums and snakes (6). The reader might irreverently query whether Addie's superlative box will make her a better layer than Cora's chickens, but then might more soberly extend the thought: will it make her a better lie-er? or liar? Whitfield, in fact, hurries to the Bundrens' so that he may confess to the "living lie" of his affair, in fear that Addie—living lie, indeed—will tell the truth on her deathbed. When she does not, the seal of the grave in fact becomes the best insurance Whitfield might ask that the lie not be repudiated.

Other effects are much more localized, based on quick repetitions within a confined space rather than on invocation of a keyword stressed earlier. Vernon Tull's narration of the night Addie dies and the work on her coffin, for example, segues into a discussion of Anse's moral uprightness compared with that of Vernon's wife, Cora, such that the discovery that Vardaman has drilled holes through the top of Addie's coffin—"When they taken the lid off they found that two of [the holes] had bored on into her face"—is immediately followed by Tull's estimation of Anse—"I think to myself he aint that less of a man or he couldn't a bore himself this long"—and then his quoting Cora's self-justification for having no sons: "I have bore you what the Lord God sent me" (73). Here, too, the apparently light, if perverse, humor of the repeated word opens into a broad consideration of the relations of individuals to their offspring or even to themselves in the face of extreme conditions or simple protracted time—how one bears what one has borne, or what has borne one—questions that are essentially those of the novel as a whole.[10]

Elsewhere, Faulkner exploits such verbal echoes to structure both quick chiasmi and tremendously distended ones. When Jewel and Darl depart early in the novel to deliver a final load of wood while Addie's health hangs in the balance, Tull confidently tells Darl, "Time you and Jewel get back, she'll be setting up" (17), while Anse frets a moment later that Addie will die in their absence: "Wagon or no wagon, she wouldn't wait. Then she'd be upset" (18–19). Anse's claim regarding the propriety of Cash's building Addie's coffin directly beneath her window—"she will rest quieter for knowing . . . that it was her own blood sawed out the boards" (19)—on the other hand, provides the ground for a bitter riff spanning hundreds of pages to bring home the dense imbrication of life and work in the Bundren family. The intensely personal—to the point of pathological anthropomorphizing—investment Cash and the others will make in the coffin leads to Vardaman's wide-eyed characterization of "Cash going up and down above the saw, at the bleeding plank" (65), and the toll that investment takes on the family's health finds expression in Darl's wry summary: "Cash broke his leg and now the sawdust is running out. He is bleeding to death is Cash" (207).

In each of these last two examples a dead metaphor—the etymological sense of "upset," the visceral meaning of "blood" ties—achieves a new physicality in what initially seem to be decidedly unpoetic circumstances. In the latter case, the mounting tension as Anse's unmarked, unselfconscious figure of speech is transposed and ratcheted up to increasing levels of audacity by Vardaman and then Darl highlights starkly the potential yield to tracking words and phrases across great expanses of text. The former case demonstrates that the same potential extends to the most pedestrian of words and usages, even absent the heightened rhetoric of Darl's and Vardaman's metaphors, the gravity conferred by Vardaman's assault on the coffin, or the explicit thematic freighting around the verb "to lie." With this in mind, I concentrate in the remainder of this chapter on what I find to be by far the most extensive, though initially one of the least obtrusive, of these systems of echo and revision in the novel: one predicated on the unprepossessing words "see" and "saw." It trades on their individual meanings as infinitives, on the second as past tense of the first, and—surprisingly, admittedly—on their ability to conjure together a sort of virtual "seesaw." The initial implausibility of this claim is belied, I argue, by the extent to which the ongoing up-and-down motion of a seesaw reverberates with the plot elements, descriptive tropes, rhetorical operations,[11] and philosophical imaginings that constitute the novel, and ultimately with my largest account of the fluctuating mode of reading the novel requires.

Darl introduces the requisite halves of this term in the book's opening chapter: "Although I am fifteen feet ahead of him, anyone watching us from the cottonhouse can see Jewel's frayed and broken straw hat a full head above my own" . . . "I pass him and mount the path, beginning to hear Cash's saw" (3, 4), the full page intervening bridged by the double reference to the brothers' relative positions, the positions again characterized by (in this case, double) inversion (Darl in front, Jewel passing him in the ellipsed portion of the text, Darl again regaining the lead). Cora uses the words in much quicker succession in the following monologue as she describes Addie surrounded by the Tull womenfolk: "She is propped on the pillow, with her head raised so she can see out the window, and we can hear him every time he takes up the adze or the saw" (8). Seeing and sawing appear straightforward and independent at this juncture, as if already flagged as signature verbs for the two characters—Cash has been introduced with the simple, repeated declarative: "A good carpenter, Cash is" (4), and Addie, motionless and "wasted away" (8), is so reduced to her gaze that in the opening forty-three pages of the novel "only her eyes seem to move" (43)—but they participate simultaneously in another, joint dynamic.

Though it seems that little beyond the simple pleasure of euphony, and the English language's own precedent in including the word "seesaw,"[12] pulls "see" and "saw" toward each other, the surrounding passages suggest otherwise. While Addie does little but see in the opening of the novel, the converse is not true; seeing extends far beyond her vision. The entire novel is crowded (even relative to other works by Faulkner) with reference to eyes, looking, watching, gazes met or averted, blindness and sight, winking and blinking and other nonverbal communication, and highly stylized visual panoramas, and it is crowned by the stubborn issue of what is usually called Darl's clairvoyance.[13]

Even against a backdrop so rich in ocular tropes, though, Cora's first section offers a particularly replete constellation. After her opening narrative of frustrated cake-baking, Cora twice consoles herself with her conviction that "the Lord can see into the heart" (7, 8). From here, her attention shifts to the room around her, where she and her daughters have gathered at Addie's deathbed. She presents an elaborate skein of both sight and sound that quickly sensitizes the reader to both, and under even passing scrutiny, ends up radically—and productively—defamiliarizing the terminology as it accretes. The women, as we have seen, are watching Addie watch Cash build her coffin, and they can hear him saw. "If we were deaf," Cora adds, "we could almost watch her face and hear him, see him" (8). They could see, that is, the saw. She continues: "[Addie's] eyes are like two candles when you watch them. . . . You can see that girl's washing and ironing. . . . Maybe it will reveal [Addie's] blindness to her. . . . 'Is she sleeping?' Kate whispers. 'She's just watching Cash'. . . . We can hear the saw. . . . It sounds like snoring. Eula . . . looks out the window. Her necklace looks real nice. . . . [Darl] comes through the hall . . . He does not look in. . . . Eula watches him as he goes on and passes from sight. . . . When she finds [Cora] watching her, her eyes go blank" (8–9). The density of visual vocabulary paves the way for the key words to begin to warble and transmute, since "saw" is also the past tense of "see." As one starts to pay close attention, the notion of seeing or hearing the saw becomes increasingly odd. Before long, it will become wholly significant in its own right.

Five pages later, Jewel ups the rhythm and the ante: "It's because he stays out there, right under the window, hammering and sawing on that goddamn box. Where she's got to see him. Where every breath she draws is full of his knocking and sawing where she can see him saying See. See what a good one I am making for you. I told him to go somewhere else. I said Good God do you want to see her in it. . . . Sawing and knocking . . . until everybody that passes in the road will have to stop and see it and say . . ." (14–15). Jewel's addition of "say" to the "see"/"saw" dyad returns us to the opening of Cora's monologue.

In recounting the trials of poultry-farming, Cora emphasizes twice, immediately preceding her enunciation of the "sees" and "saws," that it was on her "say-so" that she and Vernon Tull bought the more expensive variety of chickens (6, 7). Not only does her word-choice prepare the reader's ear for the seesaw to follow; her entire narrative presents a long series of seesawing fortunes. The "say-so" itself seesaws implicitly between Cora and Vernon (she suggests the costlier chickens, he "admits that a good breed of cows or hogs pays in the long run" [7], and they take them on her final say-so); the initial cost is meant to be offset by the eventual greater return on a good breed; the apparent wisdom of Miss Lawington's encouraging Cora in her choice runs afoul of the loss of several chickens to possums and snakes, but Cora promises that "the difference in the number of eggs would make it up" (6). When they can't afford to use the eggs themselves, Miss Lawington relays an order for cakes from a wealthy lady in town, who subsequently cancels her party and reneges on the order; meanwhile, between the commission and the baking, Cora "sav[es] out enough eggs . . . so that the flour and the sugar and the stove wood would not be costing anything" (7).

As "see" and "saw" become increasingly interlaced, such that the use of one term begins to shepherd the attuned reader's mind to the other, thanks both to the words' phonic proximity and to the trajectories of action and attention around Addie's bed, so, too, does the notion of seesawing start to achieve a degree of suggestive force. The thematic of seesawing describes far more than Cora's dogged efforts to turn each loss into future profit, along with the rising and falling luck that compels her to do so. A larger logic of offsetting, whereby the fate or value of one object or individual stands in inverse relation to that of another, informs much of the novel. Darl and Jewel jockey more or less consciously with each other for preeminent position, not only in ascending the path to the house, but more explicitly and more importantly in their rivalry for Addie's affections. Most readers gloss the latter competition as a sort of zero-sum game in which Darl, in fact, ends up with absolutely nothing.[14] Addie's own arithmetical calculation of her children's worth to Anse plainly suggests that Dewey Dell functions "to negative Jewel" (176), the child born of her affair with Whitfield. Most of the family members arguably employ a similar strategy in attempting to cope with Addie's death. Donald Kartiganer highlights the relevance of the psychoanalytic model of mourning elaborated through an extension of D. W. Winnicott's concept of the "transitional object." Winnicott elucidates the way a privileged blanket corner, or a repeated "word or tune, or a mannerism," can help a child first manage its mother's intermittent absences (Winnicott 4), softening the process of "reality-acceptance" (13) that must overcome the infant's illusion of omnipotence, its failure to grasp the distinctions between self and other. In an analogous process, Kartiganer writes, each of the Bundrens (except Darl) fixes on "a physical object . . . the coffin itself, the set of false teeth, the foetus, the fish, the tools, the toy train, the graphophone—which enables a passage from grief to recovery" ("Repetition" 38).[15] In the present context, we may substitute for the vocabulary of linear progress—"transition," "passage"—one of offsetting masses. The characters invest their objects with sufficient weight to compensate for the loss of mother or wife and to restore their lives to sustainable equipoise.

But the precarious status suggested by this new metaphorical schema—a mere balanced scale instead of the firm assurance of ground covered and the past left behind—may give us pause. Ultimately, I want to demonstrate that the perilousness of this mode of entrusting to a simple substitution the task of rendering the past past structures the novel's final moments and our response to them, and in that context to take up the notion of the transitional object again. But earlier in the novel, too, the treacherous status of any balance, literal or metaphorical, informs both plot and character development. Most obviously, Cash's extreme solicitude regarding the coffin centers on his having "made it to balance with her" (90). That balance is compromised by Addie's being "laid . . . in [the coffin] reversed . . . head to foot so it wouldn't crush her dress" (88), and Cash's woeful refrain echoes through the coffin's misadventures, predictive of each mishap (96, 144, 145, 165), until, in the course of the family's attempt to bring wagon and coffin across the rain-swollen river, his leg is broken. Imbalance then becomes Cash's own attribute, the injury requiring, in Peabody's words, that he "limp around on one short leg for the balance of [his] life" (240). Cash's equipoise is metaphorically imperiled here, a fact registered by his internal questioning of the way family and community have disposed of Darl: "Sometimes I think it aint none of us pure crazy and aint none of us pure sane until the balance of us talks him that-a-way" (233). In this last, "balance" almost means its opposite—an overwhelming preponderance; a man isn't sane or insane, but rocks back and forth, until communal consensus weighs in unequivocally, suspending him high in the air: "It's like it aint so much what a fellow does, but it's the way the majority of folks is looking at him when he does it. . . . That's how I reckon a man is crazy. That's how he cant see eye to eye with other folks" (233–34). Cash's conclusion places him in a somewhat equivocal position: aware of the potential injustice of, yet participating in, social determinations of individual status. His complacency in the face of the novel's final events testifies to his eventual acceptance of the way of the world, his smoothing of mentally ruffled edges. But the tenuously bifurcated consciousness he momentarily presents may linger in the reader's mind, cutting against the grain of Cash's own pronouncements at the end of the novel, highlighting ironies that he hides from himself and validating reactions at odds with his own.

The path to these ironies begins at Addie's bedside, at the moment where "see" and "saw" begin the process of their most thorough imbrication. In the initial moment of Addie's seeing Cash sawing, Cash also sees her seeing. "He looks up at the gaunt face framed by the window in the twilight. It is a composite picture of all time since he was a child. He drops the saw and lifts the board for her to see, watching . . ." (48). When Addie dies, Cash brings the saw with him to her bedchamber (50), and, thanks to Faulkner's penchant for neologism and functional shift, the "saw" doubles as a synecdoche for the past to which he clings, the surveillance under which he has worked. As Addie expires, and Cash "labor[s] on toward darkness and into it" (48), the saw becomes imbued with an almost mystical force, "as though the stroking of the saw illumined its own motion, board and saw engendered" (48); when she has died, it is only Cash's movements "stirring the dying light" that yield the final illusion of life (50), "so that at each stroke her face seems to wake a little into an expression of listening and of waiting" (50).

Faulkner's metaphorical transpositions begin to gain speed here, as if the "board and saw engendered" at the moment Addie dies do indeed stand in for her in a variety of fashions through the remainder of the novel, flanking the more obvious coffin and nuancing the account of the novel's mechanisms beyond that which might be garnered from the coffin alone. Cash's "saw"—functioning as a physical object with an emotional charge (as well as obvious economic value and professional utility) for the characters, and endowed with an extra, linguistic twist for the reader—becomes another site for the memory of Addie. After she has been rescued from the flooded river, a lengthy search continues for Cash's tools, which have been lost in the crossing. The last one recovered is the saw (162), through a process of instrumentalizing the hammer, the chalk-line, and the plane (insisting on their nature as mere tools, devoid of the sort of symbolic resonance now accruing to the saw), to see where the saw (its status more equivocal) would have run aground. The saw-set, on the other hand—the "device for setting the angle of the bent teeth [of a saw] accurately and uniformly" (Brown 169)[16]—is never found. The loss of the saw-set—and thus, symbolically, of orderly relation to or determination by the past—foreshadows the rising horror and chaos of the progress toward Jefferson, as Addie's body decomposes ever more obscenely and her family members increasingly pursue their own ends.

The board, on the other hand, obviously becomes a part of Addie's coffin, and shares its fate. But it also gestures toward several moments where Addie, herself, is depicted as resembling a mute piece of wood, prey to the larger forces around her and—tellingly—canted one way or another like the plank of a seesaw. A mere paragraph after her initial enunciation of the seesaw trope, Cora remarks that "under the quilt [Addie] makes no more of a hump than a rail would," her breathing and movement already dwindled to the point of being perceptible only through the gentle up-and-down evidenced by "the sound of the mattress shucks" (8). And Darl's description turns directly from the moment of Addie's final paralysis in death, following the last time in which "she raises herself, who has not moved in ten days" (48), to his narration of the wagon he and Jewel have taken with a final load of wood, wrecked in a landscape destroyed by the rain—water, earth, and sky all running together, the sole obdurate fact the wagon's cargo of dull yellow lumber unmoving and *"tilted"* (he says twice in two lines) *"at a steep angle"* (49), like an abandoned seesaw. The final lines of the monologue return to this scene, underscoring the contiguity of the two losses and the seesaw imagery that further joins them: *"ankle-deep in the running ditch,* [Jewel] *pries with a slipping two-by-four, with a piece of rotting log for fulcrum, at the axle. Jewel, I say, she is dead, Jewel. Addie Bundren is dead"* (52, Faulkner's italics).

Addie's posthumous itinerary draws the literal and metaphorical together. The series of grotesquely distended misadventures she endures on the way to Jefferson have in common the continuous careen and pitch of the coffin, like a seesaw gone crazy, from Cash's initial warning that "it wont tote and it wont ride on a balance" (96) as Jewel first lays hand on it and commands that the others "'Pick up!' . . . lifting one whole side so suddenly that [the men] all spring into the lift to catch and balance it before he hurls it completely over. For an instant it resists. . . . Then it breaks free, rising suddenly . . . tilting as the path begins to slant, it begins to rush away from [Darl] and slip down the air like a sled upon invisible snow. . . . turning, [Jewel] lets it overshoot him, swinging, and stops it and sloughs it into the wagon" (97–99). The movement continues through its travels over hill and dale ("'you and him and all the men in the world... dragging us up and down the country,'" Rachel Samson cries [117]), its tumbling escape from water ("the wagon turning over... Cash leaning more and more, trying to keep the coffin braced so it wouldn't slip down and finish tilting the wagon over... the wagon got tilted good.... Then the wagon tilted over" [152–54]) and fire ("We see [Jewel's] shoulders strain as he upends the coffin and slides it single-handed from the sawhorses. It looms unbelievably tall, hiding him... for another instant it stands upright.... Then it topples forward, gaining momentum.... Without stopping it overends and rears again, pauses, then crashes slowly forward" [222])—until it's finally laid to horizontal rest in the ground.[17]

Faulkner does not grant the reader the opportunity, however, to witness that final moment of rest and equilibrium. He elides the burial, even as he dilates on Anse's borrowing and returning the shovels used to dig the grave. Cash says only that "we got it filled and covered" in a dependent clause (237), but there is no description of the coffin's actually being placed in the ground, let alone the words said or the emotions felt at that climactic moment. Instead, Cash turns to the introduction of the new Mrs. Bundren: he refers to the latter twice, as "Mrs Bundren" (235, 236), in his penultimate monologue, relating the events just prior to Addie's interment, and he begins his last section (also the last of the novel) blatantly reiterating the ellipsis that Faulkner has already accomplished more subtly in the preceding chapters: "So when we stopped there to borrow the shovels we heard the graphophone playing in the house, and so when we got done with the shovels pa says, 'I reckon I better take them back'" (258), "there" being the new Mrs. Bundren's house.[18] Three pages later, the novel closes with Anse's introduction of his new wife, which I have already quoted in part: "'It's Cash and Jewel and Vardaman and Dewey Dell,' pa says, kind of hangdog and proud too, with his teeth and all, even if he wouldn't look at us. 'Meet Mrs Bundren,' he says" (261). Anse's avoidance of his children's eyes evidences some shame at the substitution he is foisting upon them, and even recalls Cash's metaphorical account of what testifies to a man's being "crazy," but here Cash seems disinclined to judge.

Faulkner has accomplished a sort of seesaw sleight of hand at Addie's expense, trading on the two different metaphorical modes in which the seesaw functions. We have spent the novel waiting for Addie to finally get the chance to rest in peace, for her seesawing coffin to achieve a final stasis. Instead she has been substituted for by a new object of ostensibly equal weight, aimed at restoring familial equilibrium rather than her own. The Mrs. Bundrens have been balanced, rather than Mrs. Bundren—Addie—herself, and the resolution that ought at long last to accrue to Addie instead occludes her.

As Addie goes, so too does the visual paradigm associated with her. While Cash's attention is immediately drawn by the new Mrs. Bundren's eyes, he finds neither maternal solicitude nor even stern care in this gaze, but rather "kind of hardlooking pop eyes like she was daring ere a man to say nothing" (260). Or, in the novel's tropes, to see nothing or saw nothing, meaning that the aggressivity of her stare signals an end to the entire system of remembering and marking loss for which "seeing" and "sawing" have been figures throughout the novel.[19] Cash's attitude again proves instructive. His regard for his tools has run all along in a narrow space between meticulous and obsessive, but he finally appears quite oblivious to them in the closing chapter, his focus shifting to the period after the workday, and sound replacing sight as dominant sensory input. Cash's basic nature seems to demand devotion to some material object, through most of the novel to the coffin and his tools,[20] both of which contain a "saw." But in the end, these objects are replaced by a new portable, material repository for affect: the graphophone owned by the new Mrs. Bundren.[21] Cash's admiration for it as she and Anse carry it to the wagon (261) echoes his earlier opinion that he doesn't know "if a little music aint about the nicest thing a fellow can have. Seems like when he comes in tired of a night, it aint nothing could rest him like having a little music played and him resting" (259). And he jumps forward in his recounting from his first sight of the graphophone to the following winter, where he has learned to mark time by the arrival of each new record in the mail, and pleasure by the family "setting in the house . . . listening to it" (261).

Cash seems entirely comfortable with the substitution of one Mrs. Bundren for the other and with the slightly narcotic resolution to the family's travails: Darl resurfaces in his thoughts only to be immediately rationalized away (261), and Addie doesn't even reappear. In spite of the plain-spoken sensibility of Cash's final monologues, readers tend to break from him here, feeling anger on behalf of Addie and Darl that Cash himself does not. Indeed, the very blatancy of nominating the new Mrs. Bundren so squarely in the place of the old seems calculated to provoke a different response from the reader than that which Cash displays, a response in keeping with the linguistic model at play throughout the novel. Here, surely, the word's resonance far outstrips its immediate surroundings, recalling in the reader's mind exactly that which Anse attempts to erase. Addie's failure to be properly laid to rest resurfaces now, in a final seesawing displacement: if she has been buried in the interstices of Cash's sentences concerned with other subjects, it is perhaps that she may be exhumed equally as easily, at the mere sound of what was her name.

The irony of Addie's being resuscitated by language, of which she is so contemptuously dismissive, is in keeping with that of the book as a whole; it again establishes the distance between those inside the book (the characters) and those outside (author and readers). For Addie surely reports her own experience accurately. Dorothy J. Hale's elegant elaboration of the spectrum of discursive modes at play in the novel's interior monologues—from a "public language" that would prove entirely "sayable" in conventional dialogue to, at the opposite extreme, a "private language" that wholly eludes communicability (12)—is apposite. Hale suggests that Addie's monologue "explicitly articulates her cynicism about the representational power of social language" and instead finds her searching for an internal mode of expression "that can escape the conventionalism inherent in public language" (14). Her rejection of the language's paltry-seeming words—"I knew that motherhood was invented by someone who had to have a word for it because the ones that had the children didn't care whether there was a word for it or not. I knew that fear was invented by someone that had never had the fear; pride, who never had the pride" (Faulkner 171–72)—has everything to do with her understanding of public language's inadequacy to her private experience, little to do with any actual attempt at communication, and nothing to do with the more literary functionings of language this chapter has addressed. André Bleikasten correctly concludes that Addie envisions "language as a lexicon rather than a syntax" (204), meaning that she judges language on the basis of single words, always lacking when compared to the maelstrom of emotion and event they are meant to stand for, and that she ignores any combinatory potential words might have to suggest, jointly, the enormity of what she feels.[22]

Certainly, language appears to have been of little avail to Addie. If we may surmise (and another effect of the novel's rampant discontinuities is to encourage just such a practice of extrapolation on our part) that the primary conversational partners of her adult life have been the self-righteous Cora and the taciturn Anse, neither of whom, even internally, evidences any desire to stray beyond the realm of resolutely public language, and neither of whom appears to be much of a listener, either, we may imagine Addie's frustration. As if defeated, Addie relies almost exclusively on monosyllables in the dialogues the novel reports with her children. But the whole of her chapter presents a radically different vision, a terrifyingly vivid account of one woman's experience of motherhood. To read Addie's section and to come away feeling that words are fundamentally lacking, or to conclude that it expresses the novel's views regarding language, as so many critics do, is to fall prey to the most forceful statement in the novel without acknowledging its very force. Addie's speech and the novel around it testify not only to the syntactic properties and potentials of language, but also to the great extrasyntactic possibilities offered by the dispersal and repetition of words in a poetic field, even if—or better, precisely because—they are not apprehensible by the characters doing the speaking.

The linguistic resonance functioning throughout the novel renders equally problematic readings based on what amount to "lexical" assignments of value or role to individual characters and their activities, for the novel's language exceeds its own most obvious predication. However manifestly Darl is the text's "visionary," for example, and however unequivocal the fact that he sees farther and deeper and in more stunningly replete images than any other character can—describing both scenes he does not witness and thoughts he has no explicable access to in language far more orotund and visually precise than that employed by any other character—Cash clearly has a role with respect to the visual that Darl does not approach. And, in obvious corollary, Cash's preternatural dedication to his labor, while perhaps adequately describing his character, does not exhaust the thematic functions his sawing takes on. Failure to attend to these complexities can result in overly simple binary readings and, by extension, in incomplete accounts of the novel's overall method, or value. John T. Matthews' nuanced exploration of the dynamics of industrial and agricultural modernization in the book's background, for example, falters in its final pages, as it turns its attention directly to the implications of Cash's and Darl's behaviors. Matthews indulges in the critical propensity for rendering too schematic a catalogue of authorial identifications with, and dissociations from, the novel's characters—in this case hoping that the characters might model a historically grounded and critically reflective stance vis-à-vis their surroundings and experience, a stance akin to what he takes to be Faulkner's own. Matthews suggests that Faulkner's description of the unflagging energy and unfaltering rhythm of Cash's carpentry-work "reflects the fear that humans themselves are becoming technologized" ("Machine Age" 85), citing the example of Cash's sawing "in and out of that unhurried imperviousness as a piston moves in the oil" (Faulkner 77). Matthews argues for the revelatory importance of anything that can derail the apparent unreflectiveness of that machinelike practice. He notes approvingly a variety of disruptions and disjunctions in the novel—from the broad challenge foisted on the family by Addie's death to "small snarls in the plot line" to the several literal ellipses in the text—that he sees as "sabotaging" the modernizing drive toward mechanization, integration, and commodification—forces that threaten the modernist novel itself on aesthetic and market grounds, as well as the Bundren family on economic ones ("Machine Age" 91–93). Matthews' investment, then, is in another model of analogous form, reading holes and gaps and snarls as affecting readers and characters in like fashion, and finding in that similarity the novel's moral, as well as the moral coordinates by which to judge its characters.

Matthews' earlier, deconstructive work valorized "play around voided centers of authority, being, and signified ideas" (*Play* 40); here, he is interested only in the gaps and fissures themselves, dismissing the "idle metafiction" of *Mosquitoes* and the "effete poeticism of Quentin Compson and Darl Bundren" alike in favor of "an experimentalism deeply implicated in the search for truth about the South in *Light in August* and *Absalom, Absalom!*" ("Machine Age" 93). Not only does Matthews reduce Cash and Darl to their social roles—one produces robotically, the other produces nothing but aestheticized verbal and visual filigree[23]—but he endorses, as well, a conception of language not entirely divorced from Addie's, if inverted in some of its particulars.

The empty spaces in language signal its failure to both Addie and Matthews. For Addie, they justify giving up and retreating into her private world: "I would say, All right. It doesn't matter. It doesn't matter what they call them" (173), while for Matthews these, along with the other "disruption[s]" Faulkner writes into the text ("Machine Age" 91), are the only dependable occasions for reflection in an increasingly commodified and routinized existence. "In gaps like these," Matthews suggests, "we are invited to think about problems from conflicting standpoints, to evaluate the pressures silencing discourse, as well as those producing it" (91). He lauds "hesitation" and "silent meditation" (92), but it's no more possible in his schema than in Addie's for language itself to provoke thought, for nuance or literary allusion or rhetorical brilliance to nudge one toward new insights or conclusions.

Matthews is admirably sensitive to historical allusion; his explanations of the fleeting references to the relations between blacks and whites or between farmers and their land (92), as well as to the rising Machine Age that provides the backdrop for his entire discussion, lend clarity and significance to many of the novel's less immediately scrutable passages. But that discussion nevertheless concerns itself only with those allusions that point outside the text to concrete historical situations, in what he valorizes as writing "that remains in communication with the sediment of reality it frames and forms, that forces its participants to think deeply about their lives" (94).

Thus, in terms of the critical schema with which I began, Matthews champions instances when the novel is "saying at" something outside itself or when it is not "saying at" anything, but he has no brief for those in which it is "saying" with reference to itself. This privileging of internal voids and external referents renders modernism's familiar other half—that which complements "decomposition" (91–93), dialectical juxtapositions, and alienation effects with verbal flair and poetic multiplication of sense—anathema to Matthews, as he considers the latter quite divorced from empirical reality and thus morally bankrupt (93). But in pushing the poetic aside, he wrongly scapegoats Darl for its exercise, and in scapegoating Darl, he misses the larger workings of the novel as a whole.

Matthews acknowledges the dangers of oversimplified binary thinking that would equate Cash with a traditional "ethos of use value, personalized production, and blood loyalties" (75) and label it good, in opposition to the "falsifying modernism represented in Darl's overly aesthetic and universalized responses to his material" (90).[24] Matthews recognizes the seductive power that the modern commodity, in the form of the graphophone and its recordings, has over Cash (74), as well as the fact that Cash endorses the fundamental tenets of commodification—"reification of labor into a product that can be stored over time, possessed as property, and sold when the producer decides"—when Cash accepts Darl's confinement in the asylum at Jackson as reasonable recompense for his act of arson (75). But Matthews does not extend such nuanced thinking to Darl, whom he retains as a bogeyman of bad modernism. Matthews accuses Darl of "cerebral retreats" in the face of his family's hardships, of cubist aestheticizing of his own destructive actions, of "play" with "alliterative and pictorial abstraction" and "metaphysical conceits," and of "arriving at a protective irony that is mostly verbal posturing" (88–89).[25]

Eventually, Matthews reads Darl's imprisonment at the end of the novel as figuratively confirming Faulkner's repudiation of overly aestheticist modernism (90–91). But how, then, should we read the lifelong handicap Cash is left with, or Dewey Dell's remaining saddled with an unwanted pregnancy? Do the limitations these imply represent similar judgments, less harsh than that against Darl (as they leave the characters merely incapacitated, rather than incarcerated), but of a piece? It seems more responsible to conclude that the characters' fates testify neither to aesthetic nor to moral judgments, because the book's aesthetic finally extends to a plane quite divorced from morality, independent of any character's awareness or behavior and irrespective of their individual tragedies. The litany of sins that Matthews ascribes to Darl—cerebral retreats, cubist aestheticizing, verbal posturing, alliterative and pictorial play—almost reads as a catalogue of the form and functioning of the grand metaphorical conceit of seeing and sawing and seesawing, the irony of which is not so much protective as constitutive: that Faulkner fashions his play out of the very materials so communicative of his characters' pain and suffering (Darl's far from least).

As I Lay Dying ultimately seems constructed with this end very much in mind: the lugubriousness of the Bundrens' tragedy, their continual determination by the loss of Addie and by the promise she has exacted from Anse to be buried in Jefferson, stands in such pointed opposition to the comedy, linguistic surfeit, and irreducible present tense that are the specific properties of the reader's experience. In this light, the novel's close becomes even more striking, as it effects a final seesawing of these positions. If Anse's sudden presentation of his new wife provokes shock or dismay in the reader, who has spent the whole novel becoming habituated to a world constructed around Addie, it registers the first moment when the reader feels Addie's loss in a fashion newly analogous to that which the characters have struggled with throughout.

I wrote earlier that Cash seems entirely comfortable with the new Mrs. Bundren, though in fact there is no clear indication of any of the characters' immediate responses to her appearance beyond the sudden arrested motion of "Dewey Dell's and Vardaman's mouth half open and half-et bananas in their hands" (260) as the new couple appears. But this is precisely the point. The novel stops with Anse's fiat; all we know of the characters' reaction is Cash's brief flash-forward to the family listening to the graphophone at home the following winter and his casual use of the appellation "Mrs Bundren" when Anse first borrows the shovels from her.[26] As best we can tell, though, they accept Anse's words as predicated, while we may well be inclined not to. Or, to be more exact, we are not even given a chance to, while Anse's children are not given a chance not to—we know simply that they will, that they are subject in the months to come to a normalizing of this radical redefinition that we have no opportunity to share. Thus, the novel's closing moments highlight, one last time, the fundamental divide between its readers' and its characters' experiences, predicated on a final seesawing reversal. As the reader focuses on the past and an attenuated version of loss and pain, the characters turn to the present (shading into the future), surfeit (new records continually arriving by mail-order), and aesthetic pleasure. In the single instant where our reality finally becomes truly like the characters', theirs becomes like ours.

This parodic version of the "happily ever after" of the marriage plot or the fairy-tale romance, in which characters' and readers' emotional stances can't quite be made to align, becomes a meditation on ending itself: in this novel, in the marriage plot, of the marriage plot, of any novel. By underscoring our affective relation and attachment to even a character as prickly as Addie, precisely at the moment in which she is spirited away for good, Faulkner condenses the reassurances born even of the most felicitous of resolutions with the loss nevertheless entailed. Closure itself is always potentially a wrenching experience, a perceived abandonment by characters who have become one's intimates over the course of the fiction; Faulkner yokes this experience to the larger undertaking of his novel, in which our emotional identification with the characters has already come under fire throughout from a new investment in patterns of language that do not defer to them. By hyperbolically pegging the sense of abandonment so pointedly to the novel's last words, and by making them a conduit back into the linguistic play that constitutes an enduring aesthetic invitation over-against the developments of plot, Faulkner provides both an emblem of and a response to the grander sense of abandonment that a reader might feel when faced with the forced transition from the reassuring narrators and narratives of nineteenth-century fiction to the challenges of the modernist novel. In a final complement to Sundquist's argument that Faulkner figures the "absent" author through the absent mother, the novel itself becomes a transitional object—part of Faulkner's contribution to the birth of the novel as a self-consciously aesthetic form being this complex articulation of the operational and emotional costs entailed in the demise of unselfconscious immersion in the easy mimesis of an older story-world. But the author is not a metonym for that lost world. In his case, the transitional object functions in a fashion closer to Winnicott's original sense: not as a temporary replacement for someone permanently lost, but rather as an interim stand-in that in its very existence testifies to the continuing influence and affective weight of a figure not immediately apprehensible, but very much alive.

2

YOU KNOW ME, ALICE
The Autobiography of Alice B. Toklas
(driving)

Like Faulkner in *As I Lay Dying*, Gertrude Stein closes *The Autobiography of Alice B. Toklas* with a bang, calling attention to her authorship—in her case, claiming it—in the book's final sentences. With a tone as lighthearted and offhanded as at any other point in the book, Stein writes (in Toklas's voice): "About six weeks ago Gertrude Stein said, it does not look to me as if you were ever going to write that autobiography. You know what I am going to do. I am going to write it for you. I am going to write it as simply as Defoe did the autobiography of Robinson Crusoe. And she has and this is it" (252). Here, as in *As I Lay Dying*, the book's move toward closure is complicated enormously by the sudden wavering in the relations it has established between author, characters, and reader. In Faulkner's novel, as I've suggested, the ligature of author and reader is structural, predicated on neither more nor less than a common positioning in a space where the characters' tribulations have only a partial purchase, and can easily transmute from tragic to comic. We are treated to no direct information about Faulkner, no display of his own character beyond that implied by the perspectival divergence itself, the penumbral evidence offered by the novel's multiple affective registers. Stein, on the other hand, has held herself before us constantly—her name appearing in full again and again on nearly every page. The appeal is charismatic; Stein is not merely the author, a shadowy prime mover lurking behind the book, but also an exhaustively and winningly described character in its pages. If the manifest agenda throughout has been to paint an image of Stein sufficiently gregarious and likable as to motivate a cautious reader to commit herself to the project of reading her work, the shock here lies in discovering that one already has.

Stein's strategy recapitulates, at a very basic level, that which I am tracing in more recondite and abstract byways throughout this volume. The opportunity to get to know the author is all but explicitly the purpose of her book. Authorial self-effacement and subsequent—final, showy—reinscription are highlighted unmistakably, the latter placed with as much narrative prominence as possible. At the same time, the *Autobiography*'s prose has little obvious relation to the modernist stylizations that gave rise to these critical expectations, in spite of Stein's preeminent standing (which she would be the first to affirm) as a practitioner and cultivator of modernism in the literary and pictorial arts. While I will work to attenuate the appearance of the *Autobiography*'s writing as wholly unstudied, there is no mistaking its distance from the abstruse work Stein had produced up to this juncture. Instead, the book represents a point of contact between modernist versions of authorship as they have traditionally been understood—absent centers, impersonality—and the more playful troping of the role that we associate with postmodernism. Stein frustrates our accustomed temporal-formal account of literary history because she bids explicitly for celebrity in the *Autobiography*, even while she retains the trappings of impersonality as a playful mantle—evacuating the most obvious personal and stylistic signatures until deeper consideration (of the prose's character, of the character's pose) makes them reappear. Her performance of authorial absence winks especially broadly, and (perhaps as a result) has from the start been critically undervalued, if popularly acclaimed.

The exact quality of that wink has shifted at intervals over the book's history. Today, Stein's name is emblazoned on the book's cover, and the book is her best known and most popular. Its initial readers, too—on the occasion of its serialization in the *Atlantic Monthly* in 1933—were alerted to the tale's provenance in no uncertain terms with each of its four installments, as well as in a teaser the month before the first, jauntily proclaiming: "Gertrude Stein is one of God's originals, and if she wants to call her life 'The Autobiography of Alice B. Toklas,' who are we to cavil at her?"[1] Surely even many who first read the *Autobiography* as a book were likewise well aware of its authorship, even though the inaugural edition contained no attribution to Stein on the cover or the title page.[2] But other readers were doubtless taken in by the deceptive packaging, and some were presumably left agog by the final paragraph's confession (or boast). Whether the revelation entirely surprises, or merely offers an unexpectedly neat resolution to the book's meandering narrative, it does focus attention on the subject of resolution itself. Indeed, it proposes Stein herself as a kind of resolution, as the endpoint of Toklas's long and rambling course even as she also suddenly becomes its origin. The first edition underscored this development by placing a reproduction of the opening page of Stein's manuscript opposite the final page of the published text—inviting the reader, as James E. Breslin has suggested, "to re-read the book in light of the revelation" at its close. He terms this move a "folding back on itself" by the book, and a "circl[ing] back on itself as if it were an autonomous verbal reality" (161).

Breslin employs these two topological metaphors more or less interchangeably, the first perhaps suggested by the literal operations of opening and closing a book, the second reaching toward an airier abstraction. This chapter, however, is dedicated in large part to establishing that the second metaphor is the appropriate one, not because it breaks free of the book, but rather because Stein is thoroughly concerned here with circles, and with the varying qualities of repetition they might compel or invite. Among these is, as Breslin suggests, rereading. I think he is right, too, to temper his own proposal that the final move might intimate the book's autonomy in some purely textual empyrean. While this last redirection might suggest a book not just self-reflexive but self-legitimizing or even self-authoring, it seems more importantly to underscore, again, Stein's role as author, and thus to present the reader with a host of new interpretive questions. Through 250 pages, Stein maintains a counterpoint between Alice Toklas's unassuming chatter and her own intellectual rigor; as Toklas says repeatedly, "[t]he geniuses came and talked to Gertrude Stein and the wives sat with me" (87).[3] Even though Stein's aesthetic pronouncements are adverted to with some regularity, they are woven into a steady stream of anecdotes, bons mots, and verbal portraits delivered in what painter Maurice Grosser described as "an exact rendition of Alice's conversation."[4] Such a thoroughgoing impersonation encourages the reader to relax into an appreciation of the book's most obvious narrative features, even if already privy (as we now tend to be) to its actual authorship. But Stein's closing turn complicates this easy immersion in the mimetic representation of Paris and its denizens, suddenly proposing—and potentially repurposing—the *Autobiography* as a Steinian aesthetic project. The tidy bow of the book's ending, with its self-referential concision—"And she has, and this is it"—is also a spur to its own unraveling, or to the search for a similar archness and density elsewhere in the work.

While I think there is little question that the *Autobiography* is a much looser book than either *As I Lay Dying* or *Lolita*—that it presents a resonant series of metaphors and analogues, syntactic and lexical games rather than a tight network—I also think it has nevertheless been undervalued in this regard. Ulla Dydo, one of Stein's most exhaustive and exacting critics, reads the *Autobiography*'s embrace of a readily apprehensible narrative form predicated on identifiable personages as an unalloyed retreat from Stein's radical experimentation, which had reached a new high point in the years just preceding. "Already in 1931," Dydo writes, Stein "started working more and more with single words. She concentrated on elements of language—letters, sounds, phonemes, morphemes, syllables, words, names—punning dances in the parlor of speech" (*Language* 471); and, further, "contexts of allusiveness—writing ideas, literary hints, events, letters, personal errands, people, details about art— . . . show up less and less. [. . .] It is as if her writing was liberated from the everyday world" (472). Having discussed the "Stanzas in Meditation" that emerged from this new freedom and directly preceded the *Autobiography*, Dydo asks: "what happens in the world of her words between 'Stanzas' and *The Autobiography of Alice B. Toklas*, where every word seems pinned to a fact, person or circumstance . . . ?" She concludes that "[t]he referential autobiography creates a magnificent, hollow personality, successful and famous, which explains nothing about the creative process" (489).[5]

Dydo's mistake is to equate the book's image of Stein with its entire undertaking. She is correct insofar as one of the first interpretive pleasures the work offers—far in advance of its closing gesture—is indeed the realization that, title notwithstanding, it is much more obviously an account of Stein than of Toklas. Toklas's life before the women's meeting warrants three pages, Stein's almost fifty, and a similar imbalance in attention marks much of the remainder. Dydo's adjectives are apt, too: for all that Stein traces decades of frustration at failing to find the audience she was convinced she deserved—and devotes a number of pages as well to her childhood and adolescence—an air of magnificence, success, and fame does hover around her throughout. This represents a strategic choice as well as a healthy ego, and the choice obviously paid off handsomely in the book's reception. But it has blinded many critics beyond Dydo to the ways in which "the creative process" is in fact addressed here, and to the complexity of the representations of Stein *and* Toklas that make this address possible. Prominent Steinians often simply pass the book over with only cursory attention, in order to focus on the more markedly experimental writing.[6] Others attend to its preoccupation with marketing and related demotic concerns, most often deeming the work a compromise and capitulation—to a "popular and comprehensible perspective," to commodification, to gossip and anecdote, to "chit-chat," to lies.[7] The affective register of these responses varies. Some are merely descriptive; others tend toward the evaluative, prizing pure experimentation more highly than work with too pronounced a strain of conventional narrative. In the latter case, Stein is faulted for working her way into precisely the dual expectations that I am arguing the century places before its writers. The book mobilizes Toklas's garrulousness to solidify Stein's own celebrity and ultimately to secure a larger readership and reputation. But this is itself a form of experimentation—undeniably a compromise, but not thereby compromised. Its elegant and innovative solution to the set of local demands that Stein weaves into convergence—capturing Toklas's voice, constructing an approachable text, and responding to the specific contours of what Stein saw as the misrepresentation and misunderstanding of her in America—makes it as well a crucible for the larger literary dynamics at play.

To the extent that the *Autobiography* has been read as innovative, it is in its handling of temporality and identity, grand conceptual categories that the book treats, in many respects, with an insouciance unprecedented in the genre, embracing a profoundly idiosyncratic chronology emerging from Toklas's digressive and associative train of thought in order to tell the story of what some readers see as a composite "I" generated by the fusion of the two women's characters and recollections.[8] Breslin, for example, reads the book as "not . . . a mere submission to the conventions of autobiography but an intense and creative struggle with them" (149), and concludes that "it admits the conventions of memory, identity, chronological time—in order to fight against and ultimately to transcend their deadening effects" (151). And Leigh Gilmore likewise highlights the fashion in which, "[i]n contrast to the 'faithful' autobiographer, Stein reads the network of the self-same for its gaps, discontinuities and non-coincidences and rewrites the illusory seamlessness of autobiography" by displacing the "referential anchor" of the standard autobiographical "I" onto a lesbian couple. Coupled with the work's temporal play and its loose commitment to a "'truthful' narrator," this displacement yields, in Gilmore's account, a mobilization of "the recognizable constituents of autobiography . . . against autobiography itself" (57). And Sidonie Smith fully conjoins the text's innovations regarding persona with those of temporality to argue that "[w]ith 'Alice' as narrator and 'Gertrude Stein' as abstract entity rather than psychological or self-conscious subject, the auto/biographical text is evacuated of the teleological trajectory so central to nineteenth-century notions of the universal subject" (70).

Focusing too wholly on the ways the *Autobiography* undermines chronology and identity, however, occludes the highly functional appeals it makes via these same conceptual categories. Whether one reads the entire work with a firm knowledge of its fundamental imposture, as we are likely to today, or whether one is lucky enough to be hoodwinked until the conclusion, it remains the case that until its last page, the book holds before us two women with distinct identities, personalities, and—most importantly—trajectories. Dydo's "magnificent," "successful," and "famous" are apposite here—as epithets that accrue to Stein at all points in the narration and to Toklas, at best, only intermittently and in the reduced form of reflected glory. The bravado of the conclusion depends on this distinction. If the two figures merge then, in key respects, they do so only for a single, glittering instant. The book may be a heady amalgam of individual experiences and shared ones relayed in a unified voice, but it turns, nevertheless, on the gap between being and becoming. While Stein and Toklas are essential to each other's lives from very early on—domestically and professionally joined, a recognizable (if coded) lesbian couple—they are also parties to a loose burlesque of the traditional marriage plot, arcing across the entirety of the volume. Toklas, at the start, is a naïve ingénue who meets and then falls for the sophisticated and endlessly magnetic Stein (already and always a genius); becomes her confidant and, in time, her most intimate companion; and finally, in a stunning apotheosis, is wed to her forever in the book's final scene (Reader, Stein might as well have concluded, she wrote this book for me!).

To see the book thus reopens the matter of teleology that Sidonie Smith sees as foreclosed by the play of identity, and thus compels us to reconsider the significance of Stein's construction and maneuvering of Toklas's character. Indeed, this suggests one way to read Stein's invocation of Defoe and Crusoe in the final paragraph: as a reminder that the Toklas here effectively is a character, and is managed accordingly—not least with a steady eye to the narrative arc of her career through the book. Dydo's scrupulous excavation of the Stein archive is highly instructive in this regard, revealing both the labor initially required in fashioning this character and several considerations undergirding it. She finds in the "preliminary *cahier*" with Stein's first approach to the project "three early, substantial deviations from the final text in print" (*Language* 540). While the initial two paragraphs differ from the opening of the finished work only at the level of punctuation, the third and fourth fall calamitously into Stein's voice. Where the *Autobiography* reports, for example, "I had some intellectual adventures at this period, but very quiet ones. When I was about nineteen years of age I was a great admirer of Henry James" (4), the manuscript veers toward Stein's signature style:

> I had some intellectual adventures at this time, and these adventures as I [am] about to tell you were ones that were undoubtedly much as would [interest] any one. They consisted very largely in my having begun and I did begin preparing for anything. This was not an intellectual adventure it was an intellectual [escape] as any one knowing anything could and would know how to begin.
>
> How does one begin, one begins very well.
>
> At no time does one fail in beginning very well and having indeed having begun very well one can and one does [proceed] very well to have been begun. Then and thereafter I was charming I was delicate I was delicious I was attractive and it made of me what I was and need I say what that is and that was. I may say every one does and may know what there is what that was and what that will be and as such it is completely quite completely entirely completely [undoubtedly] entirely completely satisfying as completely charming. And so my life and so it goes. (Dydo, *Language*, 541; bracketed suggestions Dydo's)

That Stein's most extended false start should be a meditation on beginning, crowned by an awkward lunge toward completion, seems to me no accident. These paragraphs not only falter tonally; with the lapse into Steinian syntax they offer, as well, something like an unwarranted X-ray of Stein's thinking regarding the work as a whole. In the following pages, I trace the ways in which, far less explicitly, the book as we know it is preoccupied with the matter of moving beyond beginning, of finding a way forward rather than falling into repetition. This entails Stein's abandoning the rich impasto of her standard prose for the thin line of Toklas's narrative speech, and at the same time conceptualizing a non-Steinian mode of repetition—which is to say a nonproductive, intellectually void mode of repetition—that Stein attributes to the pre-Stein Toklas so as to deliver her thence, over the course of the book, into a new aesthetic sophistication.

The interplay between the book's storytelling commitments and its more subtle formal experiments is essential. Indeed, they are mutually constitutive. Thus, while I welcome Steven J. Meyer's revision of the pejorative "compromise" into a characterization of the book as written "in a genuine spirit of reconciliation" with narrative ("Shipwrecked" 33), I take issue with his narrow reading of what is finally narrated. Meyer describes the concluding "transformation of the writer, but not the narrator, from Toklas into Stein" (13) as "a conversion that is only relevant to the circumstances of the act of writing and not to the story of 'living with so very many people'—the act of writing is suddenly made into the subject of writing" (16). But I think this goes too far. Key elements, both narrative and rhetorical, of the story of "living with so very many people" (70) both make the conversion possible and provide the fullest measure of its implications. For Meyer, the book becomes no more than "a continuous allegory" of the writing process (16); even describing it as "memoirs" is "misleading," he says, "for the memories it recorded, whether exact or inexact, routine or spectacular, were only an excuse for the writing" (28). The notion of reading the book for allegorical import is a hospitable one, but Meyer is too quick to propose that this single allegory substitutes itself, wholly and univocally, for the tale on which it is founded, having no relevance to the material detailed within. The *Autobiography* sustains multiple analogical readings at both local and global levels, all loosely connected and mutually reinforcing: objects and events, attributes of their description, Stein's aesthetic project, Toklas's appreciation of and participation in that project, and the reader's own interpolation all resonate with one another, all participate in the overall yoking of the book's manner with its matter. And this yoking is crucial for the book's purpose of shepherding both its putative author and its anticipated readers from an uninformed interest in modernism's key Parisian personalities to a somewhat savvier embrace of Stein in particular, and of her artistry.

The book's final sentences, as I have suggested, set Stein up at a new level as the telos toward which Toklas is moving throughout. This progress has been suggested in piecemeal fashion all along. Toklas's narrational picaresque ambles across all twenty-five years of the women's cohabitation, as well as the earlier decades of their lives, before finally arriving at the moment of her installation at 27, rue de Fleurus, a third of the way through the volume. Five chapters out of seven have already elapsed in this temporal hopscotch, as if to emphasize the comparative order and calm of lives lived in concert from that point forward. But over-against the wandering character of Toklas's narrative digressions, the construction of the conclusion as the conclusion makes clear that at one level the fullest consummation of Stein and Toklas's relationship arrives in the moment in which Stein takes the writing of the book upon herself, and completes it in the next sentence. This convergence is certainly legible as a final and unequivocal proclamation of the Gertrice/Altrude moniker that Stein took up,[9] and as a crowning gesture to the project of reconciliation with Toklas (following her discovery of a youthful affair Stein had hidden) that Dydo at one point saw as a central element of the undertaking.[10] But it's also possible to read this pointedly textual signature of extratextual attachment in more local terms, which is to say textual ones, as a point of aesthetic conflux. The *Autobiography* is noticeably reticent as to the specific details of Stein and Toklas's coming together romantically, but it does provide several stylistic measures of their progressive union.

And it is a union measured, stylistically, by progression itself. This is a question of self-definition for Stein, who of course prided herself on her trailblazing position in the history of literature as she conceived it. The *Autobiography* insists on her singular status, nominating "Melanctha," in *Three Lives* (1909), as "the first definite step away from the nineteenth century and into the twentieth century in literature" (54), and *The Making of Americans* (1906–11, published 1925) as "the beginning, really the beginning, of modern writing" (215). This bullish commitment to avant-gardism extends, over time, beyond the artistic realm. When Stein learns to drive a car during World War I, she hews to a related logic, refusing to turn back even when Toklas thinks they have taken the wrong road: "Wrong or right, said Gertrude Stein, we are going on" (173). And "even to this day," Toklas says fifteen years down the line, "when she can drive any kind of a car anywhere she still does not back a car very well. She goes forward admirably, she does not go backward successfully" (173).

I am not the first reader to read a larger significance into these lines. Breslin quotes them in passing, in connection with Stein's commitment to the modern and the new and "ongoing movement" (158). Wayne Koestenbaum, as well, draws an analogy between Stein's sentences and her driving (313–14), but in the service of a reading insisting on the immediate and immediately exhausted plenitude of Stein's writing, implicitly imagining Stein as a driver who never glances in her rearview mirror: "Self-pleased writing is not simply arrogant; rather, it earns a reader's trust by sufficing, without supplement. You are permitted to forget a Stein sentence the moment you finish reading it. Her writing perpetually toys with its own erasure: thus it always promises the reader relief from having to memorize, to learn, to sift. As she refused to believe in the unconscious, so she disavowed subtext, despite her plethora of double entendres and puns: The writing is exactly what it seems on the surface. It has no hidden depths" (312). This contrarian reading, which appears to take aim at the deep-digging consensus among major Stein critics from its title ("Stein Is Nice") onward, is powerful in its assertions, but also limited by them. One can treat Stein this way, but I am not alone in suggesting that one might, in fact, miss out on some aspects of the writing if one were to do so. Certainly the narrative elements of the *Autobiography* militate powerfully, and very appreciably, against such an approach—and indeed, while Koestenbaum quotes the *Autobiography* freely in support of his points, his principal object is what he calls "the odd Stein," not the *Autobiography*.

In nominating "driving" as a key term for the *Autobiography*, and for this chapter, I'm affirming Breslin's and Koestenbaum's senses of Stein's dedication to a relentless, propulsive movement, but arguing (*pace* Koestenbaum) that this insatiable drive, here, is not about ignoring everything external, or what has come before, and least of all the idea of a specified endpoint. Forward motion is always directed to the radical revision constituted by the book's last sentences. It becomes Stein's way, ultimately, to claim Toklas as her own, and to steer the reader into her camp as well. Appreciating this strategy requires, however, that the reader remember, learn, and sift through the text, in order to elucidate its multiple parallel constructions of advancement, from the syntactical to the characterological to the literary-historical, all interwoven with the unrolling of Toklas's temporal narrative.

Stein's continuing forward thrust emerges in myriad other sites. In the prewar years, she describes herself as having been in the habit "of beginning her work at eleven o'clock at night and working until the dawn. She said she always tried to stop before the dawn was too clear and the birds were too lively because it is a disagreeable sensation to go to bed then. [. . .] But often the birds and the dawn caught her and she stood in the court waiting to get used to it before she went to bed" (41). Elsewhere, speaking again of the "revolutionary work" of *Three Lives*, Stein describes herself as possessing "a great deal of inertia and once started [she] keeps going until she starts somewhere else" (82). Two points are important here. The first is the freedom with which Stein jumps between different registers, yoking the mundane activities and the most refined aesthetic undertakings with aplomb; the conceptual and imagistic linkages and homologies familiar from her other work are masked by the turn to a sustained narrative form, but still present. The second is the fashion in which, in the final example, she recruits even the ambivalent force of inertia to an image of herself in perpetual motion; the opposition she draws is not between stopping and starting, but between moving in one direction and starting off in another. Thus, even when her beloved car fails, her forward momentum merely shifts from physical to psychic registers. As she sits in a garage watching the automobile "being taken to pieces and put together again" (233), she is able to turn her attention to a forthcoming lecture she has been engaged to deliver at Cambridge—her grand debut as a public speaker, the prospect of which has "quite completely upset her" (232). By the time her vehicle has been reassembled, she has also composed the lecture in its entirety (later published as "Composition as Explanation").

Alice Toklas, before her departure for Paris, is painted in exactly opposite terms, moored to a staid San Francisco existence in which she is neither "very ardent in" her life nor entertaining "active desire or thought of change" (4, 5). Her "intellectual adventures," as we have seen, "were quiet ones"—the single episode she details consists of writing a letter to Henry James proposing that she adapt *The Awkward Age* for the stage, receiving "a delightful letter" in response, then blushing at her audacity and neither preserving the letter nor, apparently, following through on the project (4). The mature Stein is at pains to single James out, later in the *Autobiography*, "quite definitely as her forerunner, he being the only nineteenth century writer who . . . felt the method of the twentieth century," but her attitude toward him again distinguishes the two women. She claims not to have read James in "her formative period" and construes her youthful lack of interest as natural antagonism to a literary "parent" who might have "hamper[ed]" her development through his influence (78). Toklas's proposed adaptation would constitute fealty to the master's design, and finally she does not even go so far as to embark on the project; Stein, meanwhile, commences a career so much more thoroughly of the twentieth century as to flummox American publishers for a generation. As she says, "[t]here are many Paris picture dealers who like adventure in their business, there are no publishers in America who like adventure in theirs" (241).

Toklas, on the other hand, is herself initially quite thrown by modernism. While she is drawn away from her static life by the promise held in the "three little Matisse paintings, the first modern things to cross the Atlantic," that Stein's brother Leo and his wife bring with them to San Francisco on a trip home after the great fire (5), Paris and its denizens perplex Toklas utterly in the book's early pages. At Stein's atelier, and then at the vernissage of the Salon des Indépendants just after, Toklas is uneasy (10) and agog—alert to the "hidden meanings" Matisse and Stein seem "to be full of" (15) but, as she is quick to affirm, "not know[ing] what it was all about" (15). Even the manner in which Toklas at first attempts to parse her confusion is incorrect. Seated, at the vernissage, in front of what Stein tells her is "the whole story," Toklas sees "nothing but two big pictures that looked quite alike but not altogether alike." "One is a Braque and one is a Derain," Stein explains, and Toklas goes on to try to grasp their differences (18). Only much later does she learn that the paintings' actual significance lies not in the minor distinctions between them, but in the fact that both artists have allied themselves with Picasso rather than with Matisse.

Braque and Derain, in an implicit contrast to Toklas, have successfully apprenticed themselves to their chosen master; they model savvy reading and volitional mirroring of his work. Stein subsequently glosses this affiliation as participating in a nascent modernist juggernaut. In response to Toklas's later claim that the only thing she saw at the vernissage was that "[Picasso's pictures] were rather awful and the others were not," Stein quotes Picasso's remark that "when you make a thing it is so complicated making it that it is bound to be ugly, but those that do it after you they don't have to worry about making it and they can make it pretty, and so everybody can like it when the others make it" (23). Toklas's bewilderment, faced with Picassos, Matisses, and Cézannes at the Steins' atelier, in contrast, is rendered as an unstudied, literalized reflection, cognition and action equally stymied. Toklas descends into a sort of lexical palindrome—"Now I was confused and I looked and I looked and I was confused" (11)—which is subsequently revealed as echoing the characteristic lament of her childhood boredom: "my mother said that I always used to say, what shall I do now, which was only varied by now what shall I do" (142). For all that Stein's is an art of repetition, it does not generally embrace this kind of chiasmic structure. Rather, this figure for the pre-Stein Toklas presents her, in youth and upon her arrival in Paris, lost in herself, as listless in the second example as she is agitated in the first, but in both cases merely cycling through the same thoughts and emotional responses, rather than finding any kind of traction through them.

There is precedent for this structural shorthand. Stein suggests at the *Autobiography*'s outset that "Ada," in *Geography and Plays* (1922), offers "a very good description of [Toklas] as [she] was" in the years before her expatriation. "Ada," of course, distills this palindromic circling into a simple nominative form, and Carolyn Burke reveals that Stein has already used the name in "Two Women" (1925) for her friend Etta Cone, whom she saw as similarly trapped in a life of unsustaining, unenlightening repetition. Stein defines this state in circular terms here as well. As Burke reports: "Gertrude's last word on the Cones was 'A revolving life is a sad sad life'; what she anticipated with Alice was an evolving life, one that allowed for personal fulfillment within its own conventions" (231).[11] Burke goes on to note that the narrative in "Ada" rests on the counterpoint between the fruitless cycling of Ada's home life caring for her brother and father after her mother's death, and the emancipation, delight, and fulfillment she finds when she leaves all these duties to fall in with a new "some one"— the unnamed Stein herself (*Geography and Plays* 16): "The portrait begins with her biography and ends with an ecstatic mimesis of her fusion with 'some one,' a storyteller who loves Ada and listens to her 'charming stories'" (Burke 232). It is true that Ada's happiness in the years before her mother's death consists of sharing stories with her mother, and that the new "some one" in her life reveals herself as a new audience, but Burke does not fully explore the significance of this new love's herself being an accomplished storyteller. While Burke records the interplay of "'telling' and 'listening'" at the close of the portrait, and notes that the two "are intimately connected with 'loving,' which is also associated with Ada's escape from the demands of family life" (232), I want to add that the particularly salient qualification Stein paints herself as possessing is "telling stories having a beginning and a middle and an ending" (*Geography and Plays* 16). We can read the significance of this disarmingly simple self-description by way of the excised paragraphs from the start of the *Autobiography*—in which beginning, and even beginning very well, appears to present little challenge, but where managing to move beyond the beginning is (literally) another story. Against the palindrome, which has a beginning and perhaps a middle, but then only recurs to its beginning, Stein places the progressive structure of both sentences and entire narratives that move steadily forward.[12] Crucially, for Stein, once freed from the issueless circle of the palindrome, that movement can take the form of a degree of apparent repetition, in that (as throughout her work) repetition merely disguises redefinition and conceptual progress. Ada, thus, moves from a fearful "trembling" at the realization, while still living with her father and brother, that "she was one needing charming stories and happy telling of them" (15) to an ecstatic "trembling" in her new love life. Similarly, the renewed term is further glossed via a continuing employment of repetition and slow transmutation: "Trembling was all living, living was all loving, some one was then the other one. Certainly this one was loving this Ada then. And certainly Ada all her living then was happier in living than any one else who ever could, who was, who is, who ever will be living" (16). Here, too, Ada gains a rhetorical purchase on time past, present, and future, measured through Stein's play of tenses, in ways that Toklas will echo in the *Autobiography*.

The distinction between the actual uses to which Stein put repetition and the popular perception of her work bedeviled her continually. Alyson Tischler traces parodies of Stein's work in the American press dating back as far as 1914, highlighting "aesthetic loop[s]" and "circular... definitions" as central characteristics of Stein's prose and that of her American imitators (16). The niceties and precision of Stein's repetitions were occasionally preserved, but more often lost, in this process of translation—Stein references approvingly in the *Autobiography* Henry McBride's recognition that "the real Gertrude Stein was... funnier in every way than the imitations, not to say much more interesting" (171)—and as late as the American tour of 1934, newspaper headlines across the country announced her arrival in the same redundant and often unimaginative fashion—"Gerty Gerty Stein Stein Is Back Home Home Back," "Gertrude Stein Leaves Radcliffe in Fog, in Fog," "A Snub, A Snub, A Snub: Gertrude Stein Gives Carmel's Highbrows the Go-By." Stein was forced to clarify: "When I write a rose is a rose is a rose... I am not repeating. But, when the newspaper prints day after day that Gertrude Stein repeats, that is repetition."[13] The *Autobiography* is (among other things) a parable about bad and good repetition. Stein distinguishes between the pointless, cyclical mode of repetition that characterizes both Toklas before their liaison and the American perception of Stein, on one hand, and the realities of her own writing, on the other. However repetitive the latter may appear, however much it actually entails a degree of reiteration, it is recursive only in order to be propulsive, to serve Stein's solitary push into the twentieth century. The *Autobiography* registers this claim again and again: through self-description (e.g., as the driver who will not back up) and through its characterization of her work, but also via the shifting qualities of Toklas's own syntax and the forward momentum of her own narrative in its circuitous—but not circular—drive toward the final union with Stein. At intervals, similar strategies inform individual word choice, where partial or attenuated repetitions speak in a manner consonant with Stein's more obviously experimental work. The effects are of course more subtle, and decidedly less dense, than in Stein's other writings, but they are sited at key moments and do answer to exegetical pressure.

Stein discloses, for instance, on the first page of *Everybody's Autobiography* (the sequel volume, detailing Stein's adjustment to her newfound celebrity) that the earlier book's very title was executed over Toklas's objections: "In the first place she did not want it to be Alice B. Toklas, if it has to be at all it should be Alice Toklas and in the French translation it was Alice Toklas in French it just could not be Alice B. Toklas but in America and in England too Alice B. Toklas was more than Alice Toklas. Alice Toklas never thought so and always said so" (3). Timothy Dow Adams argues for reading Stein's insistence on the initial in light of a statement she makes in *The Geographical History of America*, that "be is for bio. And for autobiography" (24–25). This is quite plausible, and indicates in itself that the punning style of reading that critics have adopted in unpacking the more severe of Stein's texts is not out of place here. But I would add that the "b" also conducts the reader toward a sensitivity to homophonies at levels smaller than the word, that initiating an AuToBiography with the initials ABT establishes phonic relations and inversions as important from the start. The fact that any but the most masterful translation into French would lose these resonances might explain Stein's willingness to let it be Alice Toklas in French. So, too, might the ancillary pun on "be" that *Everybody's Autobiography* underscores, one that reaches back to the importance of "being" in "Ada." The important role played by minor lexical modulations in "Ada"—"living was all loving"—emerges in the *Autobiography* as well. When Leo Stein's wife arrives in San Francisco with "many stories of her life in Paris," Toklas decides to follow her there, and "in this way," she affirms in the first chapter's final words, "my new full life began" (5). The rotating consonants of "full life" (compared to mere "life," apropos of Mrs. Stein) speak to the displacement of Toklas's abode and of her affections that will constitute the renewal and the plenitude of her existence in Paris, but they also register in themselves the aesthetic qualities of that plenitude.

Most thematically freighted is Stein's strategic disassembly of Toklas's palindromic circling as a manner of registering her inborn acuity, her rising conversance with Stein's idiom, and Stein's own crucial role in this enlarging of Toklas's sphere. Over a two-page interval, the two halves of a palindrome construct a mini-narrative of Toklas's steps into her "new full life": she reports that on each of the three times when she has met a genius—beginning of course with Stein herself—a "bell within [her] rang" (5), and then that she becomes one of the select number who "rang the bell" of the Stein "pavillon," rather than being limited to knocking on the door of the atelier (7). By decoupling the halves of this potential palindromic structure, Stein intimates already the transformation she describes over the course of the book. The circles in which Toklas has been trapped give way; revolving transforms itself into evolving. Not coincidentally, the two phrases offer an account of the coming evolution in highly condensed form. The first inaugurates one of the book's most abiding concerns, recognition of Stein's singularity, while the second gestures toward the rewards that may accrue to such a perceptive individual. The space between them, meanwhile, intimates all that will follow—Toklas's forthcoming acquaintance with Picasso and Whitehead, the long-term fates of the paintings Matisse and Picasso have just finished at the time of Toklas's arrival, Stein's own work on *The Making of Americans*, art-historical evaluations of the period, and a much later conversation between Stein and Picasso ("not long ago" in the time frame of Toklas's narration) that resurfaces 187 pages on (6, 193).

For Toklas, then, these ringing bells are only the first steps of a life-altering and ultimately life-defining series of developments. The book will go on to trace her trajectory to the heart of Stein's life and livelihood, the roles—housekeeper, gardener, needlewoman, secretary, editor, veterinarian (251–52)—that Toklas takes up, and that leave her too encumbered to write her own autobiography, being precisely those that testify to her essential position in the building of Stein's career. Implicitly, the book will hold out an attenuated version of the same trajectory to the reader; the intimacy fostered here will remain at one level ersatz, secondhand, but at another just as crucial to Stein's advance, in that a broader circle of readers is exactly what she sees as necessary to confer true success upon her. It is no accident, then, that Stein builds Toklas's early palindromic circles around confusion and boredom—two highly characteristic responses of uninitiated or unsympathetic audiences to Stein's writing—and breaks the circle on, first, an intuitive recognition of her genius and, second, a foray into her foyer. To this end, Stein is quick to dispel the elitism suggested by Toklas's proud recitation of her early accomplishment in gaining special access to Stein. Six pages later, Toklas describes what the process looks like from the inside. Stein herself appears momentarily to be a formidable gatekeeper: "Gertrude Stein sat by the stove talking and listening and getting up to open the door and go up to various people talking and listening. She usually opened the door to the knock and the usual formula was de la part de qui venez-vous, who is your introducer" (13). But in fact, Toklas continues, "anybody could come." She explains that "for form's sake and in Paris you have to have a formula, everybody was supposed to be able to mention the name of somebody who had told them about it" (13). Twice more, she emphasizes that "really everybody could come in," "anybody could come in" (13), adding, "at that time these pictures had no value and there was no social privilege attached to knowing any one there, only those came who really were interested" (13).

The *Autobiography* responds to, renews, and retails that interest for a new generation, and more importantly for a populace having no intention of actually making its way to 27, rue de Fleurus. Georgia Johnston pursues a related thesis, arguing that the *Autobiography* gives the reader the potential "to read as Stein and Toklas read," to enter "the intimate circle" (596). She proposes Toklas as "the conduit through which readers move from the autobiography to other texts" (596), and observes that while "the reader will not be able to read 'the little tiny pages of [Stein's] note-book written forward and back,' the reader can go to the version of 'Ada' in *Geography and Plays* and, through that published text, enter into the reading position of Alice B. Toklas, a position of intimacy" (598).[14] I wholly agree with Johnston's estimation of the *Autobiography* both as a kind of training wheels for the remainder of Stein's corpus and as predicated on the promise of intimacy. Given the limited sales of Stein's writing before the *Autobiography* was published, however, the notion of a reader (particularly the sort of uninitiated reader Stein was courting) blithely repairing to the published version of "Ada" on Stein's cue seems anachronistic, seems to rely on the very currency Stein sought to establish (and did) with the *Autobiography*. The availability of Stein's work today allows us to read for these comparisons and crossovers freely (as I already have), but the task of the *Autobiography* was precisely to make that possible. Johnston's account, then, reads the *Autobiography* for its long-term potential, for the way its interrogation of the autobiographical "I" is complemented by its myriad extratextual references in order to instruct the reader in the possibility of associational, digressive, decentered reading practices that reach their apogee in an encounter with the book that repeatedly "go[es] outside its boundaries" (595). The interpretation I am offering complements hers, but again points to the ways the *Autobiography* has been underestimated. Johnston sees the *Autobiography* as most fully realized when it begins to break apart. I am suggesting that it directs us, too, to its own interstices, that adhering as closely as possible to the prompts to word association, digression, rereading, and reinterpreting *within* the text—at the level of individual words and even phonemes—provides the means for learning to read beyond it. Over-against—but also through—the fluid run of Toklas's chatty prose, the reader is called upon to do the sort of aural, syntactic, and conceptual manipulation more obviously demanded by Stein's more overtly challenging works; only by taking up this local challenge does the reader do full justice to the *Autobiography* itself.

Johnston concludes, by way of the conflation of "listening" and "telling" that marks "Ada," that Stein's ultimate lesson is one in which "[t]he authorial position is confounded, and the reading position becomes conflated with the authorial one"—that, in toggling between the *Autobiography* and other texts, "the reader becomes catalyst, parallel to Stein, who, as author of the autobiography, has moved herself to the margins while she is also ostensibly at the center of this text" (600). For Johnston, then, the ideal reading of the *Autobiography* is one that realizes Stein's proffered abdication, placing the reader's whim on an equal footing with Stein's own design. The minute interpretive puzzles and provocations I have been tracing pull against this dynamic, however, underscoring as they do the most local particulars of the text's design, and pointing as well to the existence and contours of the larger vision animating a work that only seems as haphazard as Toklas's train of thought. Awareness of these elements confers recognition, too, of Stein's centrality over-against the apparent looseness of the text and, at the same time, of her privileged position at one specific margin: the endpoint. Stein figures throughout Toklas's narration, and beyond it, as enigma and answer, as lure and reward, as cheerleader and mentor, as overture but also as distant horizon. The reader's freedom to range beyond the *Autobiography* and then to return is, of course, boundless, and certainly a desire for such expeditions is what Stein ultimately hopes to inculcate in the reader. But the *Autobiography* nevertheless has its own trajectory and teleology.

Johnston is right, though, to underscore the detail of the "note-book written forward and back"—Stein's own phrase in the *Autobiography* (114). Dydo describes the notebooks as "scribbled full, often starting from both ends," their pages "covered with writing, sometimes in both directions, in an uneven hand, usually in pencil." She speculates that they may sometimes have been written in the dark and notes that they also contain "letter drafts, shopping lists, guest lists, addresses and telephone numbers, doodles and small drawings, drafts of dedications for books, titles, calculations of income or expenditures, contents for proposed books, notes and jingles to Toklas, and so on." Finally, in a lovely understatement more than corroborated by photographic reproductions, she concludes that "they are often hard to read" (*Language* 27). This attribute of

Stein's practice resonates suggestively with Johnston's notion of weaving in and out of the autobiography, and with its own tremendously digressive temporal and narrative threads. Working through any of Stein's work in draft form, it appears, offers a similar challenge, requiring that one manage to read the notebooks "forward and back," a dexterousness that stands in marked opposition to the circling confusion that first characterizes Toklas's response to the inhabitants and contents of Stein's household. Toklas's skill here—her ability, at the literal level, to decipher individual words and render them into intelligible literary wholes—becomes part of her pedigree. She agrees that Stein's handwriting "has always been illegible" (76), but also holds that just as "you cannot tell what a picture really is or what an object really is until you dust it every day . . . you cannot tell what a book is until you type it or proof-read it" (113). Toklas, as one of the very few privileged to type and proofread Stein's writing, to shepherd it from manuscript to published form, knows it intimately, hard-won sentence by hard-won sentence. Her ability to make her way through this course of forwards and backs speaks to the way that an individual once constrained to the circular might navigate upon her release—offers insight as to what a circling sentence might open into after its halves have been decoupled. "Forward and back," that is, describes not only the physical structure of Stein's notebooks but also the chronological structure of Toklas's narrative. The experiences and lessons conferred upon Toklas by reading Stein in manuscript form, then, are communicated to the reader by both sentence- and book-level structures in the *Autobiography*. The bell-ringing phrases I discussed earlier offer a first hint of the temporal expansiveness that will suffuse Toklas's narration over the remainder of the book. An open circle, a voluntary forward and back, confers traction, allows the possibility of covering enormous amounts of ground rather than spinning one's wheels; it grants the expansiveness of productive reflection, of returning to an earlier moment when one wishes rather than being marooned in it.

This promise is first held out in the analogical form of Toklas's nascent grasp of modernist painting. By the end of her first evening at Stein's atelier, Toklas has been introduced to Picasso, Matisse, and Alfy Maurer, and she has been given a "card of invitation" to the upcoming vernissage of the Indépendants' exhibition (16). Initially, Toklas and the companion she brings along find themselves again thoroughly lost: "We went from one room to another and quite frankly we had no idea which of the pictures the Saturday evening crowd would have thought art and which were just the attempts of what in France are known as the Sunday painters" (17). She describes a "strange picture" by Rousseau that she "would not have recognized as a serious work of art" (17), but allows that in other cases "I say we did not know but yes perhaps we did know" (17). The example of an identifiable masterpiece she provides is, not coincidentally, a Matisse: "Then we went on and saw a Matisse. Ah there we were beginning to feel at home. We knew a Matisse when we saw it, knew at once and enjoyed it and knew that it was great art and beautiful" (17). Matisse is the artist whose work Toklas has, in fact, seen "at home" (that is, at what will become her home), as well as the one with whom she has had the most significant conversation at the atelier, the one whose "hidden meanings" have already received something of a promise of eventual elucidation (15). Indeed, not only has Stein assured Toklas that "when [she] knows France [she] will know" the significance lurking in the story Stein tells of her interaction with Matisse a year earlier, but Toklas has concluded the same paragraph with a related pledge to her reader: "Then they both began talking about the vernissage of the independent as every one else was doing and of course I did not know what it was all about. But gradually I knew and later on I will tell the story of the pictures, their painters and their followers and what this conversation meant" (15).

Toklas's narration in this phase seems almost hobbled by its eagerness to share with her reader not just "what was happening then" (6–7), but also "what had happened before, which led up to then" (7), as well as—again and again— what happened years later. "I must describe what I saw when I came" to the atelier at the rue de Fleurus, she reminds herself (7), but then must admonish herself repeatedly, as myriad extraneous details distract her, "to return to the pictures" (9), "to return to the pictures" (10), and again "this time I am really going to tell about the pictures" (10). The reader, who may well, in fact, already know something about the pictures—"now that everybody is accustomed to everything," as Toklas suggests (10)—is nonetheless shepherded into a narrative structure awarding them pride of place, such that the proffered recounting of individuals and events already begins to grade subtly into a discussion of artistic means and modes, intentions and achievements. The personalities that advertise the book give way to the aesthetic commitments attached to them, in a rehearsal of the book's overall goals and trajectory.

Equally importantly, what reads in the book's opening pages as lack of control, unclear narrative priorities, and temporal disarray is reconfigured, as

Toklas asserts an increasing narrative perspicacity, into a magisterial command, a knowledge of events past, present, and future, such that she travels through charged spaces with a godlike view of their complexities. Thus, for example, she can manage swooping chronological flights, threading them elegantly through a simple temporal and physical progress on the way (not coincidentally) to Picasso's studio:

> We went up the couple of steps and through the open door passing on our left the studio in which later Juan Gris was to live out his martyrdom but where then lived a certain Vaillant, a nondescript painter who was to lend his studio as a ladies dressing room at the famous banquet for Rousseau, and then we passed a steep flight of steps leading down where Max Jacob had a studio a little later, and we passed another steep little stairway which led to the studio where not long before a young fellow had committed suicide, Picasso painted one of the most wonderful of his early pictures of the friends gathered round the coffin, we passed all this to a larger door where Gertrude Stein knocked and Picasso opened the door and we went in. (21–22)

The *Autobiography*, unlike much of Stein's work, is not generally characterized by such long sentences. But in this and surrounding passages, wherein Toklas asserts her growing mastery of the new world she is coming to inhabit (and, by extension, of the aesthetics governing it), they come to the fore. Stein registers such length as key to her own stylistic breakthrough, to the progress of literary history and to her effect on readers, referring repeatedly to "those long sentences [in *The Making of Americans*] that had to be so exactly carried out" (41)—and affirms that "[s]entences not only words but sentences and always sentences have been Gertrude Stein's life long passion" (41). Length itself, in fact, becomes a way to link Stein's work to that of her favorite painters. The site of the exposition that spurs Toklas's transformation is the "long low certainly very very long temporary building that was put up every year for the independents" (16). This structure, as opposed to the more classically proportioned Grand Palais in which the Salon eventually came to be housed, represents "adventure" and "interest" to Toklas (16).

"Adventure" refers us back to Toklas's nonardent life and to Stein's intervention therein, at the same time as it points to the distance at which the American literary establishment has held Stein's literary sallies, which require "adventurous publishers" in order to reach their intended audience of strangers

(240). Central to the autobiography's achievement is the continuity or even the congruity it establishes between the adventure of beginning one's life anew in the artistic community of prewar Paris and that of the sentences that emerge from that milieu—even those that describe it from a vantage point twenty-five years on. The vicarious thrill of life on the Left Bank proves to be not just distantly apprehensible as a series of stories, but also more immediately at hand as an aesthetic—with the corollary that one may participate in that world, may be drawn progressively farther into it, as much by expanding one's own aesthetic horizons as by savoring anecdotes.

Toklas becomes the ideal intermediary between Stein and the larger readership she courts by being able to stand in for both, at once enunciating Stein's opinions and practices, and modeling the process of approaching them successfully. The Toklas-Stein convergence in the final sentences does not merely register as a characterological sleight of hand or a veiled statement of lesbian identity; it also signals, obliquely, Toklas's arrival at a final level of conversance with Stein's mode of textual production. "About six weeks ago," Toklas concludes, "Gertrude Stein said, it does not look to me as if you were ever going to write that autobiography. You know what I am going to do. I am going to write it for you" (252). The reader has by now grown thoroughly accustomed to Stein's idiosyncrasies regarding punctuation and capitalization, including her penchant for replacing question marks with periods. But I want to argue that her choice here marks anything but imprecision—Stein's rhetorical question, "You know what I am going to do?" is indeed best rendered as a declarative: "You know what I am going to do." Or "You know me, Alice, know me well enough to know already what I have in mind." There's a subtle pun on "know," here, intimacy proffering and grading into comprehension. This, of course, is the promise as well as the premise of the book as a whole—a promise extended to the reader even as it is fulfilled in the book's purported author. This knowledge, and this positioning, makes of Stein's tweaking of the marriage plot, and her own game of authorial hide-and-seek, something quite different from Faulkner's. The surprise ending has, like the "marriage" it announces, been prepared for throughout the book, and we have been party to its construction there. In this sense, it much more fully resembles a traditional novelistic ending. At the same time, closure here does not necessarily serve to whisk the happy couple off into an ever-after we cannot glimpse. Rather than abandoning us, Stein and Toklas usher us into their world. The experience is reassuring not because they are real people—readers, particularly at the time of the book's composition, would not have had much more access to the women's lives than to those of fictional characters—but because the stake of completing the work is the opposite of that entailed in starting it: immersion into an aesthetic space rather than a character-driven one.

3

SEE MONKEY, DO MONKEY

Lolita

(aping)

The search for the author turns in a new direction in *Lolita*: the appearance of absence, the posture of relinquishing control, falls quite spectacularly to the wayside. Visions and versions of Nabokov, and of authorship more broadly conceived, pervade the text, continually proliferating as the tale progresses. The search becomes a matter of thrashing one's way through the overgrown (even ingrown) jungle of competing accounts of what it means to be an author, and of what it means to be this author. Every character in the novel seems to be either an author or a "text" authored by another; to exist in this world is either to manipulate or to be manipulated, to tell tales or to too credulously believe them, or to spend all one's time and energy evaluating their credibility. Concomitantly, to read the novel is to be faced with a continual conflation of fictional characters and factual author, of superficial formal features and the deepest moral significances, of literary allusion and self-revelation. Interpretive categories are continually invoked, confused, proliferated, and never dispensed with. Authorial identity is erected through fiction and exposed as fiction, even as it is shaped into the sine qua non of a satisfactory reading of the novel. *Lolita* resolutely goads the reader into a search for the author, for origins and authenticity, and it relentlessly refuses not only to reward that quest, but even to countenance the assumptions underlying it.

Early in the novel, Nabokov provides the reader with the short inset narrative of Humbert Humbert's diary, along with two competing (if not particularly competitive) modes of reading it. When Charlotte Haze finds and deciphers the diary, she immediately recognizes that her own script for Humbert—itself already what Humbert ruefully dismisses as a hackneyed iteration of the suburban middle-class scenario built around a young widow's "taking a lodger" (37)—has been monstrously undermined. She accuses Humbert of the most horrible of machinations concerning her and her daughter, Lolita, and his only defense is to attempt to recast the manipulation as literary rather than literal: "The notes you found were fragments of a novel," he insists (96). Charlotte, in Humbert's lame effort at rewriting the scene, is a bad reader—"It is all your hallucination. You are crazy, Charlotte" (96)—because she cannot distinguish fact from fiction. Humbert's accusation is patently ludicrous, pretending to a thin semblance of justification only thanks to his extemporaneous definition of authorship as predicated on contingency and convenience—"Your name and hers were put in by mere chance. Just because they came handy" (96)—a claim thoroughly at odds not only with any reasonable explanation of the matters at hand, but also with Nabokov's famously Olympian pronouncements on the practice of writing. Charlotte rightly ignores Humbert's protests, but the reader should not. Humbert's allegations return to haunt him when he shifts into the unhappy reader's role, tortured and outmaneuvered in the second half of the novel by Clare Quilty's authorial production. The key terms Humbert introduces in his panicked response to Charlotte—craziness, hallucination, fragmentation, chance—resurface as Humbert struggles through the ever-expanding miasma of clues and nonclues Quilty leaves for him, structuring and restructuring an increasingly recondite and self-contradictory panoply of modes of reading and writing. These myriad accounts of authorship, in turn, precede and more importantly precondition the reader's response to Nabokov's own stentorian declarations, in the afterword to *Lolita*, regarding his novel's construction and its elucidation.

Lolita, as originally composed, already constitutes a turning-point for this study, suffused as it is with self-conscious figures of and ruminations on authorship. But the afterword recommends it especially. If Faulkner's and Stein's works are both short-order tours-de-force, gauntlets thrown down to the literary world and released to it not long after, *Lolita* is a very different beast. Composed over six years rather than six weeks, it had to wait several more years even to begin the process of American publication. After appearing under the imprint of a French publisher of both avant-garde fiction and pornography, *Lolita* endured scandal, censorship, and the threat of courtroom trial before a plan was hatched to present it to the American public.¹ A painfully and almost bewilderingly bowdlerized third of the novel made up the bulk of the *Anchor Review* for 1956. To further domesticate the work, literary critic and former *Partisan Review* editor F. W. Dupee wrote a thoughtful introduction, and Nabokov added his own "On a Book Entitled *Lolita*," forever since included as a postscript to the novel. The essay serves, then, as a bid for popular acceptance, a comparatively direct engagement with the publicity apparatus seeking to introduce both novel and author to a wary but very intrigued audience in Nabokov's adopted nation. Questions of reception and interpretation of the very text in the reader's hand stand explicitly articulated here, poised at its edge and paving the way for ever more thorough elaboration in works of the following decades.

The afterword gives the lie to its own proclamation of disinterest—Nabokov's protestation that he is "the kind of author who in starting to work on a book has no other purpose than to get rid of that book" (311)—unless getting rid of it in fact means next courting readers who might take it up. It's fair, of course, for even as imperious an author as Nabokov to be touched by market concerns, and perhaps even possible to imagine an author focused on publication but still "perfectly indifferent to the capacity and condition of his reader's brain."² But Nabokov's airy detachment is not, I think, the whole story of *Lolita*, a book so pervasively concerned with the processes of reading, and indeed with the omnipresent threat that—like Nabokov and Humbert, like Humbert and Quilty—the reader and Humbert will emerge as more aligned and identified than is quite comfortable. The afterword is the final proving ground for these fears and their potential dissolution, and as such is a recurring point of repair in this chapter. My contention throughout is that the afterword functions as fully part of the novel, and that it almost has to be read in terms dictated by the rest of the work even as it also provides new language and clues for deciphering the three hundred pages that precede it.

Nabokov's audacity—his game participation in the evisceration of the novel for the *Anchor Review* behind him, the fate of his writing career and perhaps even of his position teaching literature at Cornell hanging before him—was to make the afterword a full-blown literary performance, as complex and convoluted as the novel it accompanies. With characteristic bravado and finesse, he admits in the first sentence that the essay strikes even him as an "impersonation" (311), and then carries on with the show. Introduced under the sign of mimicry and subterfuge, then, the afterword recapitulates rather than resolves the themes of doubling and repetition, and of uncertain agency behind questionable acts, that are at the novel's core.[3] In so doing, it explodes whatever putative boundaries one might have hoped to maintain between the novel's world and ours. It represents not an afterthought or an apologia so much as the capstone of the novel's own undertakings. If Stein in the *Autobiography* represents a positive, personally ameliorative mode of seduction to and for the reader, *Lolita* presents the opposite. Stein's charm offensive is traduced into Humbert's offensive charm, the sole distraction from the perversion and perfidy that are the tale's matter. The essential question the reader faces is whether the slight divergence from parallelism in the previous sentence's formulation—substituting Humbert for Nabokov—is either legitimate or apposite. The novel maneuvers the reader into a position where trust of its author becomes very difficult, even as it emerges as absolutely essential for differentiating author from character. The reader wants the Faulkner of *As I Lay Dying*, an author powerfully divorced from his characters, but everything in the novel conspires to make Nabokov feel more like the *Autobiography*'s Stein, suffusing the book with her own concerns, in spite of having adopted the name and more or less distinct persona of another. Thus, where Stein merely invites her reader to embrace her (and her works) beyond the *Autobiography*, Nabokov instead demands such a pursuit, constructing a reader who must cling to the hope of discerning a firm, distinct, reproving authorial presence outside the text. *Lolita*'s genius lies in the interminability of this quest.

Humbert's own interpretive odyssey begins, in the period in which Quilty follows him and Lolita on the road, with his attempts to dismiss Quilty in terms redolent of his own former effort to dissuade Charlotte from her deductions. Attempting to shrug off the evidence of his senses, he ponders the possibility that he, himself, may be a "madman" (215), that to imagine he is being followed by "another Humbert" would be "too foolish even for a lunatic" (217), that "perhaps, [he is] losing [his] mind" (229). He wonders if Quilty's appearances are hallucinations (217, 241), as in the case of his earlier evanescent vision of Lolita with an unauthorized male tennis partner in the course of their first trip across the States (163). And he endeavors to reassure himself just before Lolita's disappearance that "all those identical detectives in prismatically changing cars were figments of [his] persecution mania, recurrent images based on coincidence and chance resemblance" (238). After Lolita's escape establishes the core of Humbert's perceptions as correct, he remains unable to confirm the outer edges of his consciousness as less than delusional, wondering if in his obsessive search of hotel registers along their route he is, in some instances, confusing the "verbal phantoms" of Quilty's teasing clues with actual "living vacationists" (251). Quilty becomes a sort of personification of authorial intentionality, and Humbert a reluctant convert, initially loath to credit all Quilty's manifestations as evidence of the same intrusive hand, but subsequently utterly dedicated to tracing and parsing every single outcropping of its script.

As explanatory systems grounded in chance fall away in Humbert's mind, as the notion that he has been drawing paranoid connections between disparate beings is dismissed in favor of a far broader and more encompassing paranoia, Quilty's status as an author, in myriad permutations, comes closer to the fore. Quilty's work in theater and film as dramatist, scenario-writer, and director leads Humbert to assume that his adversary has choreographed, with Lolita, the entire cross-country itinerary (248); indeed, when the two men finally meet at the novel's close, Quilty derides Humbert's murderous intent by ordering him to "stop trifling with life and death" (298). "I," Quilty proclaims, "am a playwright. . . . I know all the ropes. Let me handle this" (298). This self-identification echoes Quilty's previous adoption of the dates of Shakespeare's birth and death as license plate numbers (251), and finds more significant justification in the blurring of diegetic levels effected by his writing projects undertaken in collaboration with the anagrammatically portentous Vivian Darkbloom (31, 221).

When push finally comes all the way to shove, Quilty refuses to adhere to the dictates of Humbert's script for his demise. He casts Humbert as a functionary from the telephone company, a foreign literary agent, a Frenchman, an Australian, a German-Jewish refugee, and a policeman (295–98), continually knocking the foundations from underneath Humbert's posturing, before ultimately accepting that Humbert might actually be Lolita's stepfather (and still, nevertheless, questioning his "paternal" qualifications). At the same time, Quilty adopts numerous unhelpful accents and attitudes of his own. When the two men fall to wrestling, the pronouns shuffle over and between them (299), reducing the stereotyped figures required by Humbert's scenario—the abandoned lover seeking revenge on the wayward lothario—to "two large dummies, stuffed with dirty cotton and rags" (299). Quilty mocks Humbert's poetical inscription of his death writ, so that even Humbert's punitive "sentences" are half undone (299–300), and he absorbs the "slow, clumsy" bullets from Humbert's gun as if he were being tickled, as if they were "spurts of energy ..., ... capsules wherein a heady elixir danced" (303), recasting the supposed virility and mastery of gunplay as "feeble and juvenile" (297). Ultimately, even killing Quilty fails to satisfy Humbert; he comes to the defeated conclusion that he has done no more than reach "the end of the ingenious play staged for [him] by Quilty" (305).

It is worth remembering (as Humbert's rhetorical asides often compel us to do) that Humbert has, himself, staged this version of the play for us, that he may have taken liberties of his own in painting the sad story of his somewhat bungled revenge. In the pages that follow, I hope to demonstrate that the opposite is the case, that even many of the most libertine elements of Humbert's prose finally answer to dictates traceable to Quilty. Within his own narrative frame, Humbert's attempts to gloss "Quilty's" play, to chart the particulars of its ingenuity, are doomed to fail. When he searches for traces of Quilty as he writes his memoir, "know[ing] what to seek in the past" (255), he remains uncertain what among his manifold impressions is chance, what significant. When he looks for Quilty, he finds doppelgangers and false leads;[4] when he looks, in perverse nostalgia, for himself in the pages of the *Briceland Gazette* from the day after his stay at the Enchanted Hunters with Lolita, he finds instead—unbeknownst to him—a photograph of and an interview with Quilty (262). And the reader appears little better off. Limited by the thick lens of Humbert's perceptions and by the overweening compass of his search and self-narration, the reader is at pains to say whether Quilty represents authorship as textual coincidence, as perverse gamesmanship in the service of unruly sexual drives, as antic improvisation, or as cool execution of well-honed plots.

Nabokov keeps all these possibilities in play throughout the novel, and adds to them. Quilty offers the reader the specter of authorship in relatively high relief, but he is only one of many authors in *Lolita*. To speak only of strictly textual composition, there is his collaborator, Vivian Darkbloom; John Ray, Jr., the pedant *pendant* (as Humbert might say) from the front of the book; Nabokov himself in the afterword at the back; and Humbert Humbert, who crafts articles, poems, and anthologies in addition to the memoir itself. At different points, more or less protracted and more or less often repeated along the way, each of these authors seems to enjoy a privileged relation to Nabokov himself, such that the contradictions and mutual exclusivities of Humbert's suppositions regarding Quilty appear simple and straightforward in comparison to consideration of the full range of perspectives on authorship available in *Lolita*'s crowded pages.

Nabokov's afterword, which makes at least a brief show of earnest self-revelation, offers little help in the end. Its apparent raw emotion lies between, and is sometimes couched in, stretches of prose as thoroughly massaged and as allusively replete as any in the novel proper. Distinguishing between histrionic outburst and premeditated ruse—to say nothing of parsing the one or the other for accurate self-portraiture—proves as difficult as the endless task of readership to which Quilty subjects Humbert. Thus, for example, Nabokov's account of the novel's genesis, which casts *Lolita*'s first glimmering as the product of an elusive and inexplicable authorial alchemy worked on the detritus of the daily news—the collocation of chance and reverie—proves to be both a screen for and a method of introducing a pointed allusion that subtends much of the novel's imagery, plot, and ethics. The airy offhandedness of Nabokov's remarks grades, through a lengthy process of literary excavation, into a convoluted exploration of moral responsibility, the superficial and comparatively inconsequential issues of literary origin and originality opening into at least the suggestion of deep claims regarding Nabokov's ultimate liability for the tale he tells. Nabokov owns up to no more than a misty half-memory of the story's beginnings: "As far as I can recall, the initial shiver of inspiration was somehow prompted by a newspaper story about an ape in the Jardin des Plantes, who, after months of coaxing by a scientist, produced the first drawing ever charcoaled by an animal: this sketch showed the bars of the poor creature's cage" (311). The putative haze of Nabokov's recollection provokes multiple questions, given the degree of power and detail for which his memory was famous. Stacy Schiff's biography of Véra Nabokov, which steers more clear of the Nabokov myth than do biographies of the man himself, reveals that Nabokov was infamous among his intimates for occasional opportune lapses in his memory, and for faulty memories—in sum, for his easy willingness to alter the past for the sake of a good story.[5]

The legacy of critical response, both credulous and suspicious, to Nabokov's claim here extends far back into *Lolita*'s reception history. Andrew Field, Nabokov's first biographer, expended a good deal of effort searching *Paris-soir*, the paper in which Nabokov said he remembered seeing the article, for the reference, and then ransacking "three other Parisian newspapers that [Nabokov] occasionally also read at that time" (323). Nothing yielded the piece. Dieter Zimmer, editor of the exhaustive German-language *Collected Works*, similarly reports a thoroughgoing search with no better result (8: 686). Carl Proffer, on the other hand, opened the first book-length study of *Lolita* by debunking

Nabokov's assertion that the idea for the novel began here by quoting at length a passage from Nabokov's *The Gift*, written between 1934 and 1937 (that is, several years before the news story Nabokov references), in which a character proposes yet an earlier prototype of the Lolita story (3).⁶ Proffer merrily concludes, "Of course, it really doesn't matter what the truth is; and the real Nabokov has a perfect right to create a fictitious Nabokov if he wants to. My point is that one should always be suspicious, because casual and credulous readers will share the fate of Nabokov's butterflies" (4).

Proffer is right to enjoin suspicion and wrong to immediately turn aside, as he does, to "another typically Nabokovian piece of tomfoolery" (4). The "fictitious Nabokov" is indeed the real one's right, but he is also highly deserving of more sustained attention. Proffer's blithe changing of the subject is in keeping with his broader conclusion that while "literary associations run through the whole novel," "[i]n the great majority of cases the allusions are not 'contextual,'" meaning that "the context of the work quoted (or misquoted, or parodied) has no direct relevance for characters or situations in *Lolita*" (19). Subsequent literary criticism has of course thoroughly disabused us of this breezy stance. The lingering interest to be found in Proffer's claim arises from his terminology—"no direct relevance"—which is so strangely reminiscent of that which Nabokov himself uses in fobbing off the ape story to begin with, immediately following his brief narration of the ape's travails with the cautionary admonition: "The impulse I record [that "initial shiver of inspiration"] had no textual connection with the ensuing train of thought" (311).⁷

The lack of a "textual connection" is what makes Nabokov's comment so salient, in my view. If the basic parameters of *Lolita*'s plot have already been established in *The Gift* and have been worked through in significant (if also significantly divergent) detail in *The Enchanter* (the "ur-*Lolita*" story Nabokov wrote in Paris in 1940), what is the importance of highlighting a fictive ape from an imagined newspaper story here? Various critics emphasize the ape's situation, seeing in his artistic production limited to the boundaries of his cage, which is also to say his immediate perceptual field, a metaphor for Humbert Humbert's imprisonment within the confines of his own compulsions and the distorted worldview they impart to him.⁸ While this reading offers an excellent explanation for the cage and the drawing, it says less about the ape itself. And yet, apes are everywhere in *Lolita*. In contrast, as Dmitri Nabokov observes in his afterword to *The Enchanter*, that book is filled with all manner of bestial similes: "hyenas in every hygiene; onanistic tentacles;

the lupine leer in place of the intended smile"; resolving into a "whole leitmotif of the Wolf about to devour his Red Riding Hood" (116). That this panoply of figurative identifications is largely distilled in *Lolita* to sustained and repetitive ape imagery speaks to the importance of this particular metaphorical transposition, and of the literary reference behind it, to the novel.[9]

The issue of reference is particularly important at this juncture, as well, in that it is caught up with the question of establishing origins that marks the novel as a whole. Humbert Humbert is, sporadically, preoccupied with establishing the etiology of his own sexual obsessions, querying whether his predilections are innate or whether they were determined by the brief flowering, the frustrated attempts at consummation, and the too-quick demise of his childhood romance with Annabel Leigh.[10] That Humbert's account asks whether Annabel is the first manifestation in his life of a preexisting pattern or whether she inaugurates the pattern, when she herself is a figure predicated on an allusion to Poe's poem "Annabel Lee," means that psychology, biography, and literary inheritance are all fuddled from the start.[11]

Proffer does not, in fact, mark Nabokov's account of the story's incipience as a literary allusion at all. Elizabeth Phillips does, glossing it as a "wry reference" to Poe's "The Murders in the Rue Morgue," which turn out to have been committed by an orangutan, later recaptured by its owner and sold to the Jardin des Plantes (97). For Phillips, the allusion provides an entrée into her main thesis, that *Lolita* represents "a satire on an orthodox Freudian view of the life and writings of Edgar Allan Poe," in which the ape, according to Marie Bonaparte's analysis, is a potent father symbol, "embodying those aggressive and bestial instincts which, as primitively conceived by the child, dominate his . . . concept of the sex act" (97). Phillips provides a thorough catalogue of parallels between Humbert Humbert's life and enthusiasms and Poe's (most notably Poe's child-bride, Virginia Clemm, whom Humbert Humbert references explicitly), and she glosses numerous thematic echoes (loss and/or death of beautiful women, struggles with madness and with preternaturally persistent doubles, carefully calculated revenge, and so on) between *Lolita* and Poe's writings.[12] Alfred Appel, Jr. also references "Rue Morgue" in discussing the ape imagery in the body of the novel (Nabokov, *Lolita* lxi), linking Poe's vocabulary to that of other nineteenth-century tales of demonic doubles such as Dostoevsky's *The Possessed* and Stevenson's *Dr. Jekyll and Mr. Hyde*; Appel's gloss of this moment in the afterword, however, concentrates on imprisonment per se and does not read the story as an allusion to Poe. Appel does note that there are more allusions in *Lolita* to Poe than to any other author (330), embracing not only plot developments and rhetorical echoes, but also Humbert Humbert's self-designation as Edgar H. Humbert, and his momentary conflation of Annabel Leigh, "Annabel Lee," and Dolores Haze—the latter appearing at one point as "Annabel Haze, alias Dolores Lee, alias Loleeta" (167).[13]

That there are so many allusions to Poe, that he stands as a tutelary figure and a literary precursor behind the novel at so many levels, lends credibility to the impulse to read Nabokov's account of *Lolita*'s origin as a veiled reference to Poe's story.[14] I want to argue, however, that the novel's engagement with "Rue Morgue" is considerably more complex than the programmatic psychoanalytic satire Phillips proposes. Nabokov appears to believe that Freud is adequately dispensed with in a few well-placed asides; his use of Poe, on the other hand, embraces both protracted parody and more freighted inquiry. The myriad allusions to Poe's story prove much more than a series of nods and winks; rather, they establish the fashion in which *Lolita* takes up and works through moral questions Poe's tale might evoke in some readers' minds but that it scrupulously avoids addressing. In this way, the allusions to "Rue Morgue" begin to illuminate the stakes for the kaleidoscopic proliferation of authorial perspectives, personae, and claims with which *Lolita* teems.

The significance of Nabokov's allusion can best be determined by way of a more thorough rehearsing of the tale's main coordinates. "Rue Morgue"—commonly thought of not just as the first locked-room mystery, but as the first modern detective story—tells of the murders of a Madame L'Espanaye and her daughter in their private apartments on the fourth story of a building on Rue Morgue. In the wake of the women's screams, several other residents of the building hear the violent expostulations of two individuals, one of whom they all recognize as speaking French, while they variously characterize the other as Spanish, English, German, Russian, or Italian, each witness averring that he or she does not speak the language he or she imputes to the second individual. After the police make their way into the apartment, at length they discover the daughter deeply scratched and bruised and ultimately throttled to death, her body shoved far up the chimney. While several "long and thick tresses" of the mother's hair are found in the apartment (147), her corpse turns out to be in the building's back courtyard, thoroughly mutilated and with the throat so deeply slashed that her head falls off when the police attempt to lift her. Inside the apartment, the police find wanton destruction but no apparent theft. After lengthy investigation and multiple depositions, the police profess themselves clueless, while the papers continue to trumpet the "extraordinary" (and "mysterious," "perplexing") nature of the crime (147).

M. Dupin, a generally retiring man of letters, eagerly anticipating the "amusement" (153) to be afforded by joining the investigation but also intent on freeing an associate imprisoned (Dupin believes wrongfully) for the crime, trades on his acquaintance with the prefect of the police to gain admission to the scene of the murders. Dupin's conjectures, the reader learns later, progress unerringly; even the most solid of physical structures in and around the apartment yield docilely to the contours he has provisionally assigned them in order to account for the murderers' entry to and exit from the locked room.[15] Finally, having concluded that such an "*outré*"—"praeternatural," "brutal," even "*excessively outré*"—"*grotesquerie*" (154, 159, 161, 160, 161) could have been committed only by an orangutan (the source of the ineluctably "foreign" voice overheard by the several bystanders), Dupin places an ad in the paper luring to his apartment the French sailor who, Dupin correctly guesses, had brought the creature to Paris and accidentally released it into the night. In confronting the sailor, Dupin carefully delineates between being "in some measure implicated" in the events that have transpired and being in any way "culpable" (165), and—thus reassured—the sailor narrates the entire ugly episode, perfectly in keeping with Dupin's suppositions. Thanks to Dupin's interventions, the innocent man is enlarged, and the sailor too remains at liberty, able both to recapture the ape and to sell it to the Jardin des Plantes for a handsome fee.

Poe's story draws an opposition between brute power and ratiocinative force, between mindless destruction and the shockingly puissant ability of a supreme mind to restore order—and, thus, moral clarity—where all appears lost.[16] Too, Poe allies the rational with the aesthetic, at the level both of the formal satisfaction afforded by the mystery's solution and of various attributes of Dupin's character and predilections. Nabokov recasts the story and its moral by making Humbert Humbert the primary representative of the brutal, but also of the aesthetic and the endlessly rationalizing (if not always rational) individual. In elaborating extensively on this new premise, Nabokov reflects at length on the moral coordinates of life and art and their intersection, even as the relations between these reflections end up fashioning something much closer to a hall of mirrors than an ethical parable. Adumbrating the parallels and echoes between Poe's and Nabokov's works will not offer us a route all the way out of the funhouse, but it will illustrate a way in.

Humbert describes himself as an ape from the start. He first sees Lolita through "aging ape eyes" and tracks her breathing with his "ape-ear" (39, 48), his looks are "attractively simian" (104), he takes Rita's hand in his "ape paw" (258). So, too, he is "lanky, big-boned" and "wooly-chested" (44), possessed of a "huge hairy hand" when he masturbates surreptitiously to Lolita's presence on the couch (60) and of a "hot hairy fist" as he clutches the key to their room at the Enchanted Hunters (123), and it is again his "hairy fist" that he raises in poetic lament to the lost Lolita late in the novel (256). He also repeatedly labels himself a "brute" or "brutal" (24, 47, 193, 262, 284), and a "beast" and "bestial" (55, 59, 287); both Lolita and Quilty echo these epithets (140, 221, 298).

At the same time, Humbert does not scruple to speak of Lolita's own "monkeyish nimbleness" (58) or her "long-toed, monkeyish feet" (51), or even to call her his "monkey," *tout court* (213). He likewise relishes the image of his first wife, Valeria, and her new husband on all fours, subsisting on a diet of bananas and dates in an "ethnological" experiment (30), and he mentally accuses Charlotte of "monkeying with the furniture" (93). Nabokov himself might point out the distinctions (in behavior and in size—both of which seem apposite to a comparison between Lolita and Humbert) between monkeys and apes, as he does those between moths and butterflies, in order to establish Humbert's lack of zoological discernment (327, 376). In this fashion, the broad brush with which Humbert diffuses a trope meant more specifically for him would be corrected for, even as the distinctions between Humbert and his creator would be (for a moment) underlined. On the other hand, Humbert may be read as aware of the discrepancies his vocabulary suggests, which would hammer home the accusations he levels against himself even as it would muddy the terms of the accusation, for Humbert as self-conscious and articulate and rhetorically adroit is Humbert as Dupin rather than Humbert as ape.

At the level of action, destruction, lives ruined and lives taken, we might nevertheless remain committed to drawing the parallel between Humbert (alone) and the ape. In accordance with this emphasis on crime and guilt, the more important foil in Poe's story would not be Dupin, but rather the sailor who brought the ape to Paris in the first place. Reading Humbert as ape would then lead to reading Nabokov in terms of the sailor; each member of the latter pair might then be glossed as an enabler, proximate to the crimes committed by the members of the former pair, but not directly responsible. "You have done nothing which you could have avoided—nothing, certainly, which renders you culpable," Dupin tells the sailor (165), prefiguring the distance Nabokov initially seems intent on drawing between himself and his creation, maintaining that he begins books only to have done with them (311), and referring to *Lolita* dissociatively as "the thing" three times in the course of one page's recounting of its textual history (312). Though I have already rehearsed how the variety of ways in which simianness is distributed in the text might undermine this parallel, I want to keep it in play. For it is precisely our inability to establish any such coordinates firmly, just as—more locally—it is our inability to discern with confidence the agency properly attributed to the passive construction in the previous sentence, that makes *Lolita* so infuriating and so successful a novel—its success predicated in part on the degree to which it compels us to yearn, even clamor, for the absolutes it denies us.

The "Rue Morgue" allusion presents a fine illustration, offering a characteristically looping, inconclusive Nabokovian itinerary, in which the surface claim for the dumb literary luck of Nabokov's inspiration by a chance item in a Parisian tabloid—no clear memory of the source, no textual connection of the source to the result, the whole event predicated on the briefest visitation by an unorthodox muse from an unexpected venue—reveals itself under interrogation to be the artful key to an intricate, sustained, highly freighted engagement with a precursor text.[17] Parsing that earlier text appears to complete the loop, in that doing so yields a renewed claim for lack of agency—since Poe's story, too, relies on an orangutan ex machina in order to escape the strict confines of its locked-room setup—but then all these coordinates and inversions are thrown back into doubt by the slippery appositions and echoes that dot the novel. In like fashion, Nabokov figuratively throws his hands up "when asked to explain [*Lolita*'s] origin and growth," admitting, he says, that he can but rely on the dubious and slightly unwieldy formulation, "Interreaction of Inspiration and Combination" (311). Nabokov allows that in speaking of his work thus he "sounds like a conjurer explaining one trick by performing another" (311), but the misdirection may be precisely in the appeal to magic tricks as the defining metaphor. Instead, that bizarre and awkward word, "interreaction"—which is not in the *Oxford English Dictionary*—suggests a more chemical valence, recalling T. S. Eliot's figure of the author as catalyst in "Tradition and the Individual Talent," and with it Eliot's claims for the irrelevance of individual authorial psychology and biography to an artwork in fact structured by literary inheritance. Nabokov was no fan of Eliot's work, but—as other passages in the novel indicate—he was certainly willing to mobilize it in support of his vision.[18] Here, specific allusion displaces the mystification of an underarticulated artistic genesis, but again the allusion renews the obfuscation, and the claim for determinant forces beyond the author's control, at a deeper level.

These oscillating interpretive possibilities recall those which Quilty's actions place before Humbert: myriad details legible as chance textual collations or as fiendishly grand and mocking design. But Nabokov's introduction of the "Rue Morgue" allusion significantly complicates the depiction of authorship previously offered via Quilty. To recapitulate and abstract, Humbert construes Quilty's authorship as limited to two basic functions. On one hand, Humbert views Quilty's hotel register entries—on the far side of their deep investment in "logodaedaly and logomancy" (249–50)—as fundamentally a distorted mode of self-revelation; he nurses the wan hope that Quilty might "slip on the glaze of his own subtlety, . . . introduce a richer and more personal shot of color than was strictly necessary," and give away his identity (249). On the other hand, Humbert reads Quilty as a constructor of plot, of which his scattered roadside appearances, Lolita and Humbert's attendance of the play in Wace, Lolita's illness and hospitalization in Elphinstone, Humbert's beleaguered pursuit of Quilty's clues, and even the dénouement in Parkington are a part.[19] But Nabokov adds a major element to the schema of authorial activity articulated through Quilty: the creation of character. Unpacking the "Rue Morgue" allusion highlights the contours of this augmentation. The ape in Poe's story is not a character in any full sense; he enters and leaves as a function of plot, predicated on the pure ratiocinative force of Dupin's deductions. The plot dictates the most rudimentary, literally inhuman "character" for its logical completion; the murders arise at least tangentially from the ape's attempt to mimic the sailor's use of a straight-razor. Its failure to wield the instrument properly measures the distance between the animal kingdom and ours. In Nabokov's appropriation, this figure broadens to a tremendously fledged individual, endowed with history, psychology, *tics nerveux*, dreams and nightmares, and—far from least— the possession of articulate speech.

In "Rue Morgue," morality amounts to little more than freeing the innocent man mistakenly jailed by the police. More complex notions of guilt drop by the wayside, along with continued concern for the two dead women, in the interest of argumentative force. In order that the sailor be compelled to complete the tale, he is guaranteed immunity by Dupin at the start, and in order that

Dupin prove himself as "praeternaturally" acute as Poe desires, his reasoning—and the dispensation that goes with it—must be unimpeachable. But by presenting the inhuman monster as a full, human character, and a disconcertingly charming one at that, Nabokov shifts the ground radically, asking—or threatening—that the crime and its perpetrator be "understood" not just logically, but morally. And of course by making Humbert Humbert not just a character, but also the author of very nearly as much of the tale as Nabokov himself, Nabokov flirts with (or risks, or even suggests) implicating himself in the crimes Humbert perpetrates. Humbert joins literary creation to literal destruction, and does so with such force that readers and critics have long struggled with the question of whether a similar equation or collocation should be extended to Nabokov himself. Véra Nabokov worried that such confusions were particularly American, but Stacy Schiff points out that Nadezhda Mandelstam (Osip's wife) raised similar objections, telling Carl Proffer that "in her mind there was no doubt that the man who wrote *Lolita* could not have done so unless he had in his soul those same disgraceful feelings for little girls" (Schiff 199–200). More recently, literary critics have conflated not only Nabokov and Humbert, but also the fictive text and the real world. Linda Kauffman, for example, labels "aesthetic bliss" (which is Nabokov's terminology, in the afterword) "meager consolation for the murder of Lolita's childhood" (146), and Jen Shelton deems Lolita's tears, by virtue of their nonlinguistic status, as signatures of the real somehow quasi-impervious to manipulation by Humbert or by Nabokov (281–87).

My point in citing these responses is not to suggest that they are wrong. They are right, I think, in that they are precisely the effect the novel envisions and encourages, alongside the formalist and aestheticist defenses against which these formulations react. Such readings are mistaken, on both sides, only in presenting themselves as the final word, as correctives that eclipse those interpretations with which they disagree, rather than as elucidations of the other side of the balanced mechanism that Nabokov puts into action. The function of that mechanism is to compel a continual skittering of attention between the work of art and the man behind it, the literary "prime mover." Nabokov's own investment in himself as prime mover manifests itself particularly pleasingly in an interview with the BBC in 1962. Nabokov here proffers a startling emendation to a near-verbatim retelling of the *Lolita*-origin story, thereby flagging a clue from the afterword regarding the author-character relationship that he apparently deemed underappreciated in the years immediately following the novel's publication. It is worth noting in this context that, after a pair of early interviews that Nabokov determined laughable failures because of his inability to speak articulately without preparation, he elected to conduct all remaining interviews purely in writing, allowing himself all the premeditation and linguistic precision he needed, and thereby magnifying the importance of minor textual details and deviations (*Strong Opinions* ix). In the afterword to *Lolita*, he writes, "The first little throb of *Lolita* went through me late in 1939 or early in 1940, in Paris, at a time when I was laid up with a severe attack of intercostal neuralgia" (311). The reader, conditioned by Humbert Humbert's references to his own facial neuralgia (77, 193, 291), may skate by the specifics of Nabokov's medical complaint, but—as always in Nabokov—specifics are everything. The key here is not the neuralgic pain, but rather its intercostal location. Having failed to excite the response he was looking for, Nabokov refashions the narrative slightly in the BBC interview, with added emphasis. He now writes, "[t]he first little throb of *Lolita* went through me in Paris in '39, or perhaps early in '40, at a time when I was laid up with a fierce attack of intercostal neuralgia which is a very painful complaint—rather like the fabulous stitch in Adam's side" (*Strong Opinions* 15).[20]

Neither the Bible nor, say, *Paradise Lost* mentions any physical pain attending the removal of Adam's rib. The import in the source texts, as in Nabokov's reference, would seem to lie instead in the fact that Eve is fashioned from Adam's rib. The barest contours of the story that follows—a creature, straying from the surveillance of a potential or putative overseer, commits a horrible crime for which that overseer may or may not be held to some degree responsible—suggest another narrative analogous to the one already adduced by way of the allusion to "Rue Morgue." Eve would now take her place alongside Humbert Humbert and the murderous ape, leaving Adam in Nabokov and the sailor's slack-jawed company.[21] If we postulate Eve as a free agent wholly capable of making her own choices, this parallel parable again seems to deflect responsibility for Humbert's actions away from Nabokov. But at the same time, it raises the question of ultimate culpability, both at the level of the debates around free will that are central to the biblical narrative and commentary on it, and at the simpler level of effective causality, in that it is God, not Adam, who removes Adam's rib and makes it into Eve. Thus, while we might be tempted by a schematic rendering a threefold structure of responsibility—

Humbert Humbert	Nabokov	
ape	sailor	
Eve	Adam	God

—we would be wise to remember that the order of quickly progressing events in Eden (whether the Adam-before-Eve of Creation or the Eve-before-Adam of apple-eating) notwithstanding, Adam and Eve end up on the same plane, ontologically and morally, punished alike with expulsion from Eden and a future of painful labor. Thus it might be that Eve and Adam should contract to hold a single place in the schematic, with God to their side:

Humbert Humbert	Nabokov
ape	sailor
Eve/Adam	God

Alternatively, the fluttering possibility (or the fleeting fact) of a third figure on the line provokes new questions: might we restore Eve and Adam to the spots we accorded them originally, and then speculate on the existence of some constructive force legible to Humbert's left, or to Nabokov's right, or perhaps intervening between them? If so, does Nabokov provide a model by which to articulate it?

In fact, Nabokov's invocation of Adam points the reader back into the novel. The implicit addition of Eve and the rib in Nabokov's retelling of *Lolita*'s origin recalls another nested pair of brief narratives—again invoking Eve and the rib in metaphorical terms, but again literally describing, in the end, a man reading a newspaper. Here Humbert himself reflects on creation, albeit in vaguely hallucinatory terms. Twice in the course of the novel he reports the same situation, initially toward the end of the chapter in which he first introduces the concept of the nymphet:

> It happened for instance that from my balcony I would notice a lighted window across the street and what looked like a nymphet in the act of undressing before a co-operative mirror. Thus isolated, thus removed, the vision acquired an especially keen charm that made me race with all speed toward my lone gratification. But abruptly, fiendishly, the tender pattern of nudity I had adored would be transformed into the disgusting lamp-lit bare arm of a man in his underclothes reading his paper by the open window in the hot, damp, hopeless summer night. (20)

For a man in the grip of an overwhelming and very singular obsession, writing a 300-page narrative in the space of fifty-six days (308), Humbert Humbert does a fantastic job of not repeating himself. Its basic fervor notwithstanding, *Lolita* is an extremely disciplined narrative. The fact that Humbert retells this story—again at a highly charged moment: when he receives the letter from Lolita three years after her disappearance in Elphinstone—is itself noteworthy; the additions he makes to it are more so:

> I used to recollect, with anguished amusement, the times in my trustful, pre-dolorian past when I would be misled by a jewel-bright window opposite wherein my lurking eye, the ever alert periscope of my shameful vice, would make out from afar a half-naked nymphet stilled in the act of combing her Alice-in-Wonderland hair.... Hanging above blotched sunset and welling night, grinding my teeth, I would crowd all the demons of my desire against the railing of a throbbing balcony: it would be ready to take off in the apricot and black humid evening; did take off—whereupon the lighted image would move and Eve would revert to a rib, and there would be nothing in the window but an obese partly clad man reading the paper. (264)

Humbert's formulation at the close of the second narration again misdirects us. "Eve would revert" accords temporal and ontological primacy to the obese man, giving rise to another short-lived three-layer structure:

> nymphet   obese man   Humbert Humbert

resolving upon reflection into

> nymphet/obese man   Humbert Humbert

What do these unstable structures teach us? The conventions of authorial commentary would suggest glossing Humbert Humbert's narrative with Nabokov's, but I want to propose doing the opposite, looking to Humbert to teach us how to read Nabokov. Humbert's narrative and Nabokov's have in common the man-reading-newspaper at their cores, the creation of a fictional other creature through a process of projection, and—most tellingly—the puzzling, perhaps slightly disturbing "throb" that, in the wake of Humbert's masturbatory fantasies, may set one's own teeth slightly on edge when Nabokov uses the same term not just in describing the impetus for the first "ur-*Lolita*" short story (311), but also for the provocation to return to the theme ten years later, when "the throbbing, which had never quite ceased, began to plague [him] again" (312).

Both iterations of the balcony-window-fat man scenario differ from the three previous structures in that no crime is committed by the creature in the first position—in fact, that first position is occupied by nothing but an unwitting fat man or, qua nymphets, by nothing at all, just the momentary effects of Humbert's solitary fantasy. If, in the first iteration of the narrative, that fact serves only to disappoint Humbert—at this point he characterizes such episodes as "end[ing] in a rich flavor of hell" (20)—by the end of the novel he recognizes the advantages to, perhaps even the ideal represented by, the situation. In it he sees a sort of essentialized representation of his "nympholepsy" itself, or of what "nympholepsy" was for him before he broke all its rules in his relations with Lolita:

> There was in the fiery phantasm a perfection which was out of reach, with no possibility of attainment to spoil it by the awareness of an appended taboo; indeed, it may well be that the very attraction immaturity has for me lies not so much in the limpidity of pure young forbidden fairy child beauty as in the security of a situation where infinite perfections fill the gap between the little given and the great promised—the great rosegray never-to-be-had. (264)

In this realm of complete imaginative license balanced by actual powerlessness, Humbert projects his own sexual excitement onto the world all around him—the sunset becomes "blotched," the night "well[s]" up, the balcony "throb[s]" and then "take[s] off" (264).

But an experience so thoroughly predicated on solipsism leads to an inevitable question as to the effect of Humbert's solitary bliss. Just after the first version of the balcony scene, he asks himself, "In this wrought-iron world of criss-cross cause and effect, could it be that the hidden throb I stole from them did not affect *their* future?" (21). And he begins to provide an answer in his narration of the most profound of his "hidden throbs." The episode on the living room sofa of the Haze household, which ends with Humbert's "moaning mouth . . . almost reach[ing Lolita's] bare neck, while [he] crush[es] out against her left buttock the last throb of the longest ecstasy man or monster had ever known" (61), opens with Humbert's repeated protestations as to the care he takes to maintain a thin line between himself—his "gagged, bursting beast," "the hidden tumor of an unspeakable passion" (59)—and Lolita. He indulges in a sustained fantasy of being able, "despite the insatiable fire of [his] venereal appetite ... to protect the purity of that twelve-year-old child" (63), and so he reports the solicitude with which he maintains, here, "the physically irremovable, but psychologically very friable texture of the material divide (pajamas and robe)" between himself and Lolita (59). Even as Humbert delights in the possibility of "doing away, in an illusional, if not factual sense" with that divide, by way of a "magic friction" (59), he reassures himself that it constitutes, nevertheless, a gulf tantamount to an ontological chasm between them: "nothing prevented me," he concludes, "from repeating a performance that affected her as little as if she were a photographic image rippling upon a screen and I a humble hunchback abusing myself in the dark" (62).

At the limit, Humbert's fantasies distend yet further, beyond the carefully calibrated minimal distances or boundaries between himself and his inamoratas, beyond their fading into insubstantiality before the force of his mental internalizations. Humbert, the brute, imagines that he utterly deliquesces in the close proximity of nymphets, "dissolving in the sun" on a park bench as "a perfect little beauty ... dip[s] her slim bare arms into [him]" (20), his knees "like reflections of knees in rippling water" when he first glimpses Lolita (40), and, in a late echo, "melting in [a] golden peace" upon her revealing Quilty's name to him (272). The evaporative triumphalism of his self-congratulation after the interaction on the Haze davenport—"I had stolen the honey of a spasm without impairing the morals of a minor. Absolutely no harm done. The conjurer had poured milk, molasses, foaming champagne into a young lady's new white purse; and lo, the purse was intact" (62)—represents this conviction at its zenith.

But the novel argues, and Humbert recognizes obscurely, that the opposite is the case. Humbert's bad faith is brought home to him in a distorted mirror scene that even he recognizes as "a rather good symbol of something or other" (226), shortly before Lolita escapes from him. In Wace, Lolita disappears briefly while Humbert screens her mail, reporting on her return that she has run into a friend from Beardsley also named Dolly. Humbert recognizes this inward-turning lie as a "dead end," "the mirror you break your nose against" (225), but accepts and adopts and thereby underlines her usage of her public nickname, Dolly, in the ensuing dialogue.[22] When Lolita, attempting to concoct a passable account of how she spent the time out of Humbert's sight, claims that she and the other Dolly looked in shop windows, Humbert presses her for specifics, and together they approach the nearest display. There, the dual Dollys are doubled by another pair of life-size "dolls": two mannequins in the process of being dressed in nuptial finery, one—"stark naked, wigless, and armless"—strikes

Humbert as "sexless," but destined to be "a girl-child of Lolita's size," the other "a much taller veiled bride, quite perfect and *intacta* except for the lack of one arm." Two of the three missing arms are twisted together on the floor in what seems to Humbert "to suggest a clasping gesture of horror and supplication" (226).

Humbert's questionable taste, his sexually obsessed myopia, and his jaunty brutality are all displayed in his carefree ability to proclaim the larger mannequin virginally intact and then to add the grace note of her missing arm. It's easy to read the amalgam of the two models as standing for Lolita's itinerary in Humbert's hands, forced to become a child-bride while still at an essentially sexless age. The lurking symbolism Humbert suspects stretches yet further, however, in that the dismembered mannequins return us once again to the afterword: not only to the violence and bodily destruction wrought by the ape in "Rue Morgue,"[23] but also to Nabokov's metaphorical description of his literary endeavors. Among the closing statements in the afterword, under the guise of claiming that it is "childish to study a work of fiction in order to gain information about . . . the author," Nabokov reports a friend's concern, upon reading the novel, that he (Nabokov) "should be living 'among such depressing people.'" Nabokov demurs: "the only discomfort I really experienced was to live in my workshop among discarded limbs and unfinished torsos" (316). The bait-and-switch technique is familiar: Nabokov denies any relevance of his work to his person—in fact, to people, period—then metaphorically reimagines his novelistic practice as akin to the destructive arcs of both Humbert and the ape. The implication of the rhetoric at this moment, then, is that artistic work does not happen in a vacuum, that the human costs are pronounced.

In similar fashion, the throbs that function for Humbert, among other things, as indices of his enforced solitude—part of the lonely record of the minute attention he pays to his own body—find their way into the heart of Nabokov's statement of artistic solicitude. I have already cited Humbert's throbs on the Haze couch, in the two iterations of the balcony-voyeurism moment, and in his reflections following. They appear as well in another pledge of his meek nature—"the majority of sex offenders that hanker for some throbbing, sweet-moaning, physical but not necessarily coital, relation with a girl-child, are innocuous, inadequate, passive, timid" (87–88)—again in earnest of the pangs caused by Lolita's absence during the school-day—"I would . . . listen to receding girl laughter in between my heart throbs and the falling leaves" (184)—and in his final jailhouse exhortations—"while the blood still throbs through my writing hand, you [Lolita] are still as much a part of blessed matter as I am, and I can still talk to you from here to Alaska" (309). John Ray, Jr. vouches for Humbert Humbert in contiguous terms as the novel opens—"a desperate honesty... throbs through his confession" (5).[24]

This sublimating itinerary, wherein Humbert's base sexual transgressions are domesticated to what Ray characterizes as the admirable sincerity of his writing, reverses itself in the afterword. For Nabokov, the throb is initially "little," a mere "shiver" as he begins the short story that was in the end to become *Lolita* (311), but by the time he sets to work on the novel proper it has become a "plague" (312). Whatever hopes one may entertain of reading this language as innocuously as possible, ignoring the vocabulary's history in the bulk of the book, become increasingly difficult to sustain in the face of Nabokov's disturbingly intimate description of the role the published novel plays in his life. One may make one's peace with *Lolita* as "a constant comforting presence" (315), but it's rather difficult to wholly avoid a salacious reading of Nabokov's invocation of the "favorite hollows that [he] evokes more eagerly and enjoys more tenderly than the rest of [his] book" (315–16), and, even more, his characterization of the book's "pilot light burning somewhere in the basement," such that "a mere touch applied to [his] private thermostat instantly results in a quiet little explosion of familiar warmth" (315). It is not far from here to the "bubble of hot poison in your loins and a super-voluptuous flame permanently aglow in your subtle spine" that Humbert deems requirements for perceiving nymphets (17).[25]

Nabokov insists that he does not share Humbert's sexual proclivities (315), but he also hastens to define his aesthetic as predicated on "bliss" (314) and via a further eroticized vocabulary—"tenderness," "ecstasy"—appropriated directly from Humbert Humbert (315). The elements of that aesthetic that set Nabokov apart from Humbert—the insistence on "curiosity" and "tenderness" (315) that are so important to readings of the novel like Richard Rorty's—risk being swallowed by the vortex of Humbert's lubricity, such that the full nominative ensemble Nabokov proposes as the essence of "art"—"curiosity, tenderness, kindness, ecstasy" (315)—reads like a definition of good sex. Which may well be part of Nabokov's joke. Certainly, he embraces numerous opportunities to paint Humbert's qualities, both large and small, as reflections of his own. In the aggregate, Humbert reads as an entity midway between the underdeveloped and generally unremarkable Vladimir Vladimirovich (professor of Russian literature and accomplished lepidopterist), who appears to be the unnamed narrator of *Pnin*, and *Pale Fire*'s more-or-less mad Charles Kinbote, whose glorious evocations of the lost kingdom of Zembla function in part as parodies of Nabokov's own rhapsodies in *Speak, Memory* over the lost haunts of his Russian youth (to speak only of the narrators in the three works written in closest proximity to *Lolita*). The interests uniting adolescent Humbert with Annabel Leigh—"the plurality of inhabited worlds, competitive tennis, infinity, solipsism" (12)—are also demonstrably those of his creator. Humbert and Nabokov share, as well, several languages, favorite authors, protracted exile from European homelands, a preference for rented lodgings while in the employ of small New England institutions of higher learning, skill at chess, numerous personality traits,[26] and copious stylistic eccentricities.[27]

Perhaps most of all, Nabokov and Humbert also both espouse a militant aestheticism, one that suggests reading Humbert's "bubble of hot poison" and "super-voluptuous flame" (17), along with the "jewel-bright" world they illuminate (264), as deriving from Walter Pater's famous exhortation to the aesthetic life in the conclusion of *The Renaissance*. "To burn always with this hard, gem-like flame, to maintain this ecstasy, is success in life," Pater maintained (152), scandalizing Oxford and providing a rallying cry to generations of aesthetes in his wake.[28] Numerous critics have discussed *Lolita* as a supremely ebullient immersion in aestheticism, or as providing the ground for a thoroughgoing critique thereof.[29] Indeed, the potential for delineation between Nabokov's aesthetic and Humbert's has become crucial for many readers of the novel.[30] It is my contention that Nabokov makes this distinction unsustainable, even as all the energies of the novel are bent toward exhorting readers toward the attempt. In quintessentially Nabokovian fashion, the very index of that joint aestheticism—the "supervoluptuous flame" virtuosically associated with Humbert throughout—becomes a playing piece in a larger and even more baroque system of authorial sharping and slippages.

Humbert is of course enflamed throughout the novel, from the first moments of his narration—"Lolita, light of my life, fire of my loins" (9)—through the brief affair with Annabel Leigh—"the haze of stars, the tingle, the flame, the honeydew, the ache" (15)—his arrival in Ramsdale—finding that the McCoo house, in which he was meant to lodge, "had just burned down—possibly, owing to the synchronous conflagration that had been raging all night in my veins" (35)—and the "sun-shot moment" (39) in which he meets Lolita and his ardor, which will consume all the boundaries and baffles he has formerly maintained about himself, flares up in earnest.

Against this backdrop, the reasoning for Quilty's endorsing "Drome" (for Dromedary, for Camel) cigarettes becomes quite clear. Quilty is the water to Humbert's fire, the rain on his parade, and—like a camel—he carries water with him wherever he goes.[31] A "Drome" cigarette obviously condenses the attributes of fire and water, and it is likewise the case that while I am about to play out instances of water symbolism accruing to Quilty at some length—for the novel does predominantly tie him to water imagery—he is associated with flames at intervals as well. Thus, for instance, as he tails Humbert and Lolita with "Jovian fireworks" and "crepitating lightnings" (217), he sparks in Lolita a "private blaze" of excitement that eventually grows into a "scalding hot" fever (219, 239); a letter of his to Lolita prompts her nurse to warn Humbert not to touch the envelope lest he "burn [his] fingers" (242); and his own ranch proves late in the book to have "burned to the ground, *nothing* remained, just a charred heap of rubbish. It was so *strange*, so *strange*" (277, Nabokov's emphasis). But Nabokov's emphases with respect to the last event suggest (by way of *The Tempest*) the intervention of a "sea-change"—one we might relate to Quilty's birth in Ocean City, NJ (31)—just as the fireworks and lightnings illuminate an ongoing thunderstorm, supplying a watery residue to even the most fiery indicators of Quilty's presence. And by this light, Humbert's own seaside interlude with Annabel and his lake-swims with Charlotte begin to seem something other than wholly his own. These moments of exception, along with those in which Quilty or Humbert appears to annex his rival's talismanic forces, figure in a manner analogous to the famous pronoun slippage when the two men finally come face-to-face. Humbert's recognition of the challenges to discrete self-definition suggest a threat to his very identity—and thus to the stability of the world as he understands it—akin to that provoked in the reader's grasp of that world by ruptures to the novel's preponderant symbolic economy. But while Humbert has no external recourse, the reader may imagine calling on Vladimir Nabokov himself, an expedient perhaps encouraged by Nabokov's entrance into the concluding chapters of many of his earlier novels. *Lolita*, as I have been suggesting throughout, instead offers the afterword. In the remainder of this chapter, I sketch out the mechanisms by which the Humbert-Quilty relationship parses itself within the novel's narrative space, and then those by which it extends out to the afterword (in which, it is interesting to note, Quilty—alone among the novel's major characters—fails to make an appearance).

Let us return, then, to the fundamentals of the elemental identifications the novel sets forth, beginning with Humbert and Lolita's initial approach toward the Enchanted Hunters lodge. The ice cream parlor they stop at between her camp and the hotel is bathed in sunlight, but as they near their destination the sky becomes "gloomy," and a "steady drizzle" commences, which becomes a full-fledged rain before they find the hotel (115–17). Subsequently, Humbert first perceives Quilty in the dark on the porch, "screwing off" and then "on" like a faucet, with a "discreet gurgle" (126), and later that night Quilty's flushing toilet strikes Humbert as "a veritable Niagara" (130).[32] "A tepid rain"—which eventually leaves Lolita "drenched"—starts again just after Lolita escapes the house in Beardsley to plot the second cross-country trip with Quilty (206–7). The chase from Kasbeam, where Humbert places his first recognition of Quilty as his pursuer (247) and where Quilty and Lolita stage a rendezvous while Humbert is having his hair cut, to Wace, where Humbert and Lolita watch Quilty and Darkbloom's play and where Quilty takes Lolita on a joyride the following morning, is marked by "a number of great thunderstorms—or perhaps . . . a single storm . . . which [Humbert and Lolita cannot] shake off just as [they cannot] shake off [Quilty]" (216), and Humbert and Lolita spend the night in Wace in a "very foul cabin, under a sonorous amplitude of rain" (220). Humbert catches Lolita gamboling with a terrier for Quilty's benefit by the side of a hotel pool between Wace and Elphinstone (237), and, while Lolita escapes Humbert in Elphinstone under fair skies, Humbert himself retrospectively supplies the missing atmospherics when he recasts the scene in a poem: "Officer, officer, there they go—/In the rain" (256). "[G]ray drizzle" attends Humbert's arrival in Coalmont (where he learns Quilty's identity from Lolita), becoming heavy enough to mire both Humbert and his car in "slosh and anguish" (281) after his departure, and even the old Haze house in Ramsdale is now graced by a "torrent" of Italian music (288). Humbert observes, pointedly, that "no piano had plunged and plashed on that bewitched Sunday with the sun on her beloved legs" (288).

"A thunderstorm accompanie[s]" Humbert "most of the way" on his last morning's drive to Quilty's lair, but by the time Humbert arrives, he observes that "the sun [is] visible again, burning like a man" (293). This sudden climatic transposition—inverting that as Humbert and Lolita approached the Enchanted Hunters—gestures toward the ensuing showdown between Humbert and Quilty, recapitulating the ongoing duel of tropes marking their earlier encounters at key points in the narrative. When the two men first meet, Quilty's rhyme-strewn dialogue toys with Humbert not only in its ostensible clarifications of its bursting accusations, but also in its casual appropriation of Humbert's heat and fire to Quilty's ends:

"Where the devil did you get her?"
"I beg your pardon?"
"I said: the weather is getting better."
"Seems so."
"Who's the lassie?"
"My daughter."
"You lie—she's not."
"I beg your pardon?
"I said: July was hot." (127)

And when Quilty strikes a match, "because he [is] drunk, or because the wind [is]"—but mostly because he is trumping Humbert's tropes here—"the flame illumine[s] not him but another person," depriving Humbert of the chance to see his face when it might make a difference to the tale's outcome (127). The opposite situation pertains on the night Humbert and Lolita decide to take to the road again after their sojourn in Beardsley. When Humbert recovers Lolita after her secretive telephone conversation with Quilty, his chest fills with "a storm of sobs," and he imagines a sort of triple correspondence between the exterior weather, his emotions, and his amorous relations with Lolita: "It may interest physiologists to learn, at this point, that I have the ability—a most singular case, I presume—of shedding torrents of tears throughout the other tempest" (207). In fact, Humbert's precipitate embrace of Lolita's plan merely marks him as her and Quilty's dupe, as does the "beautifully cut aquamarine on a silver chainlet . . . a spring rain gift" that Humbert presents her with the following day (208).

Thus it is of some import that Humbert attends the "bliss" of finally having Quilty "trapped, after those years of repentance and rage" by removing his raincoat (295), that Quilty goes to the extreme, lacking matches, of "taking [a] Drome cigarette apart and munching bits of it" while Humbert menaces him with his gun (297), and that Quilty hopefully attempts to coax Humbert back into the water through both accusation—"You're all wet"—and invitation—"Come, let's have a drink" in the wake of Humbert's first shot (298).[33] Quilty's previous ability to turn Humbert's trope to his own ends appears lost. He does not carry, as the French the two men speak would have it, fire, and the talismanic force associated with the Drome cigarettes eludes him. Humbert, on the other hand, announces his next shot in apposite terms—"*Feu*" (302)—and indeed all the firepower at this point rests with him. The "old Stern-Luger in the music room" that Quilty threatens Humbert with (297) appears to be stored, appropriately, in "a kind of seaman's chest near the piano," but Humbert prevents him from opening it with a shot to Quilty's side (302). Quilty, in response, rises from his chair "like old, gray, mad Nijinski, like Old Faithful, like some old nightmare" of Humbert Humbert's (302), but Humbert "fire[s] three or four more times in quick succession, wounding him at every blaze" (303), and minutes later Quilty is apparently dead, the "bubble" on his lips an evanescent, airy recollection of his former command (304).

Humbert's long-awaited triumph—and the resulting fact that it is he who gets to tell Lolita's tale—could cast some doubt on the literary theatrics preceding. One might go so far as to suspect that the gloomy weather that attends Quilty's presence throughout is a protracted pathetic fallacy imputed to the tale's background, consciously or otherwise, by Humbert in the course of the telling. As early as his entries in the pocket diary, he plays with consonances between his mood and the weather. The infamous sun-drenched Sunday morning on the couch follows two weeks dominated on the one hand by Humbert's eager anticipation of a trip to the lake with Charlotte and Lolita, and on the other by the periodic rains that frustrate his plans. Numerous entries begin with an annotation as to the weather, which often segues directly into a statement as to Humbert's spirits, or, on one occasion, the reverse: "*Monday. Delectatio morosa.* I spend my doleful days in dumps and dolors. We ... were to go to Our Glass Lake this afternoon, and bathe, and bask; but a nacreous morn degenerated at noon into rain, and Lo made a scene" (43).

Or one might propose that Humbert insists on these elemental oppositions between himself and Quilty in order to underline an alterity between the two characters otherwise menaced by the "affinities" Humbert notes between Quilty's "genre, his type of humor—at its best at least—the tone of his brain" and his own (249), along with their common sexual tastes, overlapping career paths, and their mirrored roles in the story. The dense tropiary would thereby counter the pronoun slips (as in the wrestling scene), the grammatical pile-ups—"I said I had said I thought he had said he had never ..." (296); "All of a sudden I noticed that he had noticed that I did not seem to have noticed ..." (298)—and the ultimate fungibility that threatens Humbert even in the closing lines of the book. "And do not pity C. Q.," Humbert writes, "One had to choose between him and H. H."—a choice Humbert suggests was made for the artist over the scenario-writer, the lover over the rake—"one wanted H. H. to exist at least a couple of months longer, so as to have him make you live in the minds of later generations" (309).

But if one assumes that the narrative is reliable with respect to these particulars of weather and water, one arrives at a very different conclusion. Rather than emphasizing Humbert's control over the presentation, the barrage of waterworks accompanying Quilty then appears to testify to his own alliance with external forces much larger than he, which is to say those actually structuring the novel. There is a touch of the retrospectively obvious to this reading, given that Quilty does explicitly collaborate with "Vivian Darkbloom," who later writes a biography of Quilty suggestively entitled "My Cue" (4).[34] Alfred Appel, Jr. also quotes Nabokov as insisting that Quilty's dismissive refusal of the laurels accorded him by those who consider him "the American Maeterlinck"—"Maeterlinck-Schmetterling, says I" (301)—is "the most important phrase in the chapter" narrating, at length, the struggle between Quilty and Humbert (448). "Schmetterling" is the German for "butterfly," and thus Appel reads the moment as superimposing "the author's watermark" on the scene (449); I want to highlight the further importance of the fact that this "watermarking" (did Nabokov suggest the term?) arrives by way of Quilty's mouth (as we have already seen, Humbert Humbert knows nothing about butterflies).[35]

What implications would accrue to such collusion, what posthumous reach might Quilty enjoy? Humbert reports no release following Quilty's death: "a burden even weightier than the one I had hoped to get rid of was with me, upon me, over me" (304). A straightforward psychological reading is obviously available, but we also know that Humbert fears the ghosts of those he has harmed (87, 140), and indeed this "burden" sits upon Humbert in a fashion grammatically and syntactically reminiscent of Quilty's body in their brief tussle on the floor (299). John Ray writes in the preface that "[t]he caretakers of the various cemeteries involved report that no ghosts walk" (4), but they may be deceived. By the time Humbert makes his way out of Quilty's mansion, several guests have arrived, none of whom takes Humbert seriously when he tells them that he has just killed Quilty. And Quilty does in fact crawl onto the staircase landing, "flapping and heaving," before he collapses for good (305). The chapter's penultimate paragraph runs: "'Hurry up, Cue,' said Tony with a laugh. 'I believe he's still—' He returned to the drawing room, music drowned the rest of the sentence" (305). Tony's sentence presumably ends with the word "drunk," and its slight irony is that the phrase should end where it does, that Quilty is, instead, "still"—unmoving—period, for good. But the greater irony is that Quilty seems at some diffuse rhetorical level to be alive and kicking. "Music drowning the sentence" collapses into the briefest of spaces several freighted tropes already arrayed in the scene: the piano that Quilty hammers away on shortly before his death (and, by way of contrast, the piano music Humbert has ruefully noted the absence of in his Ramsdale days with Lolita), the "sentence" that Humbert has written for and attempted to impose upon Quilty, and—unexpectedly—a recurrence of the water imagery, overwhelming the "sentence."

That imagery surges forth one more time, as Humbert pauses to look over his manuscript just before concluding it. He reports: "At this or that twist of [the story] I feel my slippery self eluding me, gliding into deeper and darker waters than I care to probe" (308). The denial may be properly Humbert's, or it may represent an interdiction from on high: that the final darkest depths are inherently inaccessible to him because they are territory allotted only to Quilty and Nabokov. At a key moment earlier in the novel, when Humbert has given up the search for Lolita but returns to Briceland in hopes of finding a newspaper photograph of himself from their evening at the Enchanted Hunters, he comes across a small piece on Quilty in the paper, but draws no connection to his tormentor: "Wine, wine, wine, quipped the author of *Dark Age* who refused to be photographed, may suit the Persian bubble bird, but I say give me rain, rain, rain on the shingle roof for roses and inspiration every time" (262). Quilty references "the Persians" when he first meets Humbert and offers him a cigarette (127), but of greater import here are the rain, the rose—which Appel points out is consistently associated with both Annabel and Lolita (362), elsewhere calling it "the fatidic flower" (381)—and, most of all, the appeal to "inspiration," which returns us, at long last, to Nabokov's own account of the novel's writing in the afterword.

The early pages of this chapter explored the critical commonplace alleging the possibility that Humbert has at some level authored Quilty, creating him out of a bundle of paranoia, or at the very least collating disparate bits of life's detritus into a fuller and rounder character than Quilty himself presents.[36] Such a hypothesis would provide the missing third term for the graphic schema of creation/responsibility, the first line of which would run

| Quilty | Humbert | Nabokov |

But these late revelations regarding Quilty's unexpectedly long reach would reverse the assumptions of the first line, presenting us instead with

| Humbert | Quilty | Nabokov |

not necessarily meaning that Quilty has full ontological primacy over Humbert, but that he has an otherworldly hand in the text's construction, overagainst Humbert's own composition. At this level, even Humbert's early fantasies of dissolution in the presence of nymphets, his marine encounters with Annabel and his freshwater ones with Lolita and Charlotte, appear to be part of an obscurely repetitive destiny colored by Quilty's wet hand.³⁷ Such activity would put Quilty very much in the company of the Vane sisters, in the story of that name (written in 1951), and of the various deceased members of the Shade family in Brian Boyd's reading of *Pale Fire* (1962), each engaged in occult activities accessible only after similarly lengthy critical excavations (the Vane sisters reveal, by way of an acrostic unwittingly incorporated by the narrator into the story's final paragraph, their responsibility for—again—atmospheric conditions that engage the narrator from the start; the Shades manifest themselves through an array of supremely recondite rhetorical means appreciable only, Boyd suggests, on the third reading of the novel).

Boyd reads such spectral promptings as indices of the fundamental "generosity" of Nabokov's compositional method, the "sweeping surprises" it holds in store for the tenacious reader (247), the one who carries on beyond the manifold "negative ironies" so immediately obvious in Nabokov's tales (234). Nabokovian bedrock, for Boyd—after all the feints and misdirection and seeming callousness—is the "generosity of his metaphysics, his hunch that the world sets before us the possibility and the pleasures of endless discovery, inexhaustible excitement, which far from stopping even at death might then merely shift into a still higher gear" (247), testifying—finally—to "an unfathomable creative generosity behind our origins and ends" (246). Leland de la Durantaye arrives at a similar, if less cosmic, faith by the end of his book-length discussion of the novel, ultimately reaching beyond the hedged position that "*Lolita* is a moral book in the simple sense that from its first page to its last it explicitly treats moral questions" (190) to a final endorsement of the sincerity embodied by its style (194). But the final effect of *Lolita*'s style is, I think, to render all sincerity suspect, ending as it does with explicit, ardently generous statements by both Humbert and Nabokov (the former's repentance and closing address to Lolita; the latter's gloss of art itself as "curiosity, tenderness, kindness, ecstasy," and of fiction as valuable only in the event that it advances these ends; his appreciative acknowledgment of good readers; and his thoughtful résumé of the novel's key points) lagging after such a gleefully depraved narrative. The challenge *Lolita* poses is not locating Nabokov's benevolence, but believing in it. That the novel's most involuted narratives and most subtle frameworks recapitulate its surface concern with manipulation, struggle, and abuse renders Boyd's glowing conclusions quite dubious, and even de la Durantaye's more circumspect convictions less steady than one would like.

Lolita seems dedicated to the proposition that there is no such thing as Nabokovian bedrock, and—simultaneously—to provoking a ceaseless search for just such a fundament.[38] The afterword, which articulates Nabokov's devotion to a moral schema closely akin to Boyd's, is riddled with the deeply vexing vortex of frequently contradictory allusions to the novel and to previous literary works, and further complicated by a sort of backward ventriloquism whereby Nabokov appears to speak in Humbert's voice, rather than vice versa. The novel spreads authorship not just among its many characters, but also across a broad weave of precursor texts, even as it underlines Nabokov's hand, one way or another, on almost every page. The afterword answers to, but does not answer, the uncertainty and the desire for resolution fostered in the reader by these strategies. Ultimately, under scrutiny, it reveals the jockeying for authorial control between Humbert and Quilty, or between our critical construals of them, as another layer of misdirection, what turns out to be a local distraction from the last iteration of the novel's tripartite order, which runs thus:

| Humbert/Quilty | Nabokov | Nabokov |

All the dueling compositional pyro- and hydrotechnics to the side, Humbert and Quilty are both, of course, nothing but the work of Vladimir Nabokov. But so, too, the Nabokov presented to the reader both by all the glancing reflections within the novel and by the ostensibly straightforward afterword is another elaborately constructed character, charged with the creation of Humbert, Quilty, and their world, but ultimately another layer of mask between them and their ever-elusive author. The tenuous ontological status of this interstitial Nabokov illuminates the mechanism at work in the collapse of the earlier tripartite schematics. There are no midlevel executives here, irrespective of the frequency with which their specters are raised. Nevertheless, our recognition of this intermediating figure clarifies the novel's operation. For all that this middle Nabokov is another fictive creation, he stands firmly, implacably, in the way of our ever accessing the truth about the Nabokov beyond him.

Lolita is constructed as a deliberate provocation, a multitiered elaboration on the search for the author encouraged by its modernist predecessors. Nabokov adopts elements of the previous generation's rhetorical complexity, and nods at times to their themes and forms, but his larger tribute and his innovation arise in his making the pursuit of the author closer to an imperative than an option. Formalists are compelled by the nested narratives, by the tale's preoccupation with modes of writing and of being scripted by others, to attempt to trace the author all the way to his lair. Moralists, incensed by Humbert's behavior and his cheery discussion of it (or, on occasion, applauding Humbert's late-breaking scruples, or confident of having delineated the disjunction between Humbert and Nabokov), are even more driven to import culpability (or kudos) to Nabokov himself.

The afterword is a calculated response to this provocation, under the guise of earnestness constantly pointing away from itself. While the novel proper presents an endless hall of mirrors that compels readers, against their better judgment, to embark on doomed quests to isolate and describe the author somehow casting all those reflections, the afterword, conversely, purports to be the work of a sincere and unaffected Nabokov, but splinters into glittering shards at the slightest interpretive pressure. Even the lost authentic Nabokov it evokes at the close, the one who wrote in his "natural idiom, [his] untrammeled, rich and infinitely docile Russian tongue" that "none of [his] American friends" can read (316–17), the one who had at his command "the baffling mirror, the black velvet backdrop, the implied associations and traditions" of "the native illusionist" (317), is nothing but a composite of the afterword's shuffling tropes (which themselves echo and revise those of the rest of the novel): the conjurer at its start, but also the orangutan from "Rue Morgue," identified by Dupin precisely by way of its untrammeled, rich chattering in an incomprehensible tongue. Nabokov describes his current voice, too, entering into this juncture, as "rising to a much too strident pitch" (316), neatly encapsulating the varied epithets—"shrill," "harsh," and "loud"—accorded by witnesses to the ape (150). The "discarded limbs and unfinished torsos" Nabokov describes as filling his workshop (316) might invoke the magician's trick of appearing to saw a woman in half and then restoring her to health and happiness, even as it also recalls the ape's less happy experiments with dismemberment. Individually and in their ceaseless dialogue, both novel and afterword continually force the reader to ask whether she or he is witnessing real destruction or mere illusion. The work's success—that it is so precisely balanced between these mutually unsatisfying eventualities—recedes from view precisely because it is so elegantly poised. Its achievement is, in some sense, that very achievement's invisibility, which is to say its "penultimacy," the manner in which readers continually look for the magician or the beast hidden beyond the text's scrim.

4

THE GOSPEL ACCORDING TO DAVE
A Heartbreaking Work of Staggering Genius
(imbibing)

Three quarters of the way through his memoir, Dave Eggers announces to the reader and then to his younger brother, Toph, the newest attention-seeking gambit hatched at *Might* magazine, the wildly ambitious but perennially underfunded satirical magazine Eggers edits with several friends in mid-1990s San Francisco. The magazine will announce the death of Adam Rich, childhood star of television's *Eight Is Enough*, and then provide a lengthy, emotional, but only sporadically accurate farewell tribute—the most fundamental of its impostures arising from the fact that Rich is alive and well. Eggers imagines the aftermath of the hoax: Rich and the editors of *Might* together lambasting the sentimental culture of celebrity eulogy in the national news, the publicity greatly improving both the actor's and the magazine's fortunes (314). Rather than share Dave's glee, however, eight-year-old Toph—who has become Dave's charge following the actual deaths of both their parents, thirty-two days apart, roughly two years earlier (this the first of the more legitimate tragedies and disappointments giving the memoir its name)—breaks character to offer, with all the insight and rhetorical sophistication his thirty-year-old brother can bring to the writing of the scene, a withering critique. Toph reads this story as "gruesome and transparently symbolic, you people killing this contemporary of yours, a kid on TV when you were kids watching TV" (316), an attempt to punish Rich for having attained a celebrity that Eggers and his cohort feel might just as easily have descended upon them. "[Y]ou feel, deep down," Toph says, "that because there is no life before or after this, that fame is, essentially, God.... [Y]ou all want to be famous, you want to be rock stars, but you're stuck in this terrible bind, where you also want to be thought of as smart, legitimate, permanent," and thus invest in coterie writing projects rather than those with mass appeal (317).

Toph is right on the money, neatly encapsulating Dave's desirous but fraught relationship with the prospect of fame—a shimmering, elusive goal that bubbles up at intervals throughout the book in tandem with loftier aspirations both aesthetic and philanthropic. Toph is more right than he knows, though, in his loose equation of celebrity and divinity, obliquely foreshadowing the more substantive exploration of these terms, further conjoined with that of authorship, in the final moments of the book. Here, Eggers exhorts and then stages his own death in terms most visceral and literal, but also literary-critical. Eggers' overweening (at times, all but overwhelming) self-consciousness evidences a familiarity with '60s and '70s metafiction, and with the broader run of experimental narrative techniques stretching back as far as Joyce, whom he pastiches at numerous points. The text's thoroughgoing reflexivity—which is motivated aesthetically by the project of bringing this avant-garde lineage to bear on nonfiction memoir, and mimetically by Eggers' constant concern regarding the figure he presents to the world—reveals itself at the close to have an enormous theoretical stake as well. Journalistic responses to the book read Eggers' postmodernism as a compositional tic, a derivative embrace of stylistic bric-a-brac that acts as an impediment to communicating the meat of his story. The narrative's denouement, however, makes clear how incomplete this characterization is, the care with which Eggers positions himself not just with respect to his literary predecessors but also in an implicit debate with Barthes. *A Heartbreaking Work of Staggering Genius* (hereafter *AHWOSG*), like the two films I discuss in Chapter Five, emerges from an environment in which the notion of "the death of the Author" has sufficiently widespread cultural currency to bubble up in myriad unexpected locales, including narratives of widely varying generic affiliation, each wholly compelling in its own right but all joined by the fact that they take that "death" up as scriptable event only in order to interrogate its premises and refute Barthes' conclusions. For Eggers, this means conjoining his lamentation for his mother, his own fear of mortality, and Barthes' scenario to build, with the ostensible dead ends of his literary-theoretical moment, a renewed horizon of possibility, both personal and authorial.

The death of the author becomes, in Eggers' hands, nothing more—or less—than a springboard for immediate resurrection. The rhetorical trappings of this rebirth are loosely Catholic in the aggregate; more accurately, they trade on a repurposing of Catholic practices, images, and dogma to a set of ends ranging from the manifestly secular to a twilight zone of uncertain belief. This compass itself attests to Eggers' position, articulating at length and embodying in sum a common-enough Generation X yearning for a transcendent sense of self and purpose, compromised by (or perhaps even manifested in) a pervasive disaffection. Eggers inherits a Catholic imaginary, but not a regular practice or anything approaching an uncomplicated faith, from his mother (222). In retooling his religious vocabulary to personal ends far removed from Church doctrine, Eggers follows in a path that has begun to be charted in other writers of the day experimenting with the possibility of situating convictions, or at least intimations, of something approaching the sacred within secular linguistic structures. Amy Hungerford offers an extremely persuasive argument that Don DeLillo's work, for example, "imagines how religion that is abandoned in most respects can persist in a literary form" (344). Hungerford finds a common underlying logic to the elliptical conversations that fill DeLillo's novels, the idiosyncratic torsions of his prose, and his incantatory rehearsals of everyday experience: each contributes to a sense of language itself housing an enduring capacity for belief, not because it presents a conduit to God, but because in its meditative potential and its ability to slip away from conscious control it constitutes "a medium that contains the transcendent within it" (374). Eggers does not appear to entertain such a mystical relationship to his own language—his prose does not feel so obsessively worked, or reverentially fingered, as the rosaries of DeLillo's sentences—but he does share with DeLillo a renovated sense of sacramental logic. As DeLillo fashions his language into a repository for a latter-day sort of immanence, echoing the real presence of God located by the Catholic Mass in the quotidian substance of bread and wine, Eggers casts the very material of his book—the paper itself—as a Eucharistic substance hovering at the cusp of reembodying its author.

This "ontological playfulness," to use the terminology John A. McClure applies to a much larger body of postmodern texts, puts Eggers in the company not just of DeLillo, but also of Thomas Pynchon, Ishmael Reed, Leslie Marmon Silko, Toni Morrison, and the broad international swathe of magical realists. McClure suggests that these authors' "assaults on realism ... and their experiments in the sublime represent a complex and variously inflected reaffirmation of premodern ontologies—constructions of reality that portray the quotidian world as but one dimension of a multidimensional cosmos" or, later, "a richly polyontological cosmology" or "a liminal space between worlds" (143, 149).[1] He goes on to argue that "some of the very features of fiction which secular theorists have singled out as definitively postmodern must at least in some cases be understood in terms of a post-secular project of resacralization" (144). McClure allows for degrees of commitment to such a project; Eggers, as I have already suggested, sits in an ambivalent middle. Eggers' project is less to body forth whole new worlds (or tremendous ruptures in this one) than to tinker at the extremes; he does not reanimate the sacral so much as appropriate it to personal ends—no doubt prima facie blasphemous ones, but ones that perhaps vouch for a renewed possibility of faith to the entire cohort of his readership. In so doing, he turns his book's juggernaut of nearly paralyzing self-consciousness around, not rejecting its welter of reflexivity, doubt, irony, and other postmodern appurtenances, but refining from them a final apotheosis equally grand and unexpected.

Anyone who's glanced at the book for even a few minutes knows the leading indicators of its reflexivity—its hipness, irreverence, playfulness, or snarkiness (depending on the interpreter's sensibility), its exuberant or condescending piling of surplus verbiage on the reader, its seemingly abject inability even to get started. Eggers prefaces the memoir with nearly fifty small-print pages of commentary on the book to come and the process of its creation. Beginning with a set of "Rules and Suggestions for the Enjoyment of [the] Book" (vii) that end up recommending that "the first three or four chapters are all you might want to bother with" (vii), this opening section makes what appear to be various flanking assaults on the integrity of the narrative that follows. The "Rules and Suggestions" are followed by a preface that includes several pages of material excised from the main text; a table of contents that burlesques loquacious eighteenth-century conventions by reducing the components of each chapter to haphazard, gnomic particulars that prove difficult to coordinate with the works' actual interior, even after one has read it (xix–xx); twenty-two pages of acknowledgments (largely in the sense of the author's more or less rueful admissions about himself and his writing, rather than articulation of his debts and thanks); and various charts, tables, and lists repackaging the book's contents according to one or another semi-abstracted schema, including a nearly A-to-Z list recapitulating its major themes, a segment of what Eggers claims is a far larger narrative/cognitive/emotive flow chart tracing his actions and motivations throughout the book (xxxviii), a ledger tracking money earned and spent in the course of the work's gestation (xxxix), and an "Incomplete Guide to [Its] Symbols and Metaphors" (xlv). The pace of self-conscious gestures slows somewhat in the pages that follow, but Eggers continues to indulge in various formal experiments at intervals throughout, including occasional diagrams and bursts of musical notation, play with fonts, rendering of dialogue as theatrical script or putative interview transcript, intermittent direct address of the reader, and characters breaking from their generally realist presentation to comment caustically on the proceedings.

Unsurprisingly, reviews of the book make regular reference to these "postmodern literary high jinks" (Hirschorn, "One Story"), "hypertext song-and-dances" (Kantor), "postmodern pyrotechnics" and "pomo gimmickry" (Kakutani, and, mutatis mutandis, Mosle, Begley), opposing them to "straight writing" (Kantor), the "real" or the "pure" (Hirschorn, "To Be," "One Story"), to "earnest sentiment" (Kakutani), or to "genuine, unsentimental poignancy" (Mosle).[2] As the dictates of review essays in mainstream publications more or less demand, both those who applaud and those who condemn Eggers tend to move rather quickly to totalizing and somewhat reifying accounts of his metatextual exuberance. Devices are catalogued, perhaps summarized, and then set out in simple terms as that which distracts the reader from the true subject matter of the memoir. (In the more abstract language of my introduction, the repeated claim is that Eggers' aesthetic play is an impediment to the book's actual mimetic undertaking.) In positive accounts, this delay at least throws the book's emotional core into "high relief" (Kakutani), while less charmed readers find the tonal oscillation debilitating. Michael Hirschorn, for example, reads the "endless preface and lengthy fake MTV *Real World* interview" at its center as evidence that "Eggers doesn't know whether to situate himself inside or outside his narrative," and, with apologies, concludes that Eggers "ends up disappearing ever further up his own fundament" ("To Be"). I'm going to more or less invert Hirschorn's closing metaphor, but I want very much to ratify his sense of Eggers' bifurcated stance. Dan Savage offers a more sanguine version of this reaction, attributing to "Eggers and his contemporaries" the canny ability to "mock and inhabit their lives at the same time." Eggers, in *AHWOSG*, is the poet laureate of the nation of ambivalent youth; he simultaneously mocks and inhabits numerous institutions and beliefs in the course of the memoir—indeed, its very conclusion depends on precisely such a carefully performed ambivalence.

The mechanics of this performance are decidedly more complex than a simple juxtaposition or even adroit toggling between two disparate rhetorical modes. Rather, Eggers appears to display his own emotional lability as nakedly and fully as possible, not merely offsetting credence with detachment, but tipping from the most expansive optimism into corrosive paranoia without warning, punctuating his standard chummy, even philanthropic, demeanor with outbursts of aggression. Eggers holds onto his readers through a consummately skillful weaving of these two widely divergent tenors, and at base by way of an enduring charisma predicated on this very openness, as well as on his informality, enthusiasm, and humor. The aggregate strategy sounds Nabokovian, and with good reason. In an interview with the *Harvard Advocate* conducted shortly after *AHWOSG*'s publication, Eggers answers a question regarding his unorthodox approach to the project of memoir with reference to his reading in college, and lists Nabokov first among the resultant influences.[3] The precedents Nabokov sets for self-conscious metafiction (or metafact, as the case may be) are legion, of course, and Eggers adverts to many of them. Most salient, though, are several of the provocations in *Pale Fire*. Brian McHale, in *Postmodernist Fiction*, nominates *Pale Fire* as one of the limit texts that teeter at the outer edge of modernism's epistemological dominant, where "intractable epistemological uncertainty becomes at a certain point ontological plurality or instability" and tilts into the postmodern (11). His reading concentrates on the irresolvable contradictions between four different basic hypotheses we may posit for the underlying truth of Nabokov's narrative (18–19), but part of the payoff in the novel itself is the profound ontological uncertainty introduced on the last page. Here, taking a half-step beyond Humbert Humbert's ongoing helpless victimization at the shadowy hands of Vivian Darkbloom and onto the closing threshold of the book itself, Kinbote apparently intuits Nabokov's presence and even the fissile identity they share, observing: "I may turn up yet, on another campus, as an old, happy, healthy Russian, a writer in exile, sans fame, sans future, sans audience, sans anything but his art" (300–301).[4] Kinbote's sudden accession to a new degree of self-awareness has no clear warrant in the preceding narrative, but—qua ontological perceptiveness—may be forecast by his ongoing preoccupation with the materiality of literary compositions. The second sentence of his introduction to Shade's poem is already enmeshed in a description of the index cards on which Shade (mimicking Nabokov himself) drafted his work (13), cards which Kinbote ultimately wears, sewn into his clothes, to spirit them away from rival exegetes (300). Once the contents of those cards has been elaborated at length into his own manuscript, he suggests that his reader "eliminate the bother of back-and-forth leafings" between Shade's poem and Kinbote's annotations by "cutting out and clipping together the pages" (28). And he closes by constructing an index that pivots from the standard utilitarian directives regarding the preceding text to the tantalizing promise that it might reveal the location of the much sought-after Crown Jewels of Zembla, only to conclude with an endless circle of self-reference—from "Crown Jewels" to "Hiding Place" to "*Potaynik*," glossed by reference to "*Taynik*," which is defined as Russian for "secret place," and which refers the reader back to "Crown Jewels"—that does not even escape the confines of the index itself (306–14).

The index—boiling down the myriad convolutions of Nabokov's narrative into a pithy mix of user-friendliness and misdirection—predicts strategies Eggers employs through much of the front-matter of his own book, but the specificity of his engagement with *Pale Fire* becomes clearer at the conclusion of the prefatory pages. At the twenty-two pages of acknowledgments' end, Eggers writes: "Here is a drawing of a stapler:" followed by, indeed, a rudimentary drawing of a stapler. Eggers' implicit invitation inverts that offered by Kinbote: rather than being exhorted to destroy the book by cutting it apart, we are prompted to participate in assembling it. The stapler, standing just at the juncture between the apparently haphazard introductory matter and the beginning of the memoir proper, seems to promise that the myriad provocations of the opening pages might be collated in some productive fashion, that that collection might indeed be profitably appended to the narrative that follows, and that the reader might have a central role in that process. Eggers' laconic wording skirts the cool remove of the gesture's most obvious antecedent, René Magritte's *La trahison des images* (*The treachery of images*—the famous painting of a pipe accompanied by the legend "*Ceci n'est pas une pipe*" ["This is not a pipe"]), but Eggers' formulation does not simply evidence his penchant for the colloquial. Rather, in a move predictive of the strategy of the work as a whole, he trades on the two senses of "here" in order to balance between a self-evident constative utterance equivalent to Magritte's (and, indeed, less provocative for its inclusion of the word "picture") and a low-grade performative, proffering the stapler to the reader. Eggers thus yokes Magritte's reflections on the nature of representation to his own interest in presentation, in the sense both of giving a gift and of working through the implications of the form that the gift takes. Eggers, like Magritte, muses on the relation of image to real object, but the tension he elucidates there is an introduction to the larger thematics and endeavors of the book as a whole, wherein the drive toward a degree of fungibility between representations on paper and real objects or individuals will be central. "The betrayal of images" with which Magritte concerns himself is only one of the many kinds of betrayals that bedevil Eggers, and that he attempts to address by bridging the divide between image and actual rather than simply reiterating or citing it. That bridging will, too, refer back to Kinbote's ontological perspicacity and audacity, again finding a way to build on his example at the other end of the book's narrative.

There are obvious differences, as well. Kinbote, his fleeting intuition notwithstanding, remains one of Nabokov's "galley slaves" (Nabokov, *Strong Opinions* 95)—a fact that not only places absolute limits on his mobility and agency, but also highlights the fact that the reader's attention is finally drawn through the character and the text to the author standing behind it. Eggers' position differs not only in that he offers himself to the reader far more directly, but also in that his final aim seems less the ineluctable demonstration of rhetorical mastery ("staggering genius" notwithstanding) than the production of community and collaboration of a sort that would not have interested Nabokov. From the start, the self *AHWOSG* presents is one aspiring, explicitly and transparently (if not without a degree of self-mocking irony), to a high degree of intimacy, predicated again and again in the opening pages on identifications reflecting and further structuring an underlying sense of camaraderie. Thus, opposite the copyright page and in place of a dedication, or perhaps in earnest of a profound and personal dedication to each and every interpellated reader: "First of all: / I am tired. / I am true of heart! // And also: / You are tired. / You are true of heart!" (v)—and, a few pages later: "the author feels obligated to acknowledge that yes, the success of a memoir—of any book, really—has a lot to do with how appealing its narrator is. To address this, the author offers the following: / a) That he is like you. / b) That, like you, he falls asleep shortly after he becomes drunk. / c) That he sometimes has sex without condoms. / d) that he sometimes falls asleep when he is drunk having sex without condoms.... One word: appealing. / And that's just the beginning!" (xxvii).

At the same time, Eggers' embrace of the reader in the web of consciousness and self-consciousness regarding the text's attributes simultaneously creates and compromises such immediacy. On the one hand, Eggers invites the reader into his confidence to an extremely rare degree, fostering a powerful sense of complicity.[5] On the other hand, not only do all the asides and digressions forestall obvious forward movement in the book's narrative (as suggested in the reviews quoted above), but the generalized excessiveness of the approach constantly threatens an inversion from the illusion of presence to a confirmation of artifice, the latter then revealed as a less-than-entirely-successful mask for the distance that is inevitably part of the project of publication. (Likewise, the frequent direct address of the reader both makes of the mass audience a collectivity of individuals, each repeatedly hailed by the text, and testifies to the fungibility of addressees; one's position as or in that "you" is guaranteed only by one's goodwill, not by any actual privileged relationship to the text or its author.) In this light, I would propose that the more pointedly ostentatious "gimmicks" of the opening pages constitute a defensive, proactive posture. Eggers, as someone who so values and privileges personal connection, whose writing so obviously aspires to a surging and encompassing immediacy, faces a medium that beyond a certain point would not seem to allow it, that requires a retooling of lived experience into a form both digestible and marketable: more static, reified, inert. The inevitable mediation and commodification of Eggers' story in the book, then, is prefaced by a series of highlighted, hyperbolic predictive versions thereof, condensing the book's contents yet further and alienating the reader from the resulting product in humorous but pointed fashion. Thus the charts and tables, rules and recapitulations, and free-floating bits excised from the text to follow, all of which, with varying degrees of obduracy, stand in counterpoint to the swift and seemingly transparent flow of Eggers' narrative. Also included, moreover, are a complementary set of offers parodying the transactional nature of literary reading, both at the level of fantasy life (for ten dollars, the reader may purchase a 3.5" floppy disk with a digital version of the text allowing for renaming the characters in any way she likes, including making herself the protagonist—"This can be about *you*! You and *your* pals!" [xxv]) and at that of moral instruction (the reader might, on the other hand, earn five dollars by furnishing both a receipt for the book and "proof that [she has] read and absorbed the many lessons [t]herein" [xl]).

But this defensive acknowledgment—this series of small registrations of the compromised nature of the material text—seems to me only the first stage of the book's much larger gambit. Eggers is not a member of those midcentury generations that struggled long and painfully to a recognition and acceptance of representation's myriad baffles to direct presence. The ontological revelations that Kinbote and any number of less-canonized figures in self-conscious novels of recent decades (particularly in the metafiction catalogued by McHale;

see especially 113–30) at length arrive at constitute, for Eggers, neither an epiphanic telos nor an existential limit, but rather a conceptual and narrative point of departure. These literary manifestations of the thoroughly mediated world that Eggers so conspicuously inhabits within the book serve, finally, as the grounds on which to stage a showy return.

The nature of that return is profoundly inflected by the book's more obvious thematic preoccupations. These include the metaphysics of textual self-presentation just discussed, but also the more pragmatic demands of career advancement and personal self-aggrandizement, and—always lurking behind—the difficult and often forestalled project of working through the loss of his mother. (Eggers' father, alcoholic and sometimes abusive, certainly registers as part of Eggers' tragic loss, but far less as a preoccupation in the narrative of the aftermath.) If there is indeed genius to the book, I would argue that it is born of Eggers' ability to discern—or bring forth—a parallelism between these concerns, and to make them answer to a common solution. Eggers draws the first and third of these aspects of the work together in his own accounting for the apparent excesses of the book's dilatory start. Though at one point, late in the introduction, he self-deprecatingly glosses the prefatory pages as "an interminable clearing of [his] throat" and "seemingly endless screwing about," admitting that they might "very easily look like . . . a sort of contemptuous stalling" (xlii), he has already maintained that he is "fully cognizant, way ahead of you, in terms of knowing about and fully admitting the gimmickry inherent in all this, and [that he] will preempt your claim of the book's irrelevance due to said gimmickry by saying that the gimmickry is simply a device, a defense, to obscure the black, blinding, murderous rage and sorrow at the core of this whole story" (xxx). Eggers' most murderous rages themselves appear to be the products of his sorrow. In the first pages of the narrative, he imagines himself dismembering those whom he takes to be voyeurs regarding his parents' illnesses and deaths (14), and similar sadistic indulgences in defense of familial honor, safety, and memory dot the remainder of the text (e.g., 117, 160), providing much of its darker shading and grounding Eggers' narrative and cognitive wanderings in certain core emotional experiences. While Heidi Eggers expires in a paragraph break at the end of the book's first chapter (43), she resurfaces at intervals throughout, the subject of several set pieces placed at especially prominent positions in the text.

The most ostentatious of these set pieces is a description of her funeral (thoroughly displaced temporally) at the close of the book's penultimate chapter.

Eggers introduces the service via the anticipatory vision he had cherished for months in advance of his mother's demise: he pictures her presiding over the proceedings as a grand and benevolent spirit, an "ephemeral, huge . . . wonderfully glowing bright visage" floating above an "endless crowd," one that grows and grows as Eggers paints the scene for himself: "the church full like it is at Christmas, at Easter, the side aisles overflowing, the entire town there almost, all of the relatives, her brother and sisters from out East, the cousins, my father's enormous extended family from California, all her former students, all the other teachers, all my friends, Bill's, Beth's, high school, grade school, college, Toph's, their parents, the grocers, the doctors, nurses, strangers, admirers," with yet more "outside the church, a hundred on the steps, in the courtyard, wrapped around the building, down the street, a thousand or so" and finally "everyone she had ever known, millions, all with their hearts in their two hands, offering them to her" (402–3). This hyperbolic acceleration toward the universal is typical of the Eggers imaginary, and central to the book's project. The reality of the funeral is, of course, different, and lesser: "not a crowd. It was a scattered thing, a few here, a few there" (405). Eggers rockets through shock, incredulity, disappointment, and anger at the notion that his mother's life and achievements—the fact that "she gave everything for you people . . . fought for so long for all you people" (406)—should be celebrated, or even marked, by so few. In his truncated depiction of this moment, his anger overwhelms all his better emotions, crowding the eulogy he is about to deliver, along with any lingering representation of his mother, out of the scene.

We haven't been waiting throughout the entire book for the eulogy, or even for this scene, so the parallel one might be tempted to draw with the elision of Addie's burial in *As I Lay Dying* must remain a loose one. Retrospectively, though, it's easy to see this general return to Heidi Eggers' death and funeral as an important recuperation within the book's desultory temporal scheme, and the refusal to represent this recaptured moment (like the elision of the instant of her death) as significant. If Faulkner constructs his novel, however, partially in a spirit of cruel humor, denying Addie her chance to rest in peace—the lack of narrative resolution sending up her own caustic reiteration of her father's suggestion that "the reason for living was to get ready to stay dead a long time" (169)—Eggers' choice reflects a sincere anguish and, thus, a nearly opposite emotional stance. He, too, acts to keep his mother animated, but precisely in protest against the insufficiencies of her funeral, rather than in a diffuse extension of them.

The degree of his failure, in both the event and its aftermath, is underscored when Eggers disposes of his mother's "cremains." Midway through the book, Eggers reveals that his parents had decided to donate their bodies to science, in spite of his mother's "romantic, emotional, superstitious even maybe" Catholicism (222), and thence to have the cadavers cremated. Two years on, the cremains have not caught up with the peripatetic Eggers offspring. Eggers laments the fact that he "never gave [his parents] a proper burial" (222), imagining—at least fleetingly—that finding the remains of his parents' bodies, or even confronting the medical school professor who would have been charged with the cadavers, will bring him "peace" (355–56). His pursuit of the cremains becomes a leitmotif of the second half of the book. While his sister, Beth, is convinced that the cremains must have been irretrievably lost, Dave maintains that "they might still be there, somewhere" (223), and eventually does locate them on a return trip to Chicago near the narrative's end. He is shocked first by their aggregate weight (381) and then by the lightness of an individual handful (398), put off by their pebble-like appearance (which he likens to kitty litter and Grape-Nuts), alarmed by their variegated color, and fearful of their smell (395). In short, the cremains are physical, abject, base, again dragging Eggers' lofty impulses and imaginings back to earth. Ultimately, he throws the cremains into Lake Michigan, in a scene that devolves into a physical slapstick—and a sort of cognitive farce, too—as he repeatedly fumbles both the cremains and his intentions regarding them in the course of strewing them into the lake (398–401). He again imagines his mother hovering above the scene, watching, but in this case there is no comfort in that notion. Instead, she is "just there, or half there, superimposed on the blue-black sky just over [him] . . . shaking her head, disappointed, disgusted" (395). By the time Eggers finishes "winging her remains into the lake," he has labeled himself "pathetic" and his mother "aghast," his only comfort residing in the chilly, self-exculpatory but otherwise hardly reassuring assertion that, once again, "she's not watching. . . . She's gone" (400).

That Eggers should then find momentary solace by banishing the specter of his mother registers the profundity of his failure to meet his own expectations for the moment, given that his larger project (here and, more or less diffusely, throughout the book) is to preserve her memory. The repeated dynamic in these two valedictory scenes is that of the real, the immediate, and the physical rudely awakening Eggers from his loftier dreams and goals—a dynamic anyone who has read the book will remember in many other instantiations. It is, of course, the quintessential story of idealism (or youth or memory) betrayed, and as such is a recurring theme—even the dominant mode—of the memoir, which turns again and again on the tensions and disappointments that ensue when Eggers' exuberant flights of fancy and invention run up against constraints of one kind or another. From his constant romantic forays (many of which never move beyond the theater of his mind, and none of which fully takes), to myriad fleeting self- and Toph-aggrandizing fantasies, to the sustained endeavor to make *Might* magazine a financial success without selling out its principles, Eggers records a thousand small and midsized heartbreaks making up and justifying the grand claim in his title. The set pieces about Eggers' mother present some of the most condensed and freighted appearances of the theme, providing a bottom note of sincere and easily legible emotion to subtend the rhetorical whirls and feints attending the many cognate moments in the text. They also furnish a conceptual template for Eggers' construction of an alternative—a form of redress for his mother within the book, and the fashioning of a different fate for himself by virtue of the book.

Eggers' move is to take the opposition of ideal and real quite literally—to concretize the obstacle he faces as one inhering in materiality, and susceptible to redress if that materiality can be sufficiently reconceived. The cremains scene paints matter as mute, contingent, prey to small accidents and infelicities (Eggers spills bits on the jetty as he attempts to scatter them into the lake, finds other pieces sticking to his sweaty palms, and so on); the funeral presents it as limited and static (Eggers' fantasized service, attended by the millions whose lives his mother had touched, depends on a vision in which the church's "barrel vaulting would rise, and the entire roof would quietly unhinge itself and lift up, would rise straight up, and disappear and the church's huge wooden cross-supports would fly up and away" such that the church might "double in size, would triple . . . and then become bigger" [403]—but the truth, he finds, is that "the church is tiny. The pews are so low, and there are so few rows" [402], and most of them are empty [405]). Eggers' need, then, is to subject matter to his desires: to make it malleable, capable of infinite extension, and articulate, and then to populate it according to his specifications. The negative vision of Heidi Eggers as rubble, or as a spirit doomed always to fade away from an audience already too small in the first place, might thereby give way to new vision in which the material world houses the immaterial more hospitably and dependably, and fosters connections between people rather than highlighting their isolation.

Characteristically, given its pervasive reflexivity, the book itself emerges as the mechanism for this revision, an avenue not just for retelling the past but also for affecting the future. We're given a very early indication of how that mechanism will function by one of Eggers' first paratextual interventions, the copyright page. Here, Eggers segues from standard notations of the work's Library of Congress Catalog Card Number, ISBN, and print run number to a sardonic rehearsal of several numerical attributes pertaining to Eggers himself (height, weight, place on sexual orientation scale from 1 to 10), along with descriptions of his hair, eyes, hands, and allergies. Thus begins the process of effecting an equation of Eggers' text and his body, a sort of perverse polymorphousness reimagining the contours and limits of the material self—a process announced here and analogized by the several translations of the text into radically different forms in the prefatory matter, and a process we will see brought to the very cusp of realization by the book's conclusion. There's no syntactic indication at all that the copyright page is shifting from its predictable rehearsal of the text's provenance to its bodying forth of Eggers himself; in direct sequence, the one is "Manufactured in the United States of America," the other is 5'11" and 175 pounds and, the reader realizes retrospectively, also manufactured in the United States of America, a point emphasized by the page's closing assertion that the "certain, very small, liberties [taken] with chronology" are the author's right, "as an American." This last statement, and the series of small caveats that precede it, perpetuate our reflexive, uninterrogated sense of the author as standing over his text, of course, but a degree of conceptual fungibility has also been introduced. The possibility of translatability or transition between bodily forms and paper ones threads through the book to follow, from epiphenomenal details as small as the hairs Eggers trims from his head on the second page of the narrative, which become "twisted brown doodles drawn in the sink" (2), to grand metaphorical conceits wherein the book becomes a metastasizing cancerous growth, or an appropriation of Eggers' friends' lives explicitly glossed as a form of cannibalism, or the production of lampshades from human skin (424).

These transfigurations replace Eggers' earlier conception of how to reach a mass audience, one presented at great length at the book's midpoint, when he tries out for a part in the third season of MTV's *The Real World*. Painting himself to the producer interviewing him as the requisite "Tragic Person" the heterogeneous cast of the show demands (204), Eggers imagines not only that he will fill a necessary spot in the roster, but also that the show will provide him with a splendid forum in which to broadcast his grief and, furthermore, to turn it to positive ends. "All this did not happen for naught, I can assure you—" he says, "there is no logic to that, there is logic only in assuming we suffered for a reason" (236). Anticipating himself beamed into the living rooms of like-minded young people all over the world, Eggers pleads, "I will bleed if they will love. . . . I will open a vein, an artery . . . Oh please let me show this to the millions. Let me be the lattice, the center of the lattice. Let me be the conduit. There are all these hearts, and mine is strong, and if there are—there are!—capillaries that bring blood to millions, that we are all of one body and that I am— Oh, I want to be the heart pumping blood to everyone, blood is what I know, I feel so warm in blood, can swim in blood, oh let me be the strong-beating heart that brings blood to everyone!" (237). His impassioned plea fails to sway the powers that be at MTV, and Eggers does not get the part. He does, however, arrive at his most explicit articulation up to this point of the complement to paper in the book's controlling metaphor, nominating hearts and blood as means of interpersonal connection and communication. This lattice, which he has previously asserted one is "either a part of or apart from," is defined from the start in bodily terms as "connective tissue"; then as "collective youth, people like [Eggers], hearts ripe, brains aglow"; and finally as "people who have everything in common no matter where they're from," each being brought "to grab a part of the other, like an arm at the socket, everyone holding another's arm at the socket" (211). Television, inscribing both distance and a mere ocular connection in its very name, is perhaps inherently less well suited to this project than the book, with its immediate, corporeal attributes and impingements, grasped in the hand just as a nearby person's arm might be. (And, at the same time, the mimetic fidelity implied by *The Real World*'s title will prove far less conducive to Eggers' goals than will the aesthetic play enabled by his prose stylings.)

Eggers in fact spends much of the book's first chapter, which wanders in and out of the final weeks of his mother's life, grasping his mother's nose in an attempt to quench one of the prodigious nosebleeds that attend the final phase of her illness. His condensed account of the stakes—"Her white blood cell count has been low. Her blood cannot clot properly, the doctor had said the last time this had happened, so, he said, we can have no bleeding. Any bleeding could be the end, he said" (11)—establishes the narrative conjunction between bleeding and closure that carries through all the way to the final moment of the work. What the text initially proposes as the essence of wound and loss—the breaching of the individual body and of the nuclear family—is repeatedly repurposed, into an extraordinarily positive account of apertures and overtures. Eggers imagines himself and his siblings in the immediate aftermath of their mother's death as "the beautiful and tragic Eggers children, soaked in blood, stoic" (403): that is, static—objects of contemplation for the crowd gathered at the funeral. By the end of the book, though, he accords to himself the ability to "breathe in all the air full of glass and nails and blood, . . . breathe it and drink it, so rich" (433), and even before the funeral scene is finished, he has redefined blood as a space or a conduit, host to the thousands of angels accompanying the spirit of his mother: "they were all inside us, too, moving elliptically, or through our blood" (405). The angels do not reappear in the text after the funeral, but in time Eggers annexes this capacity to himself, relating at one point a "semi-conscious dream where [he] enter[s] Toph's bloodstream . . . blowing around at thrilling speeds" before "suddenly" finding himself "going through the sky," which opens out "soundlessly into ebony space" (294).

"[C]ould Toph's frame also encompass a sky," Eggers asks himself on the run (294), rhetorically, neither providing a reply nor even concluding the phrase with a question mark, pushing it halfway into a hopeful subjunctive. The answer lies precisely in the question/statement's invocation of that median zone of hypotheticals and their bounding implications in which Eggers excels, here initiating the notional defeat of a narrow logic of corporeal boundaries. Our standard assumption that bodily ruptures must be immediately staunched and sutured is briefly displaced here by a new logic valorizing the tear. Eggers makes a similar gesture at the end of the section in which he scatters his mother's cremains. Late at night on New Year's Day, on the edge of Lake Michigan, slowly recovering his calm after his frenzied completion of the task, he asserts that there is "no difference between the sky and the water," and then, in another yoking of the cosmic and the corporeal: "I am already under the water, and all of the water is inside something larger, and I look at my feet to make sure they are secure because I am inside something living" (401). The mysticism of this moment is hobbled, though, by the obscurity and indistinctness of Eggers' intimation, and also by its brevity. Eggers' vision here resonates with that of the expanding church at his mother's funeral, and it likewise turns on a literalization of the impulse behind the scattering of remains: the wish that not just Eggers' mother but he, too, might be thrust into the cosmos and unified with it. But the vision falters because matter immediately asserts itself as such; the "tiny rocks" and "pebbles" that were Heidi Eggers hit the water with a "series of pitititits," and Eggers fears they might be eaten by fish (398–401). He is left with the necessity of arriving at a vocabulary and an imaginary that can do better, and hold longer.

Eggers' difficulty here is rooted in the assertiveness of reported event; the expansiveness of his fantasies is repeatedly brought up short by the realities that provoke them. His final turn addresses this obstacle in two fashions: first, through his fashioning of narrative into performative, which thus crosses over from what is into what might be; and second, through his positioning of this performative in his final words, precisely where it cannot be overtaken or deflated by subsequent developments. As Eggers faces the apparent necessity of acceding to the realities of closure and the cessation of his voice, this strategy comes into focus. The book's last chapter dwells repeatedly on endings expressed more or less analogically. The freedom California represents in the early chapters in the book is lost by this point: San Francisco, Eggers says, is getting smaller and colder (411); memories Eggers does not want to entertain encroach on his space (429); *Might* magazine runs out of funds even as Eggers and his most of his co-editors run out of enthusiasm for the project of saving it, instead peppering the final issue with "countless references to the end of the magazine, to death, to defeat" (417). Most of Eggers' friends move to the East Coast, and Eggers and Toph, feeling "exhausted" and "hunted" (428), determine to do so as well. "[E]veryone is dying," Eggers declares, at the start of this litany of defeat (411). In point of fact, the tally is more equivocal: one of *Might*'s backers does expire, suddenly, almost inexplicably (418), but Eggers pivots from lamenting her loss—"Man, we said, you should have seen Skye"—to attenuating it—"Actually, you still can. Go rent that movie, *Dangerous Minds*. She's there, walking around, talking . . . there she is, forever, walking and talking, snapping gum" (420). Another friend, who worked downstairs from *Might*, survives a four-story fall, slowly emerging from the ensuing coma as the narrative winds down (427–28). And Heidi Eggers, whose last days are recapitulated here, runs closer and closer to her demise but again does not quite reach it; tellingly, the narrative again cuts off: "She could *not fucking believe* this was actually happening. . . . She was not ready, not even close, was not resolved, resigned, was not ready—" (432, Eggers' italics).

This constellation of anger and denial, of seeing the end (and even courting it) but not finally accepting it, replacing it instead with numerous countervailing strategies—artistic immortality, miraculous recovery, narrative truncation—attunes the reader's mind for the memoir's final set piece. The book's last pages find Eggers and Toph playing frisbee on Black Sands Beach, just north of San Francisco, recurring to an activity central to their relationship throughout the narrative, and one that has defined them in superhuman terms. Even when they first move to California, and Toph is all of eight years old, Eggers avers that "when we throw the world stops and gasps. We throw so far, and with such accuracy, and with such ridiculous beauty. . . . We throw the frisbee farther than anyone has ever seen a frisbee go. First it goes higher than anyone has thrown before . . . and then it goes farther than anyone has known a frisbee to go, with us having to use miles of beach, from one cliff to the other, thousands of people in between, to catch it. . . . No one has ever seen anything quite like it" (67–69). This preternatural ability, which already at the start draws crowds—"Busty women stop and stare. Senior citizens sit and shake their heads, gasping. Religious people fall to their knees" (69)—is central to Eggers' earliest formulations of a positive form of fame. While the Eggers children quit Lake Forest in part out of fear of becoming "this sad local legend, these sorry celebrities" (224), and elsewhere in the early pages of the book Eggers fantasizes in future or conditional tenses about the renown sure to be garnered by his prowess in various activities—as, for example, fancifully repainting thrift-store furniture (54)—only with frisbee does he shift comfortably into a present indicative attesting (albeit hyperbolically) to existing achievement and recognition. The notion of an Eggers at once all-too-vainly human, caught up in the self-aggrandizing rehearsal of his accomplishments, while also towering gloriously and benignly above those who might admire them, speaks to the further transpositions to follow, where Eggers becomes an entirely different kind of superhuman.

Describing the technique enabling his stunning throws, Eggers implicitly ties the release of the frisbee to the release he finds in frisbee, making his throws an answer both powerfully physical and inescapably phantasmal to the frustration and anger that characterize much of the book: "you whip that fucker like it had blades on it and you wanted it to cut straight through that paper-blue sky like a screen, rip through it and have it be blood and black space beyond" (435). Needless to say, the frisbee doesn't rip through the sky—"its heart breaks and it falls," Eggers says (436)—and the cosmic escape we remember from the dream of Toph's blood is momentarily frustrated. However, Eggers isn't done with the image. Here, "you" means "I" or "we," and the object of Eggers' aggression is safely diffuse, but two pages later, in the book's last lines, that is no longer the case. Eggers continues to describe the frisbee game in increasingly unstoppered prose, careening unpredictably through numerous intercalated topics (including further memories related to his mother) in sentences and then paragraphs that rush on and on, bristling with questions and taunts now directed at the reader (who is suddenly divorced from his or her accustomed position as a presumptive ally), in an ever more profane and aggressive vocabulary, before arriving at a final vision of that razor-edged frisbee ripping into Eggers himself, posed so as to recall Jesus on the cross: "if you're going to fucking sleep all day fuck you motherfuckers oh when you're all sleeping so many sleeping I am somewhere on some stupid rickety scaffolding and I'm trying to get your stupid fucking attention I've been trying to show you this, just been trying to show you this—What the fuck does it take to show you motherfuckers, what does it fucking take what do you want how much do you want because I am willing and I'll stand before you and I'll raise my arms and give you my chest and throat and wait, and I've been so old for so long, for you, for you, I want it fast and right through me— Oh do it, do it, you motherfuckers, do it do it you fuckers finally, finally, finally" (437).

The rising, pounding crescendo of pent-up energies and flows (of both language and blood) finally explodes here even as it ceases. The book suddenly falls silent with these words, and with this fall suddenly transmutes the rabid dissatisfaction of its rawest, most engulfing emotion into its grandest, most sanguine metatextual maneuver. Partial quotation can't do justice to the experience of page after page of Eggers' prose, hustling the reader into an unwitting complicity in which one finds that one has effectively whipped the blade through Eggers' body, as witnessed by the cessation of the narration,[6] before one even realizes what is going on. The result is, initially, thoroughly disturbing. In effecting the climactic joint expiration of author and text, Eggers literalizes Barthes' death of the author even as he upends Barthes' claims: the reader is not liberated, but instead conscripted into facilitating this bizarre ritual suicide. Eggers has imagined his violent death at the hands of one or another anonymous urban assailant—a carjacker (386), a man with a gun waiting outside the doors of an elevator (xxxiv), a sniper outside his office (305)—at intervals throughout the text. Here, he finally achieves it, transposing the paranoid fantasy (born of his parents' experiences) of being fate's victim into one in which he is very much in control, and achieving that control by making the assailant not a stranger barely sketched in the third-person, but instead his intimate: the reader, us. The book ends, and the eager, friendly, hortatory figure who has shepherded us through nearly 500 pages is lost in the space of an instant, his closing diatribe—unwonted as it is, unprecedented in its unequivocal aggression directed at the reader—lays the blame quite clearly at our feet. He has died for our shortcomings, our failure to attend to him sufficiently.

But this snarling turn, for all that it emerges from Eggers' eminently palpable frustration and disillusionment, is also a coolly studied, calmly plotted form of recruitment, through which Eggers recasts a death he feared would be random and pointless into a singularly significant event testifying to his own unparalleled status. If the death of the author appears to yield, in his hands, not the generative matrix Barthes anticipates but rather the death of the textual engine as well, it also mobilizes the book in different terms, consolidating several thematic strands and simultaneously poising itself to leap free of thematic analysis. Eggers' final step in redefining the stakes of bloodletting and the limits of the material self is to instrumentalize the inevitable cut that is a book's closure, tying it to an implicit laceration of the body that frees the blood beneath with all its coursing symbolic freight. Positioned as for a crucifixion, the beneficent blood he has long waited to pump to a needy world freely flowing, Eggers ushers in a new Eucharistic calculus. Trading on the interweaving of bodies and paper throughout the text, the ending's sudden, simultaneous chopping into both the book's narrative and Eggers' body positions the book *as* his body, held in the reader's hand like a communion wafer, and already figuratively consumed on this, its last page. Dave's discussions with Toph and John regarding his work as a kind of "cannibalism" (318, 424), his insistence to John that anthropophagy is not just the truth of human relations but also the height of his own aspirations—"I would feed myself to you," "I'll make you stronger" (425)—his strident questions on the book's penultimate page—"Don't you know that I am connected to you? Don't you know that I'm trying to pump blood to you, that this is for you" (436)—co-opt Jesus's words at the Last Supper. "Take, eat; this is my body," "drink . . . this is my blood," and "Do this in remembrance of me"[7] become directives to the reader regarding the book itself.

Thus the reader is cast not only as the agent of Eggers' demise, but also as that of his resurrection. Continuing to follow the Christological model, we can hear in Eggers' closing "finally, finally, finally" an echo of Jesus's last words as reported in the Gospel of John: "It is finished" (19.30). But just as Jesus's death signals the end only of the opening act of the narrative of Christianity, so Eggers' conclusion here reads compellingly as overture, packing crucifixion and communion into a single moment larded with as much promise as pathos.

Eggers' rhetorical transformation of the book into a version of himself recalls Jesus's performative refashioning of the food and drink before him into his body and blood, but the significance goes beyond that simple fiat. In recent decades, commentators have routinely read the celebration of the Eucharist as performative: in taking communion, individuals actively fashion themselves into members of the Christian community.[8] A more limited tradition also reads the Eucharist as functioning proleptically, somewhere between promising and ensuring the Second Coming, which would find its avatar here in the notion of an Eggers resuscitated or reconstituted by the reader's participation in the book.[9] Eggers' sudden worry on the penultimate page—"where is my lattice? I am not sure you are my lattice"—is answered twice over. Readers become members of the lattice, by analogy to the Christian communion, and in so doing—reversing the vector established earlier by Eggers' heart as a universal engine of life force, pumping blood to all—recall the newly moribund Eggers back to life.

The teeming profanity of Eggers' final paragraph, the insistent in-your-face interpellation of the reader as "motherfucker," serves, then, to underscore Eggers' innovative use of a particularly exigent hailing as an avenue into, and as quickly back from, death. Garrett Stewart, elaborating various influences on the nineteenth-century novel's use of direct address, highlights the epitaphic mode (stopping the reader in her tracks, as a monitory tombstone engraving might a traveler [41]) as "exaggerat[ing] to unmistakable clarity the tacit temporal lag of all reader apostrophe. No one is ever there directing a text toward us by the time we arrive on the scene of reading" (41). He adds: "The novel thus takes rhetorical form, in part, as a kind of open letter from beyond the grave of presence" (44). Eggers straddles this grave, the book's manifold interpellations of the reader finally boiling over just as its ontological status teeters at the edge of redefinition. The transit thus effected, from the self-conscious involutions of the work's beginning to the thunderclap of its close, accords with that which Hans Ulrich Gumbrecht imagines in *The Production of Presence: What Meaning Cannot Convey* (2004). Pacing Eggers' individual trajectory at the level of cultural analysis, Gumbrecht issues a grand appeal for moving beyond our current unquestioned fealty to the regimes of hermeneutics, epistemology, and interpretation, with their inherent privileging of subjectivity and self-referentiality, in favor of a renewed engagement with (or, as he maintains, a refreshed recognition of our ongoing engagement with) the bodily and the nonconceptual. In a late statement that communicates much about the inherent difficulty of pursuing this argument as an argument, let alone an academic one—although Gumbrecht writes in a heavily personalized, frank, and occasionally confessional tone that is not entirely unrelated to Eggers' own—Gumbrecht suggests that "it might indeed become important and helpful—not only for some romantic intellectuals—to have *concepts that would allow us to point to what is irreversibly nonconceptual in our lives*" (140, italics his).

Rather than articulating such a category analytically, Eggers produces it as an experience; the obsessive hermeneutical wrestling with his own self and its representation, and the reflexivity throughout, do not point to so much as vector the reader toward the book's final move. The endlessly self-conscious territory of Eggers' prefatory pages, which must be worked through before he can start, and the endlessly knowing world of *Might* magazine, which must fold before the book can close, emerge finally as baffles and buffers that Eggers employs in a highly directed fashion entirely at odds with their initial appearance. They represent both the first step in conditioning or even constituting the reader's desire for a more direct connection with Eggers (as evidenced by the critical response) and the building blocks of that connection, in that they introduce the processes by which the book begins to entertain notions of transformation and transfiguration. Gumbrecht's approach is more literal, appealing on one hand to the mute physicality of the book itself, any book, as evidenced by "the presence-dimension of the typography ... and even of the smell of paper" (109), and on the other to "the rhythm of language" (109), with its implicit exhortation to, or ghostly trace of bodily performance in, the "presence effects of rhyme and alliteration, of verse and stanza" (18). Some attention, even fleeting and intermittent, to these corporeal elements of literary praxis, Gumbrecht suggests, might begin to make the faintest of inroads against our alienation from "everything that could not be described as or transformed into a configuration of meaning," our "'loss of world' that explains why the only value (at least the highest value) that many humanists can find in the phenomena they are dealing with is the motivation to enter yet another loop of 'self-reflexivity'" (92).

Gumbrecht opposes what he labels our contemporary "meaning culture" to medieval "presence culture," with its "core ritual" of the Eucharist understood as producing "God's Real Presence on earth and among humans." In the medieval practice, "Christ's body and Christ's blood would become tangible as substances in the 'forms' of bread and wine," "'really'" present, rather than merely commemorated as subsequent Protestant theology maintains (28).

Citing "the Aristotelian concept of the sign—which," he says, "is not based on the distinction ... between a material signifier as surface and an immaterial meaning as depth"—as central to medieval thinking, Gumbrecht proposes that such a culture had "no problem with bread being the 'form' that made the 'substantial presence' of Christ's body perceptible" (29). This is the gesture Eggers recapitulates in the "form" of the book as material body.

Eggers in fact swamps the Gumbrechtian binary, building a presence effect out of innumerable hermeneutic somersaults, but it is an effect that looks ludicrous under even a little hermeneutic prodding, whether approached from the end of the book—suicide by frisbee?—or from the start, in which Eggers has admitted to the "easy and unconvincing nihilistic poseurism," the "self-righteousness," the "solipsism," and (most pointedly for the final pages) "the self-canonization disguised as self-destruction masquerading as self-aggrandizement disguised as self-flagellation as highest art form of all aspect" of the book (xxxv–xxxvii). If Eggers has fashioned himself into a hyperbolic version of the Author-God Barthes is intent on dethroning ("Death" 53), he has also told his own gospel in such fashion as to leave it at least almost as deflationary as it is vaunted. Dan Savage, I noted, characterizes *AHWOSG* via Eggers and his cohort's ability to "mock and inhabit their lives at the same time." Eggers manages to do the same with his afterlife.

Somewhat more positively: annexing the trappings of Catholicism, a ritual system that does not compel his belief but that presents him with a ready-made shell for belief, Eggers arrives at a structure hospitable to the causes in which he does have faith: his own ability to write a work of both heartbreak and genius, and his potential as a figurehead—even a leader—for his generation. But absent the hallowing effects of institutional sanction and longevity, or a clearly defined mission or credo of his own, Eggers is left urging faith in the secular and the individual itself, in what is in many respects a cult of an extremely mercurial personality—if indeed a cult predicated in large part on the charismatic appeal of that very mutability. On the model of the gospels themselves, Eggers turns the backward-facing genres of memoir and elegy into a forward-looking document, bodying himself forth as celebrity, author, even icon, where none was before, but he does so without the gospels' unalloyed conviction regarding the godhead thus effected.

"*And that will heal you?*" asks his interlocutor in *The Real World* interview's closing question, specifically referring to Eggers' impassioned plea to make him the "center of the lattice," "the heart pumping blood to everyone." Eggers' response—"Yes! Yes! Yes! Yes!" (237)—channels Darl Bundren's final words in *As I Lay Dying* as he is shipped off to the asylum in Jackson—"Yes yes yes yes yes yes yes yes" (254)—and those in which Marion Tweedy accepts Leopold Bloom's suit at the end of *Ulysses*—"yes I said yes I will Yes" (644)—and in so doing helps us read one more layer into the conclusion. Darl has been driven crazy by the complications attending the burial of his mother (for whom he alone in the family has found no substitute, no transitional object) and is lost in schizophrenic dialogue with himself; Molly's monologue, on the other hand, closes with this moment of committing herself to the course toward motherhood, to inner and outer dialogue with Bloom and ultimately with her daughter Milly. Eggers' crowning gesture in *AHWOSG* is itself in dialogue not just with this promise made at its midpoint, then, but also with the terrifically fraught evocations of maternity closing these precursor works, with the final entry in his own "Incomplete Guide to Symbols and Metaphors" on the penultimate page of the prefatory matter—"Me = Mother" (xliv)—and thus with his mother.

Eggers' last move puts his rhetorical faith in his mother's religious faith, and in so doing co-opts and refutes not just the death of the author but also that of the author's mother, finally overcoming the abject realities of her demise in this glorious fantasy of his own. In fact, Eggers intimates along the way that many of his defining authorial traits—his consuming self-consciousness, his superego, his superciliousness, his first sense of the superhuman—derive from her relentless surveillance. "Did her eyes make me this way? The way she watched, stared, approved and disapproved?" Eggers asks, feeling her gaze upon him as he prepares to scatter her remains, and then begins to answer: "Oh, those eyes. Slits, lasers, needles of shame, guilt, judgment— Was it a Catholic thing or just a her thing?" (395). This last turns our attention to the conclusion, as does an earlier account of her zealous policing of his youth. In the course of the MTV interview, Eggers affirms his suitability for *The Real World* experience in part based on the fact that he already feels he's being watched at all times, and surmises that he owes this sense to his mother's "amazing eyes, these small sharp eyes, always narrowing to a squint and tearing into you; she never missed anything, whether she was there seeing it or halfway around the world" (212). Her divine acuity thus provides the imagery ("tearing into you") that sparks Eggers' ascension, even as her rigorous surveillance offers both an earthly analogue to the omniscient Catholic God and a model for Eggers' own critical incisiveness: "When I watch people I too look through them. I learned that from my mother.... I know everything about people when I look at them for only a moment" (213). Feared but loved, resented in her presence but mourned in her absence, Heidi Eggers is effectively the god her son can commit himself to and the one he can become—the mediating force between humanity and divinity, and between the authorial hagiographies of old and the empty space accorded the author by poststructuralist theory.

5

THE DEATH OF KEVIN SPACEY

Seven and *The Usual Suspects*

(envisioning)

The first of the many messy corpses in David Fincher's *Seven* (1995) is not the work of the film's villain. Rather, the dead man's wife has concluded a lengthy domestic argument with a double-barreled shotgun blast. Nothing new, the neighbors report, except for the resolution—and indeed the simple detective-work at the crime scene is the last instance of routine police activity before the plot begins in earnest. As such, the film's opening minutes seem a detached bit of setup, their primary purpose simply to introduce Detective Lieutenant William Somerset (Morgan Freeman) and to establish his alienated status on the police force from which he is about to retire. While the officer who precedes Somerset to the scene is content to label the woman's act a "crime of passion"—invoking the quasi-judicial formulation distinguishing a sudden act born of jealousy and rage from a premeditated murder—and to have done with it, Somerset responds, "Yeah? Just look at all the passion on that wall." In the moment, the significance of Somerset's rejoinder remains unclear, but the status of passion—as intense emotion and impulsive individual action, as well as in the etymological sense of being acted upon—turns out to be central to the film's dénouement. Its last scene reunites the key terms hovering, two of them (jealousy and rage) unarticulated, at the start: serial killer John Doe (Kevin Spacey) caps a sequence of murders based on the Seven Deadly Sins by unexpectedly claiming Envy as his own failing and nominating Wrath as that of Somerset's volatile young partner, Detective David Mills (Brad Pitt). Doe thereupon goads

Mills into killing him in a moment of passion thoroughly premeditated and engineered by Doe himself. The oxymoronic notion of planning a crime of passion, of not merely foreseeing but choreographing the instinctive responses of another individual, is exactly the point. *Seven* is ultimately all about the confusion of active and passive roles, about agency co-opted in nefarious ways. Its specific perversity lies in the fact that Doe's script for Mills requires Doe's own death—that his agenda is accomplished only by this apparent self-sacrifice, which actually represents an apotheosis of both self and design. The film's larger stake is attested to by the trouble it takes to present that design in particularly literary terms, metaphorically casting the serial killer as an author, such that this slippery act of self-immolation constitutes a subtle meditation on Roland Barthes' "The Death of the Author." It is joined in this reflection by *The Usual Suspects*, released a mere month earlier and also starring Kevin Spacey as an evil genius *cum* author-figure, a consummate puppeteer who devastatingly manipulates all the other characters from behind the scenes as if endowed with a lofty or even atemporal perspective—almost an ontological privilege—that none of them shares, and who also, in the final minutes of the film, effaces himself only to assert his power more wholly.

This striking consonance tempts one to make strong claims for historical causality, and I do think both films respond to the suspicion attending overweening authorial claims, particularly those made by white males, in the wake of the "culture wars" of the '80s and '90s. One way to read the Spacey character's unflinching instrumentalizing of all other persons in each film, his willingness to dispose of any individual without a second thought, is as a consummate failure of empathy for any other subjectivity. And the corollary way to read Spacey's casting is as predicated on the unrelieved banality of his appearance (his middle-class, middle-aged, ordinary-white-guy looks) in conjunction with the body of work he amassed over the first half of the 1990s playing an unremitting series of driven, calculating, erudite, caustic characters of ferociously creative intelligence.[1] But I am not interested in dilating at length on such etiological suppositions, and even less in teleological claims for the necessity of marching through the century to precisely this endpoint. Rather, I want to read both films on their own terms, as relatively mainstream Hollywood entertainments that nevertheless betray a lively, incisive, and innovative self-consciousness regarding their material properties (and regarding shifting norms in the viewing and circulation of films) tied to a sustained exploration of the dynamics of storytelling. That the latter follows the collation of authorship and authority familiar from any number of academic discussions in the preceding twenty years is in keeping with the yield conferred by watching both films with Barthes' pungent language in mind. But the films offer a new purchase on the questions I've been asking throughout by turning away from the book as such—although steadily bearing it in mind, from the ominous empty volume that introduces *Seven*'s opening credits to the studied interweaving of screenwriter's and director's voices (per Barthes' repeated underscoring of the etymology linking "text" to fabric)[2] over the close of the *Usual Suspects* DVD's commentary track.[3]

Casting their imaginaries in visual terms, and diffusing the notion of creative agency across enormous teams (director, writer, cinematographer, editor, actors, and so forth), the movies achieve the opposite of the shuddering conclusion of Eggers' work. Instead of collapsing the text's actual author into his self-representation with terminal results, the films insist on the discrepancy between these figures—on what can be gained by an exploration of authorship that does not constantly threaten to blur ontological lines, instead always keeping the "author" before our eyes. Because these author-figures remain, finally, no more than characters contained by the diegetical frames of the movies in which they appear (with, at most, a winking metaphorical relation—rather than an operational linkage—to the actual creators of the works), the stakes of their "deaths" play out quite differently than those we have seen in the previous chapters. The "death of the author," which Barthes proposes as global metaphor for a range of literary compositional strategies and postures, here becomes a singular moment contained within the space of individual cinematic stories. This dramatization highlights not only the films' aspirations as a form of literary criticism, but also the fresh approach that their form allows: a theorization by way of narration. Authorial design, projected as criminal intrigue, ensnares readers now presented within the narrative as police detectives, and authorial death demonstrably only draws that snare tighter.

Seven offers a first nod toward these layered significances right at the start, in the scene mentioned above. Here, in the film's second release on DVD (the "Platinum Edition," featuring a new bonus disk of supplementary materials and commentaries that function, in their aggregate, as a "critical edition" of the text), the film's editor reveals in a laconic aside that "this dead guy on the floor *is* the writer"—Andrew Kevin Walker, author of the screenplay.[4] This harnessing of neo-Hitchcockian cameo to poststructuralist in-joke is left without exegesis; its significance becomes clear only through the freighted echo found in John Doe's death (an echo unremarked on the DVD) bookending the film. The dialogue after this first iteration, however, proves instructive. The camera leaves the corpse to shepherd Somerset into the scene, placing a crayoned picture by the dead man's child in the foreground as it does so. Somerset leans down to examine the drawing, and provokes his colleague by asking, "Did the kid see it?" The other officer spews profanities in response: "What kind of a fucking question is that? You know, we are all gonna be real glad when we get rid of you, Somerset, y'know that? It's always these questions with you. Did the kid see it? Who gives a fuck? He's dead. His wife killed him. Anything else has nothing to do with us." Again the questions and statements are left hanging without direct answers, but again their predictive value is considerable. *Seven* ratifies the sagacity of Somerset's query at numerous levels, elucidating the mechanics and the price of seeing things, and impugning the notion that any professional or personal detachment might guarantee a safe remove from the grisly tableaux it sets forth. Figuratively, the "kid" who at length sees too much is Mills, the junior partner, more green than he knows and more at risk than he is willing to admit. Yet more abstractly, by reinterpreting Barthes' theoretical claim by way of a narrative cinematic context, the film asks—as does *The Usual Suspects*—what it might be like, and what it might mean, to look the author in the eye—or, at the limit, to behold the death of the author.

Barthes fudges on the exact time of the author's death. Early in his essay, "[n]o doubt it has always been so" (49); midway through, it stands nascent in the "prehistory to modernity" located between Mallarmé and surrealism, and finds an analogue in Brecht's dramaturgy and contemporaneous reading practices (50–52). By the conclusion, the death teeters between logical proposition and exhortation, its realization still uncertain: "The birth of the reader must be requited by the death of the Author" (55). In contrast, *Seven* and *The Usual Suspects* make the death of the author into an identifiable event, while subjecting it to generic conventions of the police procedural.[5] These films code interpretive effort, *pace* Barthes, as a search for the author, and that search as akin to a police investigation, the resolution of which is contiguous with authorial death—literal in the first case and figurative in the second. Both films, however, present the climactic moment of revelation as yielding an immediate return to obscurity. Seeing the author is less about absolute clarity than about merely discerning, belatedly, one's place in his plans; to see his death is to witness those plans' completion, and in so doing to confirm both the author's essential inaccessibility and his enduring postmortem sway.

The decision to render the author as an arch-criminal is obviously a freighted one (the alternative might be a studiously benign, if ceaselessly manipulative, figure like Audrey Tautou's Amélie, in Jean-Pierre Jeunet's 2001 film of that name)—one that responds to the particularly virulent ways in which America's "culture wars" took up Barthes' own pathologizing vision of the author. Barthes maintains that "criticism still largely consists in saying that Baudelaire's oeuvre is the failure of the man Baudelaire, Van Gogh's is his madness, Tchaikovsky's his vice" (50). He ties these antisocial traits to the very pillars of his society, however, allying the "modern character" of the author with positivism and capitalist ideology (49–50), the sacred and the theological (51–52), and the paternal (52). He likewise refers to the author's "reign" (50) and "empire" (50, 52), blending his two rhetorical strains in the contention that "the image of literature to be found in contemporary culture is *tyrannically* centered on the author" (50, emphasis mine). All of this underscores his claims for the subversive (50) and finally "properly revolutionary" (54) character of nonauthorial writing.[6] The films conserve Barthes' sense of the author's power and of his turpitude, conflating these with a strikingly baleful construal of the literary academy's sometime demographic profiling of "dead white males" in discussions of canon-formation, its discomfort at the notion of seating blanket representational authority, with its implications for ideological resonance and institutional structures, in historically situated and limited individuals of a single stripe—individuals whose influence only grows stronger when hallowed by death.[7]

In *Seven*, the author's work consists of a series of dramatic set pieces whose immediate impact is visual and visceral, each the aftermath of a gory murder staged by Spacey's John Doe as a sort of installation artwork left for the police to discover. Doe sets himself the project of responding to the iniquities of the modern city by killing seven individuals in seven spectacular ways over seven days, making of them an "example," punishing each victim for embodying one or another of the Seven Deadly Sins. (The one-week time frame suits both dramatic economy and advertising copy, while also according to the number of Deadly Sins; it also adds to the Satanic aura of a character whose genius for destruction in this way stands counterbalanced to the weeklong project of divine creation.) Thus, for starters, Doe force-feeds his initial victim, the morbidly obese man he nominates for his admonitions regarding Gluttony, to the point of intestinal rupture and death. The revelation of this murder falls on the first day of world-weary Detective Somerset's last week on the police force before his anticipated retirement to the country, also the first day of the brief introduction to the beat that he will provide for the hotheaded and ambitious young Detective Mills. The film follows Somerset and Mills through the ensuing week, shadowing their investigation as they slowly build from the shocking provocation of Doe's first crime to an integrated sense of his larger endeavor.

That larger sense arises in part by way of various allusive literary flourishes illuminating the textual lineage essential to Doe's work. Doe leaves a quotation from Milton ("Long is the way, and Hard, / that out of hell leads up to Light") at the first crime scene and rewrites Shakespeare (offering a lawyer who, in Doe's words, "dedicated his life to making money by lying with every breath that he could muster, to keeping rapists and murderers on the streets" his life and freedom only if he cuts away from his own body "One pound of Flesh / No more No less / No cartilage, No Bone / but only flesh") at the second (Greed). When, midway through the film, the police break into Doe's apartment, it becomes clear that canonical texts do not just represent showy fillips in his public work, but that they are central to his private ruminations and his underlying motivations. Mills randomly opens one of the hundreds of composition books in Doe's apartment to an entry that fiercely, if bathetically, echoes *Macbeth*, perhaps even eclipsing the nihilism of that play's closing moments: "What sick ridiculous puppets we are, and what a gross little stage we dance on. What fun we have dancing, fucking, not a care in the world, not knowing that we are nothing, we are not what was intended." (The puppet metaphor is apposite to Doe's schema, but as his bitter, judgmental tone implies, Doe does not fully include himself in the first-person plural he employs. As suggested by his intimations here of privileged knowledge of an otherwise occulted divine intentionality, by the end of the film he will claim for himself some access to a higher plan, one he sees as in accordance with his own monstrous impulses and one that demands that he be more puppeteer than puppet.) The detectives track Doe to his apartment by way of the books he has borrowed from the library: Chaucer, Dante, Milton, Aquinas, Sade, Capote. The film presents these works as a particularized canon; the police find Doe because, once it becomes clear that Doe is basing his crimes around the Seven Deadly Sins, Somerset is able to identify the literary and philosophical works that Doe must be reading. As a convincing display of real-world detective work, this moment falls somewhat short. But it is tremendously compelling in bodying forth a notion of the force and import of canonicity: sociopathic fiend and cultivated police officer can easily agree on the Western world's key texts on sin (a collation that significantly overlaps the core of the Western canon, *tout simple*). Into this lineage, Doe seeks to add his own work.

The opening titles present that work to us by a literalizing synecdoche: the first shot of the sequence, and one frequently returned to, is of a large and entirely blank book with fluttering pages, recalling the credit sequences superimposed on cue cards or magically turning storybook pages of classical Hollywood films. Numerous shots follow of smaller composition books, which Doe has assembled and filled with all manner of disturbing matter. While the composition books are wholly diegetic, and will reappear in the scene in Doe's apartment, the large book is not. It seems more symbolic, then, of Doe's larger "work," his grander composition; the empty book seems poised to be filled by the events that make up the film to follow. We get an early indication of what those events will be like, and of what lies behind them, when Doe's hands intrude into the frame—highlighting and taking notes, pasting pictures and text into the smaller books, but also razoring their own fingerprints off. We learn later that Doe has been doing this slicing for years, as well as checking library books out, banking, renting rooms, and making all his purchases under the assumed and pointedly anonymous name of John Doe, thereby living entirely beneath the radar of assignable identity as he works toward the revelation of his masterpiece, toward releasing his work for public consumption.

Doe reads as a radical literalization of modernist impersonality, best legible through the canon (the lettered Somerset can follow the steps of his game in ways that Mills and the police captain cannot), adopting a preexisting symbolic system (the Seven Deadly Sins) as a structural armature for his undertaking just as Joyce uses *The Odyssey* and Eliot uses Frazer, deeply committed to the erasure of his own personality in the interest of what he terms his "work." Even the excision of his fingerprints reads not only in the eminently pragmatic terms the film explicitly suggests, but also as a grotesque parody of Joyce's artist-god, indifferently paring his fingernails at some remove from the world he has wrought. By adding a degree of what may or may not be religious humility via his invocation of the Seven Deadly Sins and later of Sodom and Gomorrah, and ultimately, in his willingness to sacrifice his life to the completion of his oeuvre, Doe attains a level of self-abnegation greater even than the "continual extinction of personality" (40) and "surrendering [one]self wholly to the work to be done" (44) proclaimed by Eliot in "Tradition and the Individual Talent." At the same time, he envisions for himself a quintessentially titanic modernist impact on the interpreters who will follow in his wake. "It doesn't matter who I am; who I am means absolutely nothing. I'm not special. I've never been exceptional. This is, though, what I'm doing, my work," he tells Mills and Somerset as they drive to the movie's final scene. And to Mills' brash rejoinder—"the funny thing is, all this work, two months from now, no one's gonna care, no one's gonna give a shit, no one's gonna remember"—he calmly responds: "You can't see the complete act yet. But when this is done, when it's finished, it's going to be—people will barely be able to comprehend, but they won't be able to deny... I'm setting the example. And what I've done is going to be puzzled over, and studied, and followed, forever." The echo of Joyce's famous boast regarding *Ulysses*—"I've put in so many enigmas and puzzles that it will keep the professors busy for centuries arguing over what I meant"—is unmistakable. Joyce goes on to say, "that's the only way of insuring one's immortality" (Ellmann 521); Doe's revision is to demonstrate the role of death itself in the pursuit of immortality. From the empty referents of his "name" through the numerous privations he embraces in the pursuit of his goals, Doe adopts the modernist dicta of willed impersonality wholeheartedly, as an *ars vivendi* rather than as a mere set of rhetorical postures. As a result, he can literally slip into the skin of his "characters." Having removed his fingerprints—not just from his work, but from his fingers—he momentarily commandeers those of another. When the police trace the message written in bloody handprints on the wall of the second victim's office to the room where they expect to catch the killer, they find instead his third victim (Sloth)—minus the hand Doe has cut off him in order to be able to leave the misleading fingerprints at the second crime.

The revision of expectations here is crucial. The police, confident that they have located the killer, turn out in force—a phalanx of squad cars squealing into action, filmed with the adrenaline-pumping dynamism that would traditionally signal the movie's climax. Their failure to apprehend their quarry makes it plain that they have seriously underestimated him. The "drug-dealing pederast" they identified via the misleading fingerprints is merely being used as a lure by a criminal of a wholly different magnitude, one with the resources, skills, patience, and as Somerset puts it "intestinal fortitude" to keep a man bound and wasting away, hovering at the edge of death, for exactly one year. A criminal, as well, with a particularly sick sense of humor. The message printed on the wall of Greed's office—the apparently straightforward "help me," a plea familiar from the Son of Sam case and since then become a sometime staple of the serial-killer genre—turns out to be a complexly layered taunt. John Doe, we learn, does not have a split consciousness, does not suffer from remorse or wish he could stop killing, is not in any danger of losing control. He merely ventriloquizes, here, either the cliché of a "lesser" type of killer that does not in fact fit him—or the voice of his captive avatar of Sloth, who does remain barely alive, even if already in captivity and beyond help.

That this hapless victim calls himself Victor might seem an ironic coincidence, even within the carefully scripted world of this film, but for the fact that Doe reveals a penchant for indulging in cruel puns at his "characters'" expense, yoking his deadly serious subject matter not just to an obvious project of aestheticization but also to a more clandestine series of verbal hijinks, further burnishing his modernist pedigree. In addition to making Victor his fall guy and to rechristening himself John Doe in a mocking parody of the legal proceedings he will elude (precisely by becoming John Doe, the unidentified corpse, rather than John Doe, the anonymous defendant; in this sense, the entire trajectory of his plan is announced from the start), he also literally cuts off Pride's nose to spite her face (leaving the narcissistic model whom he has elected to stand in for this sin the choice of either living disfigured or committing suicide). And when Mills, recalling the library records from which the police learn Doe's "name," pointedly addresses Doe as "John," Doe responds by forcing a different "john"—a prostitute's customer—to kill the prostitute, his figure for Lust. This sequence of crimes also marks an augmentation in Doe's precise bodily choreography of his victims. Pride and Lust move beyond the "hand puppet" he has made of Sloth to something more like marionettes: Doe leaves Pride with a phone glued to one hand and a bottle of pills glued to the other, knowing which she will choose, and he outfits the john with the bladed-phallus leather gear that kills the prostitute. "He had a gun and he made it happen," the man says repeatedly. "He made me do it. He put that thing on me and he made me wear it. Then he told me to fuck her. And I did." The final stage of this progression is the showiest: Doe, in captivity, handcuffed, and unarmed, is still able to dictate Mills' actions.

The complex layers of Doe's gambit require that his pursuers comport themselves, increasingly, not just as detectives but as bona fide interpreters of Doe's texts. Somerset advocates a search for significant marginalia that have been overshadowed by the theatrical trappings of each murder. "Even though the corpse is there," he tells Mills, "look through it, edit out the initial shock. [The] trick is to find one item, one detail, and focus on it." But where Somerset hopes to catch Doe out via the telling, overlooked detail, we find that he's always been preceded by Doe, set up to find just what Doe wants him to and thereby to be led deeper into Doe's machinations. Doe represents a postdeconstructive fantasy of authorship, in which all apparent lapses or oversights in his work turn out to be integral elements of the undertaking. The very effort of detection becomes an essential part of Doe's schema: he forces Gluttony to eat a clue, knowing it will be found in the course of the autopsy, just as the "help me" scrawled in Victor's prints at the second crime scene is essential to bringing the police in timely fashion to the third. In fact, then, the irony entailed in the "help me" is not, in the final analysis, that John Doe doesn't want help or is only invoking a trope of previous serial killers, but rather that—unwittingly and unwillingly—the police will help Doe accomplish his purposes; ultimately they will become necessary agents (albeit with no effective agency of their own) in the completion of his plans.

By the time Doe surrenders himself into police custody after the completion of five murders, Mills has learned enough, and has been thoroughly enough interpolated into Doe's modus operandi, that he echoes Somerset's convictions from the start of the film. Earlier, Mills overconfidently dismisses Doe's theatrics and the notion of an ordering intelligence behind them, telling Somerset, "C'mon, he's insane. Look! Right now he's probably dancing around in his grandma's panties, yeah, rubbing himself in peanut butter!" But Somerset warns Mills against the "mistake" of calling Doe "a lunatic," and goes on to affirm that "[t]his guy is methodical, exacting, and worst of all, patient." Thus, as the movie draws toward its finale, in spite of the evidence arrayed before him, Mills complains that "there's no way [Doe] will just turn himself in. It just doesn't make any sense." The captain adopts Mills' former perspective, matter-of-factly concluding, "Well, there he sits; it's not supposed to make any sense." Somerset rightly responds, "He's not finished." Mills agrees, but neither of them registers the rhetorical echo some minutes later when Doe's lawyer offers them the chance to escort Doe to the location of the two final bodies: concern for justice, public relations, and simple closure conjoin to overcome the detectives' wariness regarding Doe's proposal, and Mills speaks for them both when he wearily says, "Let's finish it." What they do not realize is that they will indeed be full participants in what little closure the end of Doe's spree will afford: that Mills will, at Doe's behest, commit the final crime.

Doe engineers this collusion by making Mills' wife, Tracy (Gwyneth Paltrow), the victim of the penultimate murder, an "adjustment" specifically motivated and made possible by Mills' cocksure mode of detective work. Doe poses as a news photographer at the third crime scene, and his attention is drawn by Mills' volatility and belligerence. In the course of a shouted altercation, Mills gives his name to Doe, making it all too easy for Doe to find his way to Tracy. Not only does Mills' inability to see the whole of Doe's gambit make him the perfect pawn, but Doe's plan trades on the anger that metaphorically blinds Mills at key moments throughout the film, giving Doe the inspiration for the dénouement. At the close, Doe exhorts Mills to "become Vengeance... become Wrath"—to kill him in response to learning that he has murdered and beheaded Tracy—trading on a slippage between blind justice (which Mills sees himself as serving) and blind vengeance (whose vassal he becomes), completing the series of murders even as he incarnates the seventh sin. Somerset warns Mills, "If you kill him, he will win," but Mills is unable to stop himself, and even as Doe embraces death Mills becomes a character fully authored by him and then reduced to nothing.

Faced with the destruction of his family, following protracted taunting by Doe in the police car on the way to the empty field where the final scene takes place, Mills quite reasonably loses track of the consequences of his actions. A certain blindness, however—born of a mixture of naïveté, impetuosity, and self-righteousness—characterizes much of his behavior. At various points he misses the intricacies of polite social behavior, of professional conduct, of interactions between other individuals, of the limits of the law, and, in the first part of the film, of the complexity of John Doe's endeavor. In some instances that blindness is willful, as when Mills kicks in the door of John Doe's apartment immediately after Somerset has pointed out that they have no probable cause to enter; at other times it is merely the effect of his personal drive and his desire to see justice served.

Somerset adopts blinders much more consciously, as when he counsels Mills to bracket shock and emotion in order to "remain focused on the detail," but the plot of the movie depends on the fact that he can no longer sustain this approach—that he sees or has seen too much, and now feels that he must leave the city behind. Tellingly, when forced at one point to reiterate the strength of his resolve to the chief, he does so by reference to a mugging the night before, in which the thief followed up taking the victim's wallet and watch by stabbing him in both eyes. The gratuitous savagery of this act seems offset only, and only extradiegetically, by its implicit reference to what Carol Clover has glossed as horror film's long tradition of carefully thematized assault on the eyes.[8] While this brief reference by Somerset contains *Seven*'s only account of an actual, physical ocular threat, a general constellation of visual menace haunts the film from start to end. Somerset's first question—"Did the kid see it?"— inaugurates a chain that includes all the gruesomely theatrical murders to follow, as well as Doe's extensive and disturbing photographic portfolio documenting his work, the elaborate set that is his apartment, the general darkness that pervades the mise-en-scène, and the aggressive opening credits (on which more shortly).

But visual menace is, in part, what audiences come to a certain brand of film to see. *Seven* is not exactly a horror film or a slasher flick, but it owes a great deal to each. It comes on the heels of two decades of increasingly acrobatic and imaginative murder sequences, in teen favorites like the *Friday the 13th* and *Nightmare on Elm Street* series, and in higher-brow reworkings of the form like *The Silence of the Lambs*. *Seven* both caters to and problematizes this desire for the outré and the grotesque, making the aestheticization of murder and death its explicit concern, rather than its unacknowledged spur. The character in the film who matches the viewer's insatiable—or at least presumptively unsatiated—appetite for these panoramas is John Doe. In keeping with the quasi-divine status Doe arrogates to himself, and in contradistinction to the partial blindnesses that characterize Mills and Somerset, Doe sees everything. He photographs each murder exhaustively, he foresees each step of the plot, and he sees Mills' vulnerability and how to take advantage of it. And, before all of these, he sees—and dilates upon—all the depravity of the city. As he explains in the squad car, "We see a deadly sin on every street corner, in every home, and we tolerate it. We tolerate it because it's common, it's trivial. We tolerate it morning, noon, and night." Screenwriter Walker echoes the pointed visuality of Doe's characterization in explaining the film's genesis on the DVD: "The inspiration for the Seven Deadly Sins and the inspiration for the idea for this whole movie was just the realization that in New York . . . you pretty much could just walk down the street and go, 'There's one, there's another.' You could kinda point out each of the sins . . . see them, in kinda these really overt ways." Doe's intolerance manifests itself precisely in the fact that he doesn't look away, that he stares all this and his own horrific response to it in the face. Similarly, when he is held in an interrogation room at the police station, he calmly meets the detectives' gazes through the one-way mirror that they, on the other hand, hide behind. The movie elides these kinds of all-seeingness: that which looks unflinchingly at what the rest of us turn away from, that which obsessively records all that it sees, and that which sees what others cannot—all the angles, the future. It positions them all in a common space beyond the pale, and asks the audience to accept a syllogistic logic inverting the textbook "All men are mortal" example. In its place, the movie proposes something along the lines of: A. No man can look all this evil in the face; B. John Doe looks; therefore, C. John Doe is no man; he is something both greater and worse, something demiurgic or, as Somerset suggests late in the game, Satanic.

The film's closing scenes offer a commentary on the wages of meeting that gaze. On the lengthy car ride from the urban precinct house to the desolate field where the action concludes, the blocking and montage repeatedly emphasize Mills' turning to look Doe in the eye and taunt him, while Somerset, Perseus-like, sees him only in the rearview mirror. The distinction follows the requirements of Doe's demand that only the two detectives accompany him to view the final bodies and the fact that one of the two must drive the car, but it resonates further. Doe arranges for Tracy's head to arrive by special courier, in a plain cardboard box, at the deserted site outside the city where the dénouement plays out. Wheedling and insinuating, he provokes Mills—who teeters between curiosity, dawning revelation, and denial—into shooting him upon learning the box's contents. The final scene shows Mills bundled into the back of a squad car, jaws slack, eyes wide and unseeing, as if blinded, at last, in a far more profound fashion. To face Doe directly, rather than warily circling around him as Somerset does, is to see and then to have sight taken away in the space of an instant. (Likewise, the movie's climax, saturated with desert light, is far brighter than any previous scene, but this bit of epilogue is again plunged in darkness.) The original ending (used at the producers' test screening, and included on the DVD) aimed to put audience members in Mills' position. This version goes to black terribly abruptly, seconds after Mills shoots Doe, its jagged framing and editing markedly in contrast with the polish characterizing the rest of the film. It is as if—after playing throughout the film with the dynamic between the desire to see and know more, and the horror of actually doing so—the audience is finally faced with the price it must pay for that knowledge and vision, and is blinded as swiftly and surely as the mugging victim described at the start. If Mills, in the final cut, has been written into a sort of latter-day Oedipus, blinded as a direct result of his own sleuthing (or a Pandora finagled into opening a box partially of his own making), this version of the film puts the viewer in virtually the same position, rendering all but explicit a series of loose parallelisms between all of the following: Mills' desire to know what's in the box, and our own; Mills' appetite for action, and ours for both action and aesthetic titillation sliding into grotesquerie; the larger project of detective work; and the drive toward narrative closure.

The DVD reports producer Arnold Kopelson's pithy reaction to this ending: "Oh my god, you took a perfectly good genre movie and made it into a foreign film!" The final version of *Seven* thus concludes, instead, with a relatively normalizing (and nominally reassuring) coda. The police chief promises Somerset that the force will "take care of" Mills, and Somerset responds that he will "be around," before adding in (unprecedented) voiceover: "Ernest Hemingway once wrote, 'The world is a fine place and worth fighting for.' I agree with the second part." In repudiating the first of Hemingway's contentions (while ignoring the irony and nuance characteristic of Hemingway's deceptively simple prose) but affirming the second, Somerset accepts the negative vision of pervasive sin that is the movie's premise—but also presents an escape from the inexorable wages of the audience's own sin constructed by the original ending (a path likewise attested to by the critical distance suggested by voiceover, and by the temporal remove it implies). The voiceover ending offers a smooth exit to the viewer—an exit modeled on the one it implies for Somerset himself, who has otherwise been rendered fundamentally irrelevant by the concluding action. When Somerset discovers Tracy's head in the box, he realizes that "John Doe has the upper hand," and repeatedly calls on Mills to drop his gun. Mills, refusing, not only capitulates to Doe's script for him, but also effectively screens out Somerset (and, by extension, the broader social and judicial apparatus awaiting Doe), enabling Doe to evade societal accountability and collapsing the struggle to a conflict between two men that is recapitulated in the stark final opposition between seeing everything and seeing nothing.

Much in the film likewise militates against the viability of Somerset's middle way. His plan to move to the country is predicated on the degree to which his views lean toward Doe's—a fact he acknowledges on several occasions, telling Mills at one point that he doesn't "think [he] can continue to live in a place that embraces and nurtures apathy as if it was a virtue." The screenplay included on the DVD-ROM renders the parallelism even more explicit, calling on Somerset to observe that "if you don't ignore everything and everyone around you, you . . . you become like John Doe." Ignoring everything is, obviously, the opposite of what the film encourages in the viewer, and the suggestion remains even in the revised version that if its contents have not burned us out, as they have Mills, they will leave us instead like Doe. This monitory note is articulated most clearly from a position buried deep within the opening credits, where it will be found only by those who return to the start of the film for more. If the soft landing of Somerset's voiceover epilogue reaffirms and reassures us in our common humanity, the opening credits seem to have been created with an eye to the more-than-human ability to rewind and review, and to parse at ever-more-minute levels, that video technology makes available—in particular, the frame-by-frame advance that is the common province of digital video systems. It is here, in the interstitial domain that will be discovered only by the obsessive (and/or scholarly) viewer, that the film dictates its final warning.

The opening credits are the scariest part of the film. Filmed on multiple stocks using antiquated cameras, with light sometimes intentionally allowed to leak into the chambers, the handwritten names and titles flash and scrape and sputter, blur and slide in and out of focus, inverting themselves and jumping outsized across the screen for split-seconds. Other words appear to be scratched onto the film itself. The whole is so artfully synchronized with the abrasive soundtrack by Nine Inch Nails (and with interspersed images of Doe's hands mutilating themselves, even as they assemble books filled with pictures of mutilated others) as to make one's entire body and mind feel simultaneously under siege—by way of the vulnerable eyes. However unsettling the images in other horror films, and even with the long-standing precedent of chase scenes filmed on hand-held cameras, one is accustomed to a basic stability and legibility in the opening titles.[9] *Seven* refuses the viewer that oasis of calm. Some of the fluttering brightness we fleetingly perceive here is the product not of random leakage of light into the camera, but of a methodical intercutting of words into split-seconds of the film. The credits close with the words "NO KEY" held just long enough to be perceived, if not wholly processed, without technological intervention. This taunt serves to engage the viewer in his or her own round of detective work, and points the way to the more fleeting interjections just previous. Frame-by-frame replay of the entire credit sequence, slowing the images down so that one can see everything, reveals the messages "THIS WILL BE YOU" (provocatively placed between the "casting" credit and the "costuming" one) and then (alongside the "writing" credit, such that this collocation recalls Walker's echo of Doe's justification for his actions): "REPENT." A call to repent would seem on first blush to equate the viewer with Doe's various sinners, but the film provides no syntactic referent for the "this." Instead, it would seem to refer to the immediate surroundings—that is, to John Doe at his work. Indeed, we read these words only by according ourselves the semidivine ability to slow down the passing flux of events; in so doing, we make ourselves into unblinking John Does. As Doe gleefully says to Mills in the squad car on the way to the final scene, "I can't wait for you to see, I really can't," knowing full well how unsustainable that sight will be. When the film is over, and scrawled onto our memory banks whether we like it or not, we find ourselves in a position to reread one of its other graphic gambits: the liberty it takes in referring to itself as "SE7EN." The top two-thirds of the numeral are washed out, allowing the bottom of the diagonal stroke to register subliminally as part of the "v" it replaces, even if the angle and placement of the line are not quite correct. But the more important subliminal reading is that which the brain might perform by simply allowing the faded and misplaced numeral to drop out entirely, reducing "SE7EN" to "SEEN." In fact, posters in advance of the opening labeled the movie "seven," a format preserved in the current single-disc DVD packaging. But the credits, more recent posters, and the collectors'/enthusiasts' two-disc Platinum Series use "SE7EN," underscoring the relationship between repeat viewing, greater knowledge, and infected sight.

The conclusion of the film's story converts to narrative form the notion that the apparent death of the author might simply be part of his plan, and that searching for the author would enable that plan to come to its fruition. A project of authorial self-effacement, by this logic, may well be quite the opposite of ceding control to the reader. The particular menace of *Seven* is its insidious suggestion, hidden at the very start, that this relationship may not remain agonistic—that beyond a certain point, reading begins to resemble authorship. In fact, Roland Barthes effectively concedes this point—even proclaims it triumphantly, if not in so many words—in the final paragraph of his essay, positing a reader every bit as mystical and idealized as the author Barthes works to supplant, indeed a reader even more alive to the myriad cultural tributaries feeding a work than is the author himself: "The reader is the very space in which are inscribed, without any of them being lost, all the citations out of which a writing is made; the unity of a text is not in its origin but in its destination" (54).

Barthes recognizes immediately that "this destination can no longer be personal," that his formulation requires a reader who is "without history, without biography, without psychology; he is only that *someone* who holds collected in one and the same field all of the traces from which writing is constituted" (54, emphasis Barthes'). What kind of "someone" this might be, what kind of individual resembles a space more than a localizable or describable human consciousness, is not a question Barthes undertakes to answer. Nor does *Seven*; for all that it has conducted us to the brink of this realization, it remains otherwise too invested in the monumentalizing tropes of modernist authorship to work the implications out further. *The Usual Suspects*, on the other hand, is crucially concerned with the tenuousness of the authorship it depicts, doing so in such a fashion as to yield considerable insights about readership as well, and about the interplay between the two. Here, again, the film proposes to its viewers a criminal mastermind, one whose manipulations are more occulted but putatively much farther-reaching than those of John Doe, again one who similarly seems able to maneuver all necessary individuals into exactly the positions he desires. But where *Seven* presents characters and viewers with a series of horrifying corpses united by a rigorous conceptual program bespeaking a sustained and singular intention, *The Usual Suspects* is grounded in rumor and suspicion, tale-telling and flashback, such that its central question is whether the many scattered events it depicts are in fact attributable to the machinations of one man or if they even happened at all. Over the course of the narrative, different characters credit the possibility of such an overlord to varying degrees; many see him as nothing but an explanatory myth, "a spook story that criminals tell their kids." However, by the film's end, it seems much more probable that the character played by Spacey—the ostensibly meek, palsied, and endlessly digressive short-con operator Verbal Kint, to the eye by far the least threatening of the five career criminals arrested seriatim at the start and banded together thereafter, a character apparently recruited to the film more for his capabilities and perhaps his entertainment value as a narrator than for any palpable menace—is in fact the movie's arch-villain, the underworld kingpin Keyser Söze.

Unlike John Doe, there is no whiff of God about Söze beyond that which his power implies. He does not act to make a larger point, but merely to advance his own interests at all costs, including indiscriminate murder, such that more than one character draws explicit parallels between Söze and the Devil. Near the end of his film-length questioning by New York Customs agent Dave Kujan (Chazz Palminteri), Verbal narrates his version of the scene with which the movie starts: the shipboard shooting of Dean Keaton (Gabriel Byrne) by Keyser Söze. Verbal describes himself as witnessing the killing from a hidden vantage point. But Kujan pushes Verbal, not believing in Keaton's death (he has successfully staged it once before, to escape a conviction, and it is Kujan's dogged pursuit of Keaton, a former cop ousted for corruption, that has brought the customs agent to San Pedro): "You had a gun! Why didn't you help him? He was your friend!" "Because I was afraid, okay, afraid," Verbal replies. "It was Keyser Söze, Agent Kujan. I mean the Devil himself. How do you shoot the Devil in the back? What if you miss?" In this context, the audience realizes that San Pedro Police Sergeant Rabin (Dan Hedaya), briefing Kujan earlier, is more correct than he realizes when he explains Verbal's invulnerability to prosecution: "I'm telling you this guy is protected from up on high by the Prince of Darkness."

Kujan remains convinced, however, that Keaton is not dead, that Verbal's testimony, based upon an obstructed point of view, is not sufficient proof. He takes up the legend of Keyser Söze, and by the end of the film browbeats Verbal into what appears to be a grudging, fearful acceptance that Keaton might be alive, might even be Söze. Kujan remains noncommittal as to whether Söze exists at all, but reading Keaton as some kind of criminal mastermind offers what is to Kujan the only convincing explanation for Verbal's survival: that Keaton intends Verbal to vouch for his death to the police, in what would read as a canny counterpoint to Doe's embrace of his own demise. "He programmed you; he programmed you to tell us just what he wanted you to," Kujan maintains, elaborating the evidence of Keaton's character and capabilities over a suggestive montage of his actions and dialogue from earlier in the film, ending with a revised version of the moment of his "death"—Keaton now the upright, healthy figure shooting some other man collapsed on the deck of the ship.

The notion of Söze's programming Verbal's speech, and even leading him to doubt the evidence of his own senses—"because you're a cripple, Verbal, because you're stupid," Kujan insists—does reinforce Söze's status as an author along the lines of John Doe. But this proves to be only the first of the movie's surprise endings. Verbal leaves the room in which Kujan has been interrogating him; Sergeant Rabin, whose office it is, returns to his desk, and Kujan and he engage in bantering conversation regarding the chaotic clutter of the space.

Kujan turns to survey the bulletin board that has been behind his head (and therefore before Verbal's eyes), and discovers that many of the names and other particulars Verbal has fed him actually come from items on the bulletin board. The film presents another montage, this time collating items from the board along with elements from the film and bits of Verbal's speech, and concluding with a third version of Keaton's death, in which Verbal now pulls the trigger. As Kujan chases after Verbal, a fax arrives in the police station with an artist's rendering of an eyewitness description of Söze by the ship's only other survivor—a picture of Verbal—as Verbal walks away from the police station, shakes out his ostensibly palsied hand, smoothes his crippled gait into a confident stride, and climbs into a waiting car driven by the man he has identified, in the flashback narration that makes up the bulk of the film, as Söze's lawyer, Kobayashi. Christopher McQuarrie's screenplay envisions Verbal shedding his identity with relish—his "hand flexes with all the grace and coordination of a sculptor's"[10]—pointedly likening him to an artist. With this flourish, Verbal himself—in a still more figurative instantiation of the death of the author than Doe's—effectively ceases to exist, making good in unexpected fashion on his skeptical dismissal of Kujan's conviction that catching Söze merely requires perseverance: "You think a guy like that comes this close to getting caught and sticks his head out? If he comes up for anything, it will be to get rid of me. After that, my guess is you'll never hear from him again." Before climbing into the car, Verbal pauses on the sidewalk to light a cigarette, with no visible hurry, even turning to gaze back in the direction of the police station's doors. We have previously seen Kujan emerge from those doors in chase, casting his eyes about in a search for Verbal. As the car drives away, the camera pans from it back to Kujan, emphasizing his position only a few yards away. Revelation, even in the bright light of Los Angeles at midday, again brings with it—indeed is immediately superseded by—a renewed blindness. Standing tall, in plain sight and close proximity, Verbal is nevertheless invisible to Kujan, inapprehensible in multiple senses of the term.

With Söze's emergence on-screen, however, the nature of his authorship threatens to transmute. If the story Verbal has told is substantially accurate, merely incomplete in accounting for his own actions in setting up situations in which he seemed to be only a relatively passive participant, then Söze remains a figure of awesome reach and power. But it's clear now that not all of the story is true, that some part of Verbal's authorial activity consists not in strong-arming reality into the configurations he desires, but in cobbling together the available detritus of reality into an assemblage that will hold together just long enough to satisfy his purpose. He appears now as a *bricoleur* of extraordinary skill, weaving, in textbook Barthesian fashion (53), a "fabric of quotations" into a compelling narrative. Stanley Orr, who also characterizes Verbal's speech as *bricolage*, emphasizes Verbal's employment of what Barthes elsewhere labels the "reality effect" issuing from the inclusion of small and seemingly irrelevant pieces of information in the rehearsal of a tale (69). I would underline the importance of Verbal's embrace of the myriad source texts around him in constituting this specious reality. Kujan, like Somerset, is clearly a very skilled reader. But Verbal bests him by being a better one, more sensitive to the specifics of the situation, more attuned to the details spread before him, and—most importantly—more aware of how thoroughly imbricated the processes of reading and writing may be. Kujan, focused on a concrete set of past events and a narrator whom he judges as simply needing to be pushed beyond a strategy of obfuscation, misses the fact that Verbal is a sort of textual generator, constantly reprocessing the disjecta of Rabin's bulletin board not just into temporizing digressions but also into the heart of his narrative. If a significant portion of Barthes' career was spent demonstrating the extent to which writing is constituted by preexisting writings, Verbal emphasizes the act of reading at the core of that process. With the surprise ending, what has been a thriller transmutes into a sort of detective story, though not so much a whodunit as a question of just what was done. As director Bryan Singer says on the DVD, "This film is about an experience. This is not an Agatha Christie mystery."

The film imparts that experience through studied misdirection. With enough perseverance, one realizes that the gold watch and lighter Söze possesses in the opening scene are those that Verbal receives as he leaves the police station at the close, and that this pairing explains the import of Verbal's clumsy fumble (posing as palsied) when he tries to use a lighter during the questioning. Similarly, all the shots of Söze on the boat linger on his legs and feet, emphasizing the confidence and regularity of his gait, in direct opposition to the images of Verbal limping and dragging his crippled leg. The visuals accompanying Verbal's narration of Söze's origin story run in the same vein. While Singer uses a variety of formal devices to suggest a paucity of information—shooting fewer frames per second and holding each image longer, blurring and jumping from shot to shot, bathing the whole in a muddy yellow light—the film actually greatly exceeds the specifics of Verbal's words.[11] Verbal of course makes no mention of it, but Söze walks here with an almost absurdly loping stride and has exceedingly long hair and a lean, toned body (while Verbal is stooped and pudgy and balding, with his hair cut shorter than Spacey has worn it in any other film save *Seven*). Retrospectively, one realizes that it would have been easy to identify Söze simply by looking for the character in the film least like him, as if Singer and McQuarrie were paying homage to a dogmatic structuralist playbook in their casting choices and storyboarding.

The filmmakers' liberties are matched by Verbal's own: flashbacks he introduces encompass events he didn't witness; sometimes he narrates scenes he didn't see. He reports whispered dialogue he could not have overheard on a crowded city street, and meetings within the hull of a ship he was not yet on. On the other hand, while it becomes clear that Verbal has drawn names for his minor characters—Redfoot, Kobayashi—and supposed activities from his past—picking coffee in Guatemala, participating in a barbershop quartet in Skokie, IL—from bits of text around the office in which he assembles the tale, the extent of his lies cannot be ascertained. By this point, our seeing is revealed as an armature of Kujan's belief, and thus of the self-consuming credibility of the movie's narrative. But what we are then to believe, ourselves, is finally left a deeply vexed question. We recognize the man driving the car that awaits Verbal when he leaves the station as "Kobayashi." Verbal may be only changing names, or he may be making episodes up wholesale. Or, as Söze, the man with his fingers in every pot, he may actually know or fully control things one assumes he could not. "This whole thing has turned political," Sergeant Rabin tells Kujan when he first arrives in San Pedro, to explain the degree of protection around Verbal. "The mayor was here last night, the chief; this morning, the governor called." Söze apparently has everyone in his pocket; his network of informers and pawns—or of people who can realize his designs in minute detail—could extend practically infinitely.

The status of authorship wavers, then, between the omniscient, omnipotent, eminently proactive force *Seven* constructs it to be, and a mere finessing of details—an opportunistic, retrospective narrational perspicacity. While simply introducing the second possibility radically revises our sense of the first, unmasks it as perhaps nothing more than a fiction created for credulous ears, the drift of the movie's narrative instead imparts the sense that the second might issue into the first. In the opening scene, Keaton lies helpless on the deck of the ship (we learn later that this is because Söze has shot him in the back a moment earlier). He dispiritedly lights a cigarette, and then ignites a trail of gasoline leading back to the leaking barrel behind him. But the makeshift fuse is disrupted by Söze, standing on a deck a level higher, who urinates across the middle of the path and prevents the flame from continuing along. Söze descends unhurriedly to Keaton's side, talks with him, shoots him, and then relights the fire, all while Verbal ostensibly watches (as the camerawork and his narration to Kujan later suggest) from behind an enormous tangle of ropes on the lower deck.

The camera lingers on the ropes repeatedly over the course of the film, beginning long before we know their significance to the plot. Their knotted mass obviously figures the complexity of the tale; less obviously, its teller. Stanley Orr notes that Verbal's little-used last name, "Kint," is an anagram of "knit," and proposes this affinity as an explanation of the name's etymology (69). If this reading is correct, though, we should add that Verbal is mis-knit, tangled. Likewise, in the holding cell at the start of the movie, McManus (Stephen Baldwin) refers to Verbal's contorted body in asking him, "What about it, Mr. Pretzelman, what's your story?" and this phrase is one of the last that resurfaces over the bulletin-board montage at the movie's end. The suggestion would seem to be that Verbal doesn't so much hide behind the tangled ropes as incarnate the tangle himself. By the end of the film, however, the viewer knows that Verbal is in fact "hiding" behind the ropes, or, better, that Söze is hiding behind the tangle that is Verbal. Söze, initially perched loftily above the action before entering it in pointedly condescending fashion, enjoys a removed perspective here analogous to that which turns out to be his throughout the questioning. Kujan needles Rabin for the clutter in his office at the end of the film, calling him a "slob," to which Rabin replies, "Yeah, but it all has a system, Dave. It all makes sense when you look at it right. You gotta, like, stand back from it, you know." Kujan's recognition of the trick Verbal has played on him, precisely by standing back and creating a system out of the mess, immediately follows.

Söze's descent reads like an author coming down from the empyrean to dispense with a particularly pesky character, then moving on to other projects, momentarily slumming at the level of his characters as Söze does in imaginatively placing himself behind the ropes, or more broadly with the entire Verbal persona. (His ability to start and stop at will the fire that Keaton initially ignites is in keeping with Rabin's description of Söze as "the Prince of Darkness," ironically "up on high.") In the early drafts of the film, Singer and

McQuarrie report on the DVD, the mass of ropes was instead the base of a crane. As such, it would have suggested to the viewer figuratively placed there the possibility of ascending to an elevated perspective. Eliminating the crane and replacing it with the ropes intimates that one will always remain enmeshed, moored to the deck, but some trace of the crane persists. Most of the film does seem dedicated to the tangle, not just cognitively but affectively. In keeping with its poststructuralist leanings, it eschews for a very long time a single center of gravity. Its stars are all character actors, and only gradually do some among them become preeminent in our attention. Meanwhile, the regular toggling between the heist plot Verbal narrates and the police procedural that elicits the narration, with their distinct conventions and the opposed identifications they elicit, keeps the viewer off-balance throughout. Our fundamental position in attempting to make sense of the story's convolutions is parallel to that of Agent Kujan, though, especially in the fast-paced closing minutes, and our sympathies might be expected to lodge finally with him. But they don't; by the end of the film, everyone sides with Verbal. Even as the last scene shows him abandoning his sad-sack disguise and reverting to something sinister and magisterial, there remains about him an aura of the approachable, the underdog, the lovable.

The Usual Suspects' ending is essentially that of *The Autobiography of Alice B. Toklas*. The unimposing hanger-on in a field of heavies, a chatty individual providing a narrative and affective bridge into a world heretofore occluded from our vision, reveals himself in the final moments of the piece to be the magisterial and forbidding figure at the center of the tale. And, as in *The Autobiography*, the author is thus humanized. But if Stein makes herself and her work approachable by detouring through Toklas's persona, it is with an eye to focusing attention thereafter on the remainder of her oeuvre. *The Usual Suspects*, on the far side of the poststructuralist critique of authority, makes identification with the author safe again by concentrating on the very process of tale-telling and deemphasizing, in the final going, the acts that tale narrates. In this fashion, the film affectively decouples two definitions of "authority" that have been conjoined since Barthes' writing: the *OED* distinguishes broadly between "power to enforce obedience" and "power to influence action, opinion, belief." The latter, in its softer forms, is nothing more than expertise, and thus admits of dispute and resistance, while the former—at least at the limit—need not. Barthes' objection is, at base, to the former: the author's power like the state's. This is

Keyser Söze's power, while that of suasion is Verbal's. Differentiating thus between aspects of the same character might seem like sophistry, but this limitation is the flip side of the perspectival benefits conferred by the ontological shift in these films, in which "authors" exist on the same plane as their "characters." The argument I have been pursuing throughout this book, however, is that our disciplinary abhorrence for authority as enforcement has left us hostile to authority as knowledge—forgetting that submitting to authorial authority does not mean becoming a Nabokovian galley slave but simply recognizing how much an author knows about the rules and expectations of his or her work. This boundary is, of course, toyed with in every text I treat, but it is also the engine that drives them all: invitation, however powerful or persuasive it may sometimes seem, is not the same as compulsion.

In *The Usual Suspects*, the distinction plays out in the quality of response its revelation elicits. The fact that Verbal, as Söze, seems to have killed his mates, to say nothing of a shipful of other men, seems immaterial. While Doe's savagery is part and parcel of his artwork, Verbal's gives way to the art of the story, an art in which our interpolation as recipients can easily transmute into the fantasy of sharing in its construction. Or at least of giddily floating away from the ropes, the halt steps and crabbed posture, the ground itself, with its creator. Instead of being compelled to the authorial space, as in *Seven*, we are instead invited there, on the strength of a canny combination of narrative prowess and individual charisma. For, if the movie's conclusion leads us to believe that Verbal Kint is a performance by Keyser Söze, through the first hundred-plus minutes of the plot's unrolling it plays the opposite way. Thus, we are thoroughly conditioned to ignore the affective reversal that ought to be triggered by the final revelation. Instead, we imagine the pleasure of such grace under pressure, of cobbling a story together so eloquently, of such control and aplomb while in a position of apparent powerlessness. Keyser Söze, then, reads as a bravura performance by Verbal Kint. And if the most weak and passive of the movie's characters can transform himself so, who is to say that a reader, too, might not be able to refashion himself as an author?

The two closing montages model for us, and enact within us, the electric experience of intellectual discovery that might spark this transfiguration. While extended montage sequences are more typically used to condense narrative time, often streamlining a sequence of physical development (the quintessential example might be the training regimen in *Rocky*), the montages at the end of *The Usual Suspects* run closer to the speed of thought—effectively condensing not the characters' time but the viewer's, and swiftly shepherding him or her through cognitive developments rather than bodily ones. The quick recapitulation of key moments strewn throughout the film allows for a speedy comparison and mental recalibration, taking the place of what might otherwise be a laborious process of rewinding and fast-forwarding through the film in order to locate and review salient instants. The work of home video replay, and that of the rereading, critiquing, and theorizing it enables, is built into the film itself. Worthwhile films have always rewarded multiple viewings and *The Usual Suspects* is no exception, the interpretive aid proffered by its final minutes notwithstanding. But it represents something new in its self-consciousness about the form that reviewing might take, just as *Seven* pointedly places material specifically directed to the new capacities of a home viewer in its own opening montage.

The fall of 1995, in addition to the opening of these two films, also marked the moment when the future of DVD technology became reasonably clear. Rival consortia—led by Sony and Philips on one hand, and Toshiba, Matsushita, and Time Warner on the other—announced with fanfare their agreement on a single standard for a long-playing video CD, heading off a repeat of the VHS-Betamax videotape battles of the 1980s and making good on the promise heralded by the groups' separate efforts through the early 1990s.[12] While the timing does not allow for an argument of direct causality in the production of these two films, it does speak to a general air of expectation, to the promise of a dramatically expanded cadre of cinephiles poised both to be fashioned by and to take advantage of the marriage of laserdisc features (the book-like attributes of chapter breaks, easy access to any point in the narrative, and digital reproduction capable of supporting close reading) to VHS prices, to say nothing of the community of discussants about to be created by the Internet. *Seven* and *The Usual Suspects* intuit this new audience, one dedicated to repeat viewings, given to focused consideration of discrete passages and of collated details, and ready to embark on the mash-ups, reedits, reenactments, and of course endless debates that now abound in cyberspace. The films' conjoint trajectory represents a recuperation of the author from the imperious monster of *Seven* to the voluble trickster of *The Usual Suspects*, which is also to say a recuperation from the towering eminences of early-twentieth-century literature to the ever-inflating free-for-all of the Web. The unremarkable face and physique that make Spacey an ideal vehicle for the malign anonymity of John Doe also allow for a maximum of viewer identification with the strange mixture of pathos and sass he brings to Verbal Kint.

Verbal's collation of a wash of textual and pictorial detail spread before him into a coherent narrative—indeed, into any number of narratives, always threatening to spin off into irrelevance but for Kujan's keeping him on task—registers the teetering point between readership and authorship Barthes dreamed of a generation earlier. The reader "without history . . . biography . . . [or] psychology" who "holds collected into one and the same field all the traces from which writing is constituted" is obviously no human reader at all, or at least no single individual. The vast collective that peoples and powers the Internet itself is as close as we are likely to get to realizing Barthes' vision. Barthes imagines the reader as a "site" for infinite exegesis: "a text consists of multiple writings, proceeding from several cultures and entering into dialogue, into parody, into contestation; but there is a site where this multiplicity is collected, and this site is not the author, as has hitherto been claimed, but the reader" (54). A single site, collating all the fonts and fruits of artistic endeavor, remains a Borgesian fantasy; but a loose concatenation of sites jointly achieving the same draws increasingly nigh. What Barthes did not stop to consider, though, is that his ideal reader's expository heroics would of necessity occasion more writing: appreciations, elaborations, repackagings, rebuttals—the very "dialogue," "parody," and "contestation" that he describes as "the total being of writing" (54).

Barthes is strikingly prescient regarding this societal shift, anticipating our metastasizing exegetical culture to a degree that would probably surprise even him, and that would likely pit his democratic commitments against his mandarin sensibilities. But he did not predict the ongoing centrality the notion of authorship would maintain in this vastly expanded conversation—authors of every sort as subjects of inquiry and analysis, authorship as a status conferred on the largest number of humans in history by the innumerable perduring soapboxes the Web provides, authorship as a perpetually contested state thanks to the ease of appropriating material from one site and pasting it into another. Nor did he foresee the continued weight that authorship would have, in the face of this new welter of communicative possibilities, in publishing and marketing decisions at large houses and small, staid and avant-garde. Most importantly in the current context, Barthes did not imagine that authorship, as a conceptual topos, would yet fascinate and engage us sufficiently that it might travel quite far from the literary-critical arena in which and regarding which he staged his objections—far enough to settle as thematic stake not only in literature of myriad stripes, but also in cultural artifacts where it might have seemed to have no place at all. The death of the author is the surest sign of his or her life, and abiding authority.

EPILOGUE

I closed the final chapter with an invocation of the infinitely elastic, because immaterial, realm of the Internet—and with it, new twenty-first-century critical and authorial potentials—anticipated by the Kevin Spacey films. Having reached this endpoint in the current moment, I would like to reflect briefly on a few historical developments implicit in the foregoing, before closing with consideration of two further formal dynamics that thus become visible. To begin, I want to highlight the films' attention—their vaunted expectations notwithstanding—to the material means of their circulation, the specific appeal to DVD or a like digital technology with powerful freeze-frame and searching capabilities inscribed in the modes of vision they enable, the ways in which their formal self-consciousness regards not just representational choices but the physical vehicle of that representation as well. This move is consonant with Dave Eggers' rising insistence and finally dependence on the physical book in his readers' hands. Where Faulkner intermittently suspends the regime of representation to convey through blank spaces in his text the silences and absences at the heart of the adze's rhythmic repetitions (5), the shape of Addie's body "where [she] used to be a virgin" (173), and the slow "clopping" of a solitary cow across Jefferson's empty town square (251), momentarily forcing our consideration of the emptiness of an expanse of un-inked page, Eggers turns our attention to the page itself. Over the course of the century, the hiccup Faulkner foists on the smooth stream of literary discourse transmutes into a discourse that itself finally requires us to remark on its material substratum; the paper that signifies as the absent or inarticulable in Faulkner is, for Eggers, a presence stepping beyond articulation. Formal self-consciousness is a constant throughout, of course, but the closing years of the century yoke that consciousness to an active and highly literal reflection on the processes of distribution and reception, such that physical material becomes (ironically) a primary means of expressing self-consciousness. The care with which Stein enumerates in the

Autobiography the small and embattled print-runs of her other works anticipates this concern, as does Nabokov's effective injection of a temporally discrete paratextual *apologia* into the heart of *Lolita* (or his reservation of key interpretive clues for an essay "on a book entitled *Lolita*"). But their evident awareness of the realities of publishing does not yet quite translate into the mutually dependent thematizations of textual materiality, commodification, and interpretation that mark the works in my last two chapters, and that mark them as typical of the end of the century.

Likewise, the obvious consonances between Stein's appeal for a broad readership and Eggers' should not blind us to the distinctions between her self-nomination as "the only one" "in english literature in her time" (77) and Eggers' as the center of a "lattice" of "people who have everything in common ... people [who] know all the same things and truly hope for the same things" (211). Eggers' closing move to make the book in his reader's hands a transubstantiated version of himself follows through on the imagery of this earlier passage, in which he imagines the lattice as a "connective tissue" made up by "everyone holding another's arm at the socket" (211), just as his cheeky opening assertion of similitude—"the author is ... like you" (xxvii)—anticipates it. Self-proclaimed genius notwithstanding, Eggers' rhetoric and the arc of his final apotheosis emphasize this contiguity; even his most singular qualities represent a prodigious distillation of a generational ethos. Stein's adoption of Toklas's unassuming voice does not require such an assertion, and indeed it's nearly impossible to imagine her making one. Rather, like Nabokov in his afterword, she weaves bad publicity—incomprehension, scandal, mockery—into her book to good effect, but never fails to position herself above the media fuss and the public it bespeaks, however solicitous of that public she may be. The Spacey characters finally reproduce this dynamic too, even though the demotic trappings of the Doe alias and—much more—the Kint persona appear to place them, for long stretches, in the popular sphere Eggers so pointedly inhabits. This ambivalence in their depiction, though, lends a special quality to the dizziness with which we must process the revelations that close the two films. Both, along with *AHWOSG*, explore the fashion in which contemporary celebrity often seems to emerge out of nowhere, throwing the most anodyne of individuals into the limelight.

Loosely mediating between these first two subjects—the text's material substratum as emptied or as full of the author, its representations of the author as discrete and unique or as almost one with his surroundings—are the evolving qualities of the master tropes I've nominated for authorial presence in the texts, and the related matter of the proliferation of authorial stand-ins within them. Various critics have proposed one or another of *As I Lay Dying*'s major characters as figures for Faulkner, based on analogies between the characters' positions and commitments and the author's (Addie's maternity or her philosophy of language, Darl's aestheticism and clairvoyance, Cash's investment in a well-wrought object, Peabody's and Tull's outsider perspectives, and so on; I have added the possibility suggested by Anse's unexpected closing departure from the lassitude that characterizes him through most of the novel). Choosing any one of these seems to me immediately suspect, because reductive; a seesawing between them would be more accurate, but my larger argument is that Faulkner consistently oscillates in and out of any identification with his characters at all. In insisting on seesawing as the best authorial signature here, I am affirming the importance of Faulkner's impersonal construction of his own presence, which then sets a baseline differentiating his work from all those to follow. Stein, I've argued, inhabits *The Autobiography* in Toklas's person as well as her own, and the text's drive is from the one to the other. By *Lolita*, the myriad obvious parallels between Humbert and Nabokov are complemented by the slippages between the latter and Quilty, Vivian Darkbloom, and John Ray, Jr., even as the central trope of aping is flanked by fire and more importantly water in their many instantiations as authorial inscriptions—showily projecting the author's hand as immanent throughout Creation. Eggers' controlling vision of himself as feeding, as well as feeding on, everyone and everything around him both elaborates and parodies Nabokov's stance, as does the fact that even a memoir featuring Eggers on every page intermittently transmogrifies numerous friends, relations, and strangers into obvious figures for himself. Poststructuralist criticism has often read such multiplications as a sign of the destabilization and breakdown of the author. While I affirm the shift in formal means over the course of the century, the force of my readings is directly opposed to this larger claim, demonstrating instead that there is no correlation between the number of authorial tropes or personae populating a text and the status of the author. Rather, those figurations themselves figure in broader textual systems coalescing around the performance of an authorial death that is never fatal.

There is, however, a related move that is far more consistent in these texts, involving not the author's self-depiction but rather one or more figures for a maternal other (sometimes, more broadly, simply the feminine) in each. *Seven* offers the most uncompromising illustration. I recorded in Chapter Five the debate between Detective Mills and John Doe as to the posterity the latter will achieve, Mills contending that "two months from now . . . no one's gonna remember" and Doe claiming that when "the complete act" is accomplished it will be "puzzled over, and studied, and followed, forever." The movie appears to ratify Doe's position, both in the final act's horror and in the wholesale co-optation of Mills that leads to its achievement. Mills' uncontrollable wrath is engendered, in part, by the fact that Doe reveals to him what Tracy had not yet told him herself: that she was pregnant. The film thus suggests a stark equation: that Doe's immortality is achieved at the price of Tracy's incipient maternity, or—more abstractly—that artistic self-creation stands in a zero-sum relationship with biological procreation. The literary tradition provides ample precedent for, at the very least, this collation—evidenced as well, Susan Stanford Friedman has noted, in our reverberant vocabulary of production and reproduction, mental conception and physical conception, and the presumptively male "pregnant mind" as opposed to the inherently female pregnant body (75). Friedman's subject is the explicit employment of childbirth as a metaphor for literary creativity in writers ranging from Philip Sidney to Denise Levertov, and she argues that while "the metaphor draws together mind and body, word and womb, it also evokes the sexual division of labor upon which Western patriarchy is founded," in which men make art and women are confined to making babies (75). While she goes on to adduce various theoretical accounts of "womb envy" as a central motivator for male artistic endeavor (84), the works that result from that competitive impulse do not, in her telling, trade on violent suppression of the maternal in any way commensurate with John Doe's, whose actions throughout the film are, of course, sui generis.[1]

Doe's extraordinary blend of sadism, savagery, and depravity is unique within the context of my book, too. I invoke his hyperbolic example, though, because the bald counterpoint here highlights the degree to which a less virulent eradication of the feminine—most often the maternal—nevertheless runs throughout my texts, connecting Addie Bundren's death to Stein's offloading almost every traditional female responsibility onto Toklas, Humbert's need to dispense with Charlotte Haze in order to realize his designs on Lolita, Heidi Eggers' succumbing to cancer, and the relentless macho posturing in the almost unremittingly male world of *The Usual Suspects*, before finally arriving at *Seven*'s apocalyptic conclusion.[2] A steady concomitant of the refutation of authorial death, it would seem, is a literal or figurative death of a mother. Why this should be so, as against the simpler and less troubling expedient of adopting and adapting the childbirth metaphor, is the subject of the following pages. But we must begin by charting the fashion in which the passing decades appear to register a growing discomfort with coding magisterial aesthetic performance as a hyperbolic masculine riposte to feminine fertility.

In Faulkner and Stein, the logic of substitution is relatively simple and—more importantly—less obviously freighted with moral stakes than is the case in the subsequent works. Deborah Clarke, pursuing an argument related to mine in the aptly titled *Robbing the Mother*, observes that Faulkner's "greatest novels often rely on the presence of disruptive femininity" (6), and that *As I Lay Dying* in particular demonstrates that "even killing the mother does not silence her" (36), that "Addie's corpse stands beyond the control of either literal or symbolic discourse" (39). There is ample support for such a contention, but the specific force of the closing words of the novel is to attenuate it somewhat. Here, as I've suggested, Addie's loss is measured most poignantly for the reader at the same time that Faulkner's authorial control and playfulness are perhaps most powerfully condensed—into, not coincidentally, the name "Mrs Bundren." This final demonstration of authorial prowess asserted, as it were, over Addie's dead body at least momentarily overshadows her lively postmortem discourse at the heart of the novel. Whatever further seesawing one might imagine between these two forces, the essential point is the suggestion of seesawing itself, the fashion in which the two voices are thus set in opposition here. Stein ends her autobiography quite similarly, with the catalogue of occupations at which Toklas has proven herself "pretty good"—housekeeper, gardener, needlewoman, secretary, editor, and vet for the dogs—and the difficulty of adding being an author to doing all the others "at once" (251–52). Again, the suggestion is that one can maintain the household of an author, or one can be an author, but not both—precisely the conundrum that leads Stein to write the autobiography on Toklas's behalf in the first place, and to imagine from the start that it might be entitled according to gender roles: "The wives of geniuses I have sat with" (14). Stein's self-identification as, in many respects, male is evident throughout the book; Stephen Scobie indeed argues that to "function as a genius [is] in Stein's own terms, as a writer, and as a man" (128). That some of Toklas's responsibilities might also be coded male, that procreation does not figure anywhere in her tasks, and that Stein is not unaware of elements of her own femininity all obviously attest to the complexities of applying this heuristic to this household, but again the point is the matter-of-factness with which Stein assumes that genius is masculine, irrespective of the ancillary activities of either the author or supporting persons.

Lolita initiates a turn in this logic, precisely by questioning its ostensible self-evidence as logic. Humbert's aesthetic of course depends on the refusal of adult female sexuality in its entirety in favor of the pubescent nymphet, at the limit imagining that he might trump both taboo and time by engendering on "a difficult adolescent" Lolita of whom he would otherwise have to rid himself a "Lolita the Second," and then impregnating the latter with a "supremely lovely Lolita the Third" on whom he might—"bizarre, tender, salivating"—practice "the art of being a granddad." Even Humbert recognizes this dream as "insanity" (174), but the novel for a long while obliges him in its hostility to mother figures. As if in anticipation of his later proclivities, it disposes of Humbert's own mother with unsurpassed efficiency—"(picnic, lightning)" (10)—and does not scruple to do much the same with Charlotte, subjecting her as well to a freak accident when Humbert cannot bring himself to murder her on his own. Finally, John Ray, Jr. reports that Lolita, too, "die[s] in childbed, giving birth to a stillborn girl," and thus paving the way for the publication of the book (4). But by making the effacement of the maternal (to say nothing of the depredations of the female more generally) a vexed plot point, rather than an effective condition of the narrative in the first place as—mutatis mutandis—in Faulkner and Stein, Nabokov subjects it to a more overt ethical calculus. For all that Humbert's moral compass is profoundly compromised, his resistance to killing Charlotte still registers; while he opines at the end that he would "have given Humbert at least thirty-five years for rape, and dismissed the rest of the charges," including Quilty's murder (308), he still thanks God for his failure of nerve where Charlotte was concerned and counterpoises the "innocuous" behavior of the sexual deviant with that of the killer (88). The novel obviously undermines this opposition—as it does all Humbert's protestations—in myriad fashions, but here one might defend Humbert by arguing that it codes removal of the mother not just as criminal but also as criminalizing: that only in the wake of Charlotte's demise does Humbert become the rapist and murderer he emphatically says he is not at this earlier juncture. Humbert is of course able to adopt this stance precisely because "fate" (which Nabokov repeatedly conjoins with the authorial hand) eliminates Charlotte for him, but by effecting Charlotte's death so insouciantly a mere nine pages later, the novel suggests some recognition of the bad faith involved in using all three of these maternal deaths as a means of moving the story forward.

The Usual Suspects effectively thematizes this very action; the version of Keyser Söze's origins Verbal relays to Agent Kujan paints Söze as only a "small-time" dope runner until the moment his legend begins to take hold. Pressured by a rival Hungarian gang to give up his territory, his wife and children held at gunpoint to enforce compliance, Söze instead "looks over the faces of his family" and then turns his gun on them. Having "show[n] these men of will"—his rivals—"what will really was," he allows one to escape to tell the tale, waits until "his [own] wife and kids are in the ground," and then goes after the gang: "he kills their kids, he kills their wives, he kills their parents and their parents' friends, he burns down the houses they live in and the stores they work in, he kills people that owe them money. And like that, he's gone, underground, nobody's ever seen him since, he becomes a myth." The larger-than-life villainy and brutality, and the consummate untouchability, that constitute Söze as a transcendently powerful author-figure and that drive the film are predicated on this repudiation of wife and children. The film recapitulates this dynamic more diffusely across its narrative, which is suffused with testosterone and in which any sign or imputation of weakness is invariably (save by Kujan) rhetorically coded as either gay or feminine, functionally equivalent terms here for victims and losers. The only actual female speaking part of any significance is Edie Finneran, Keaton's girlfriend and his aid in leaving his criminal past behind. Verbal derides this romance as a "good little scam," and quickly draws Keaton out of her orbit and back into action, suggesting that her presence in the film, as in Keaton's life, is but a structural cliché. But by the end of the film she is revealed to be the "extradition advisor" for a Mexican mobster acquainted with Söze's appearance and possessing "intimate knowledge of his businesses"—"the one guy," in Kujan's words, "that could finger Keyser Söze" to the Justice Department. In her private life, then, Edie is an obstacle to Verbal's plan—the construction of the band of outlaws the film will follow—while professionally she is poised to destroy Söze himself. Kobayashi reveals that Edie is in his power at one point in order to cow an uppity Keaton and a trigger-happy McManus, but ultimately Kujan announces that Söze has had her killed to protect himself. This is precisely the extreme to which Humbert cannot bring himself, a pragmatic brutality revealing—like Söze's origin story—in its schematic rigor.

A yet more virulent hostility toward the female attends *Seven*, culminating in Tracy's murder but evident already in the two preceding. Doe's first three victims—Gluttony, Greed, and Sloth—are men, and at least in the first two cases men who do indeed seem embodiments of the sins Doe attributes to them. But as Doe turns to female victims the balance shifts: Pride may indeed be a woman "so ugly on the inside that she couldn't bear to go on living if she couldn't be beautiful on the outside," as Doe contends, but setting a prostitute, rather than one of her customers, as an avatar of Lust is likely a misogynist displacement. This choice in turn anticipates the even more profound illogic of Doe's making the innocent Tracy suffer the consequences of the sin he nominates as his own: envy for the "the life of a simple man." Doe is willfully inflammatory, of course; he has altered his plans in response to the opportunities presented by Mills' character and is intent on provoking the homicidal rage that will perfect the sequence of his crimes. His phrasing underscores the degree to which Tracy is a mere pawn in his design, Mills its object. That Doe's substitution is so blatant seems to me the best justification for reading the misogyny as his rather than the film's as a whole; the slippage can hardly fail to spark a recognition of his "wielding of women as mediators of male transactions." These words are Eve Kosofsky Sedgwick's, of course, in the groundbreaking *Between Men* (102), first published in 1985 and quickly reissued in 1992. I suggest that its relation to *Seven* and *The Usual Suspects* is somewhat akin to that enjoyed by "The Death of the Author." Sedgwick's title and catchphrases do not have quite the cultural cachet of Barthes', and it would be more difficult to argue that her analysis directly gives rise to the films' scenarios—but perhaps only because it offers a crystalline formulation of a far more widespread and long-standing dynamic (literary and otherwise). The clarity with which the films reproduce the core of Sedgwick's thesis might argue for reading them as pure products of these long-standing social and narrative conventions, but both films' overall intelligence and self-consciousness make a more positive reading available. Thus, while we could view the extraordinarily masculine orientation of the two films, and the Spacey character's willingness in each to dispose of mothers and other women with serene indifference in pursuit of his authorial agenda, as no more than an extension of the calculus we have seen in the earlier works, we might do better to treat the films as drawing those earlier assumptions into a light harsh enough to begin to dispel them through a fuller elaboration, and indeed extension, of the transactional logics in play.

Dave Eggers, who inherits neither the gendered conventions of serial killer, heist, or cop movies nor a conception of titanic authorship (or even, finally, of gender relations) uninflected by late-twentieth-century doubts and ironies, furthers this project considerably. His fantasies of excellence are less traditionally masculine, inflected as they are by notions of nurturing and connectivity, and by his own experience of acting in the place of both mother and father to young Toph. Structurally, nevertheless, the model we have seen is maintained: Heidi Eggers' death, too, is essential to her son's authorial apotheosis. As *AHWOSG* presents the story, she provides occasion, material, and impetus for his transformation from a talented but not yet tremendously distinguished college student to the creator of the staggering work before us, and finally to the demigod whose transcendence is effected by our reading. But if Eggers indeed capitalizes on her unfortunate fate, he does not initiate it in either the cold-blooded or the complacent fashion of his various predecessors. At a deep emotional level, he appears not even to accept it. Indeed, as I've argued in Chapter Four, while Eggers' bid for immortality has its own ego-driven components, it is also clearly a recuperative act, a memorial to his mother as much as a hagiography of himself, a resuscitation of her through the performance of his own death and resurrection. Eggers understands the enabling effect of his mother's death, thus, but through his identification with her finally approaches an escape from the mood of psychosexual anxiety and the logic of alterity that govern the earlier works. He elaborates this move in a short-lived postmortem: a forty-eight-page appendix to *AHWOSG* that briefly supplemented its paperback publication in 2001. It consists mostly of annotations keyed to individual words and phrases in the main text, either setting the record a little bit straighter or adding material pertaining to the work's reception over the intervening year. Eggers here reports coming across a letter his mother wrote to him and his siblings "a year or so before everything got hairy," and describes himself as "stunned by how many echoes [he] hear[s], stunned by how clearly and deftly much of [his] book, its themes and even its punctuation, is hinted at in her short note." He then proceeds to reprint the note in full, "because it is a nice note," and because he hopes we "will like it and hear a voice that should immediately sound familiar and good" (42). The tropes of identification and the affective bonds that structure Eggers' appeals on his own behalf are thus extended to his mother, in the same mix of brief declaratives and optatives that he recurs to at key moments in the main text.

Eggers reanimates, though, not just his mother but also his text, demanding new attention to its style and reevaluation of that style's stakes. I am going to argue that this is no coincidence, that the ends to which mothers are brought in all these texts have much to do with the ends of the texts themselves—that Eggers, once again, dramatizes interpretive exigencies envisioned but left implicit in all the earlier works. His "stunned" response, and the rereading it encourages, echoes that occasioned by the surprise ending with which his book proper concludes, and points toward the importance of surprise endings as a constant throughout the texts I have discussed. Each text concludes with an unexpected turn that significantly revises or even upends that which has preceded it, thereby requiring rereading as a component of any good reading.[3] In this way, each ultimately recruits the energies of plot to urge the reader beyond plot, into an exploration of the stakes of formal play and experimentation over the course of the text. Thus, while my argument has been that mimetic and aesthetic regimes are in productive tension throughout these texts, I want to underscore now the texts' most emphatic insistence on this doubled interpretive charge as they conclude. The demand once again belies Barthes' proposal that the two modes of literary delectation must be antithetical, and it complicates as well our dominant understanding of the force and function of narrative endings. Both Frank Kermode's *The Sense of an Ending* (1967) and Peter Brooks' *Reading for the Plot* (1984), the two most prominent discussions of the structure of narrative design in the last half-century, generally conceive of narrative as vectored toward the coincidence of conclusion and revelation. For Kermode, "the provision of an end . . . make[s] possible a satisfying consonance with the origins and with the middle" (17), and Brooks likewise describes reading as "seeking in the unfolding of the narrative a line of intention and a portent of design that hold the promise of progress toward meaning" (xiii). Both critics recognize that twentieth-century writing complicates such claims; Brooks suggests broadly that with modernism enters "an era of suspicion toward plot" and thus a felt obligation to "show up [plots'] arbitrariness, to parody their mechanisms while admitting our dependence on them" (7), or to deflate them through anticlimactic endings: "no spectacular dénouement, no distribution of awards and punishments, no tie-up, through marriages and deaths, of all the characters' lives" (314). The works I have discussed exemplify a broad countertrend, however, embracing every element in this catalog—but with only a very nominal, indeed temporary, sense of finality. Rather than eschewing the novel's traditional mechanisms of closure, these works force such mechanisms into non-closural ends, undermining not only their clichéd functions but also the attendant assumption that order and resolution are temporally defined.[4]

Indeed, to push from the end of the text back into its heart divorces the characters' temporality from what we might call author-time, or—more pointedly—author-timelessness. We can elucidate by digging deeper into the echo of

Macbeth in John Doe's notebook. Doe writes, "What sick ridiculous puppets we are, and what a gross little stage we dance on," further diminishing the account of agency in Macbeth's bleak contention that "[l]ife's but a walking shadow, a poor player / That struts and frets his hour upon the stage, / And then is heard no more" (5.5.23–25). In making Mills into his puppet, Doe exempts himself from the "we" in his statement, and from the limitation to a mere "hour upon the stage." The sense in which Mills' existence is "the life of a simple man" expands from a description of character and behavior to include ontology as well: this is life as we know it in its basic form, sustained through all its teeming generations by simple, even unconscious, processes (Mills, again, is unaware of Tracy's pregnancy). To attain immortality, to achieve something greater than Macbeth's "signifying nothing," is to supplant biological conception with artistic preconception and an enduringly engaging artistic concept, and thus to overcome one's immersion in and subordination to temporal progression itself. This larger stake reveals the insufficiency for these texts of likening literary creation to childbirth, or of reading their artistic production under the sign of "womb envy." The logic of the womb, tied as it is to orderly succession of the generations, is precisely what the authors want to overcome. The point is not the artist's giving birth to the text, but rather the text's confirming and sustaining the life of the author. Thus, it seems, the resistance to the figure of maternity; while the texts do not shy from sentimentalized or otherwise emotionally fraught presentations (just as they complement the other linguistic and theoretical gambits I've traced with rich plotting and characterization), the underlying logic construes the maternal as a figure for life itself viewed as a form vectored toward its own cessation and replacement, and thus a figure that must be displaced by that of the undying author. So, at least, in the masculine tradition I trace here. The complexity of Eggers' gender roles and emotional commitments carries him some distance toward circumventing this dictate, and I wonder whether a counterhistory of female repudiations of authorial death over the course of the century would yield a very different dynamic. I leave this question to others, noting in passing, though, that even as Stein fits the pattern I've traced through her male-identified behavior and the division of labor with Toklas, she differentiates herself here.[5] There is no strong figure for maternity in the *Autobiography*; instead, as I've noted, Stein builds the book around complicating a different master trope for relentless forward motion—driving—and then annexing it to herself, rather than merely standing against the flow of time as do her peers.

Stein nevertheless positions herself in opposition to the temporal swirls and eddies of her book's narrative; she still sets author-time against character-time and narrative time, and she still likewise demands rereading as the avenue to grasp the fullness of her achievement. In this, the *Autobiography* stands aligned with the rest of the works herein, and we can call on them jointly to extend Kermode's famous analysis of the "fictional difference" with which we supplement the repetitive sound of a ticking clock, such that "we agree that it says *tick-tock*" (44). Kermode argues that this move "humanizes time by giving it form," and thus models "what we call a plot" (45). He does not speculate on the implications vis-à-vis humanity of plots, such as that of *Ulysses*, "containing a good deal of *tock-tick*" (45). Too, his thinking appears to remain temporal here, but it makes available the kind of conceptual analogue I have proposed, in which the *tocks* closing the mimetic succession of narrative events and providing certain kinds of resolution at the same time transmute into aesthetic *ticks*, requiring that new aesthetic *tocks* be discerned within the field of preexisting mimetic *ticks*. *Ulysses* pushes Kermode to entertain such possibilities through its embrace of "randomness," featuring "coincidences, meetings that have point, and coincidences which do not" (113). Joyce provides us with the experience, Kermode recognizes, of "fiction fitting where it touches" (113), of "concords"—which Kermode introduces under the sign of origins and endings (4–5)—flowering throughout. Outside of Joyce, though, Kermode reads such multivalent syntheses as the work of the poet, who "finds his brief fortuitous concords, . . . 'the freshness of transformation,' the 'reality of decreation,' the 'gaiety of language'" (the quotations are from Wallace Stevens) as distinct from the work of the novelist, who responds to "need" and the "nature of reality" as a "*donnée*" (133). Joycean language-play (and its echoes and analogues in the works I have treated), thus consigned to the poetic side of this equation, largely escapes Kermode's analysis. When Kermode does consider puns and other linguistic ambiguities, he too turns to the inexorable temporal logic of *Macbeth*, in which he sees them as absorbed into plot: the play "is about failures to attend to the part of equivoque which lacks immediate interest" (84) and constitutes "an enormous dramatic extension of the double-take" in Macbeth's long-delayed apprehension of the true significance of the witches' prophecy (53). What I have traced, instead, is the inverse: plot absorbed into puns, variously verbal and conceptual.

For a long while Brooks reproduces the narrative/lyric binary: "meanings developed by narrative *take time*: they unfold through the time of reading"

(92, emphasis Brooks'), for example, but lyric poetry "strives toward an ideal simultaneity of meaning, encouraging us to read backward as well as forward (through rhyme and repetition, for instance), to grasp the whole in one visual and auditory image" (20–21). Ultimately, however, he explores the pertinence of this idea of "repetition" in narrative, building from poetic devices (99) to plot elements (101) to "more subtle kinds of interconnectedness" in modernism and postmodernism (113). In his final pages, Brooks applies this analysis specifically to the notion of a teleological reading: "Since ends have ceased to be simple . . . the end that narrative seeks, in its anticipation of retrospection, may disappoint and baffle. Yet this may only make it the more necessary to construct meaning *from* that end, moving back to recover markings from the past, reconstructing the outposts of meaning along the way" (323, emphasis Brooks'). This conception is quite similar to mine, and it is surely no coincidence that it is Faulkner (in *Absalom, Absalom!*) who pushes Brooks to entertain the possibility that "[n]arrative plots may be no more—but of course also no less—than a variety of syntax which allows the verbal game—the dialogue really—to go on" (305). But for Brooks, this is a dialogue between reader and text, or, in various reformulations, reader and "the agency of narrative," reader faced with "the urgency of narrative act" (305). A certain possibility is elided quite subtly here, but elsewhere it becomes clearer. Brooks observes that "narration [in *Absalom*] as elsewhere in Faulkner seems to call upon both the individual's voice and that transindividual voice that speaks through all of Faulkner's characters" (294), which would put Faulkner, appropriately, in a lineage stretching back to Flaubert, who in *L'éducation sentimentale* presents us with moments that "tend to compose themselves into an aesthetic vision that does not belong to any character within the novel, but rather to an impersonal person, the composer of tableaux, the author" (212). As with Barthes' fastidious demarcation of the "figure" of the author (and perhaps directly alluding to it),[6] Brooks hastily revises this statement: "what seems to arise . . . at the end of this education . . . is again the figure of the novelist, or, to put it less in terms of person, the figure of novelizing, of the narrative act" (212). Brooks swiftly assimilates what looks like an authorial signature—or specter—to a postulated intratextual force, a narrative agency untethered to an extratextual agent; even his first invocation of the author limits him to his textual function: "an impersonal person." The alteration is consonant with his larger project of resolutely translating psychological drives from human functions to textual ones (xiv), and represents a significant step toward cementing the death of the author as a critical truism.

My counterargument is twofold: first, that the break and rebound from plot to rereading uncovers the work of a motivated and anticipatory intelligence; and, second, that this pivotal moment is staged—throughout the century—in such fashion as to underscore authorial identity and identification through the consistent production of especially prominent authorial avatars and signatures in the last moments of our texts.

At the start of the book, when he remains much more invested in notions of linearity and closure, Brooks expresses his "simple conviction . . . that narrative has something to do with time-boundedness, and that plot is the internal logic of the discourse of mortality" (22). Channeling Kermode's general eschatological orientation, and explicitly elaborating Walter Benjamin's conclusions in "The Storyteller," Brooks argues that "only the end can finally determine meaning, close the sentence as a signifying totality"; and again, "death . . . writes *finis* to the life and therefore confers on it its meaning" (22). I am willing to grant this construal as an account of how we read human lives, but its applicability to literature—precisely because we reanimate the field at every pass—seems to me only partial. Rather than death's conferring meaning, it would seem that a certain idea of meaning has here predicated a certain conception of death. But what if this narrative "death," this apparent conclusion, is only a performance, at length a preamble? This is my point, in another guise: before, beneath, and beyond—yet eminently accessible—is more life. A text's end is never dead, and an author who plays dead therein or thereby is supremely, and appropriately, confident of vitality.

REFERENCE MATTER

NOTES

INTRODUCTION

1. Of course, there is precedent for such duality before the twentieth century in what Robert Alter calls "the other great tradition," the line of self-conscious writing stretching as far back as Cervantes and embracing Fielding, Sterne, Diderot, and so on. This tradition has come to the fore, however—indeed achieved preeminence—in "literary" fiction over the last century.

2. Clara Claiborne Park has ably attributed that extremism to an assault on the most venerable institutions of French culture and the networks of power subtending them—"the death of the Author" as a pointed overthrowing of the "immortals" of the Académie Française. Michael North adduces an additional set of determinations in the essay's original context: not in *Mantéia* in 1968, but in the Fall–Winter 1967 issue of *Aspen*, a short-lived multimedia arts magazine, alongside, inter alia, aleatory music by John Cage and Morton Feldman, films by Robert Morris and Robert Rauschenberg, and recorded readings by Marcel Duchamp, Richard Huelsenbeck, Alain Robbe-Grillet, and William S. Burroughs.

3. The argument to follow parallels in some of its conclusions Burke's own reading of Barthes' ultimate reconciliation with the notion of the author, a development Burke sites in the overall progress of *S/Z* and in Barthes' late autobiographical works (44–59).

4. Kevin J. H. Dettmar offers an excellent précis of this development in *The Illicit Joyce of Postmodernism* 15–26.

5. The earlier essay glides surreptitiously between hortatory and triumphalist modes, a manifesto largely presenting itself as a history. It records numerous imperatives, but it also records most of them as accomplished, irrefutable, henceforth immutable: "*writing* can no longer designate an operation of recording" (52), "the *scriptor* no longer contains passions" (53), the "destination [of a text] can no longer be personal" (54), "[w]e are no longer willing to be the dupes" (55), "[w]e know now that text consists . . . of a multidimensional space" (52–53), "literature (it would be better, from now on, to say *writing*)" (54, emphases Barthes', throughout). The essay presents, with supreme confidence, a new literary world in which certain behaviors are not just the only ones desirable but also the only ones possible.

6. Quoting *Sade, Fourier, Loyola* 8.

7. DiBattista distinguishes her work from "conventional biography" because her focus is not on "the historical person"—"the author's imaginative personality, not her animal life, underpins it" (9).

8. "The Reader's Share," *Times Literary Supplement* 11 July 1975: 751.

9. Jennifer Wicke goes a step further in *Advertising Fictions: Literature, Advertisement, and Social Reading* (1988), arguing that our conversance with advertisements itself helps us to understand even the most recondite literature, her prime example being *Ulysses*. Thus, for example: "what I want to complicate is the certainty about the status of advertising as an ideological production, where advertisement is almost always figured as 'other.' More salient critiques of advertisement require an analysis of its affinities to a host of cultural practices—among them, literature" (11).

10. Critics vary in their estimation of just when middlebrow begins to take hold. For alternative chronologies, see Lawrence W. Levine's *Highbrow/Lowbrow: The Emergence of Cultural Hierarchy in America* (1988), and Joan Shelley Rubin's *The Making of Middlebrow Culture* (1992).

11. For instance, within texts earlier discussed, see Rainey 3, 173; Jaffe 33, 177, 185; and Turner 38–39 and passim.

CHAPTER ONE

1. There are, of course, other novels and even other Faulkner novels where characters share a name. Faulkner's innovation here is in making this move the jaw-dropping conclusion of the novel, all but entirely refusing it the normalizing contextualization that helps the reader to arrive at an acceptance of, for example, the two Quentins in *The Sound and the Fury* or the two Catherines in *Wuthering Heights*.

2. Quoted in the "Editors' Note" to the Vintage corrected text, 264.

3. Minor discrepancies do exist between the holograph manuscript and carbon typescript, and again between the typescript and the book as originally published. See McHaney.

4. Thanks to Joseph Jeon for the several parallels observed in the first half of this paragraph.

5. André Bleikasten is particularly eloquent in this respect, speaking of the novel as presided over by "the demon of analogy" (*Faulkner's* 39) and later as "a protean world where no thing is a single thing . . . where all things come to resemble and mirror one another in infinite regress" (*Ink* 168). In both cases, though, Bleikasten is primarily concerned with the workings of simile and metaphor, the richness of the novel's symbolic turns. While he notes that figurative language springs from all parts of speech in the novel (*Faulkner's* 40), he does not address the connections born of purely linguistic similitude that I focus on.

6. Critics have proven deeply divided as to whether Faulkner ratifies Addie's claim. Many do indeed read Addie as articulating Faulkner's own view, prominent among them Deborah Clarke, Donald Kartiganer (*The Fragile Thread*), Paul R. Lilly, Jr., David M. Monaghan, Eric J. Sundquist, and Olga W. Vickery. Others, including Bleikasten, John T. Matthews (*Play*), Stephen M. Ross, and Karen R. Sass, see the bulk of the novel,

and even Addie's own monologue, as a strong repudiation of her beliefs. Harriet Hustis advances the revisionary thesis that neither of these responses adequately reflects the actual purport of the novel, that Addie's view of language is necessarily limited by internalized patriarchal norms. Hustis describes herself as exploring "Addie's capacities as a female subject who grapples with her desire for alternative images of relationship and communication, with a view to opening new avenues of interpretation for *As I Lay Dying* as a whole" (11). While I believe the interpretation that follows would satisfy Hustis's exhortation, it is sparked by formal peculiarities of Faulkner's writing throughout the novel, rather than by Addie's particular complaint.

7. Arguments focusing on the novel's notorious blank spaces and its other disjunctions might be construed as exceptions to this norm of reading for what words "are trying to say at," though in practice that horizon of attempted articulation remains central. The most powerful of these discussions, in my view—John T. Matthews' *"As I Lay Dying* in the Machine Age"—is the subject of the final portion of the chapter.

8. Sundquist (who presents the most succinct and eloquent articulation of this approach to *As I Lay Dying*) reads language in the novel as focalized by loss, striving for an impossible recovery, and ever doomed to "fail to describe or fill the blank space that only the act of conceiving the need for a word can make manifest as irreparably lost or passed" (38). Thus Addie's posthumous monologue is "one of the most emotionally charged pieces of writing in the novel and perhaps the one that comes closest to stating internally a theory of its narrative form," and that narrative form is itself predicated on grief (36). The novel's comedy serves only as threat to its ritual force (42), or at best as a temporary release (43)—the latter claim, in his usage, eliding the distinctions between characters' and readers' experiences. For example, Sundquist instructs us to read Vardaman's boring holes through the top of Addie's coffin and into her face as "an act of love whose grotesque expression is at once perversely comic and at the same time utterly sincere" (42). But this is not the perverse humor of a little boy breaking rules with the knowledge that he can claim ignorance later on. For Vardaman the gesture is nothing but sincere; for the reader, even grasping Vardaman's sincerity and the concerns it expresses, the act registers as loving, horrifying, and yet comic. Sundquist also quotes Darl's evocation of Anse's face as if "carved by a savage caricaturist [in] a monstrous burlesque of all bereavement" (42), but the image seems more concerned with describing in Darl's standard oblique fashion the fact that the rain pouring across Anse's features magnifies his tears, such that his face appears to be "streaming slowly" (78), than with actual burlesque humor.

Olga Vickery takes a step toward making such distinctions, proposing the novel's eight nonfamilial narrators as "reverberator[s]" who "offer release from the tension through humorous or ironic remarks. Because only the actions of the Bundrens and not their thoughts and emotions are perceived, they become grotesques. What is horror and pain for the family becomes farce for those who are not themselves involved and who merely observe with the physical eye" (65). There is some immediate intuitive sense to this claim, and the character sketches with which she accompanies it are quite deft, but I think she gives short shrift to Moseley's and Peabody's outrage, the sense of powerlessness shared by Tull and Samson and Armstid, and so on. While these characters indeed generate a great deal of the book's humor, I again feel that they do not much appreciate it. Rather, Vickery's analysis highlights the reader's position and dilemma—at a qualitatively different degree of remove than even these characters' and thereby, unlike them, wholly unencumbered by the Bundrens' misfortunes, but at the same time far more deeply privy to those misfortunes' contours and emotional effects.

9. Sundquist, too, in the course of building to a thematic claim (rather than a pointedly linguistic one), argues that "the connection between sexual 'lying' and lying dying is an intimate one" (37).

10. Faulkner also chooses this moment to highlight the near-perfect anagrammatic relationship of Bundren and burden—"the only burden Anse Bundren's ever had is himself," Tull says in the midst of these ruminations (73)—the latter, it might be worth noting, ultimately coming from the same Indo-European root as "to bear."

Two of the novel's more brief reflections on maternity reinforce these connections. Cora describes Jewel as "the one she [Addie] labored so hard to bear" (21), and Peabody's passing thoughts echo her concern in his own more sardonic idiom as he arrives as the Bundrens' hilltop home: "Anse has not been to town in twelve years. And how his mother ever got up there to bear him, he being his mother's son" (42).

11. Among these I include the plunges from the sublime to the banal and sometimes back, the sudden reversals between the comic and the tragic, and the pervasiveness of chiasmus as structuring device in the previous examples.

12. The word itself was born out of such an impulse toward euphony centuries earlier, as—in the words of the *Oxford English Dictionary*—"a reduplicating formulation symbolic of alternating movement," its earliest form "used as part of a rhythmical jingle, apparently sung by sawyers, or by children imitating sawyers at their work."

13. Robert J. Kloss offers an extensive catalogue of descriptions of eyes in the novel (and of critical endeavors along similar lines), but he reads their importance in psychological, emotional terms having to do with intersubjectivity and the mirroring of one character's gaze by another.

14. Elizabeth Hayes discusses this tension with great thoroughness, elucidating Darl's existential musings and Faulkner's revisions to his manuscript as highlighting Darl's consciousness of his own isolation in comparison with the strength of the bonds between Jewel and Addie.

15. Each of these objects is associated with Jefferson, Addie's home town, where the family is headed for her burial. In some cases, the stake is merely getting to town with the objects intact (the tools, the coffin); in others, the object is one available for purchase in town. For Dewey Dell, the town druggists offer the hope of an avenue to end her unwanted pregnancy. Bleikasten (*Ink* 177–83) and Vickery (61–63) make similar arguments without using the psychological terminology.

16. A fine set of teeth, we might note, seems one of the novel's indices of health and happiness. When Jewel imagines himself alone with Addie atop a hill, the rest of humanity below, his scenario is of "rolling the rocks down the hill at their faces, picking them up and throwing them down the hill faces and teeth and all by God" (15), and Anse's

lack of teeth causes his face to "collapse" (17). New teeth, in Anse's mind, not only will "be a comfort" (111), but will restore him to his proper place in the Great Chain of Being, able to "eat God's own victuals as a man should" (37).

17. That in this last stage of the journey the coffin's movements exceed those of a seesaw, turning all the way end-over-end, seems in keeping with the absurd escalations of the Bundren family's misfortunes in the latter portion of the novel.

18. "Graphophone" was the brand-name employed by a popular maker of phonographs, but it seems to have become a generic term. See Luce (87) and Brown (94).

19. And *Sanctuary*, written before *As I Lay Dying*, though published after, testifies to just how aggressive Popeyes can be.

20. When the coffin has just been completed, near dawn on the day after Addie's death, and all the other men are exhausted and hungry, Cash disappears, and the narrative focus shifts to reveal him carefully cleaning and storing his tools (80). After the river-crossing, as Cash awakens very sick at Armstid's after having been operated on by a veterinarian, his first (barely audible but much repeated) concern is for his tools. Darl brings them where Cash can see them, and then "shove[s] them under the side of the bed, where he [can] reach his hand and touch them when he [feels] better" (186).

21. Kartiganer, in his most recent work on *As I Lay Dying*, notes the same itinerary from coffin to tools to graphophone. He sees it, though, from a perspective aligned with that of the characters, as Addie's "being decomposed by the very narrative line she has composed" in demanding to be returned to Jefferson, consonant with the objects' dissolution from metaphors (which speak directly to Addie) to metonyms (defined merely by contiguity), and hence testimonial to the diffusion born of new objects and actions and affections. He also reads the group as "a random series of signifiers," rather than one with linguistic and thematic determinants ("Farm" 295).

22. Critics who base their accounts of the novel on the fragmentation evidenced by its many discrete monologues, rather than on the aggregate, recapitulate Addie's conception of language on a larger scale.

23. "Darl's cubism substitutes formal intricacy for the reality of a blazing barn; it converts the issue of his agency in destroying property into a question of geometry" and "Darl's playful musical effects conspire to make Addie's expressions meaningless" ("Machine Age" 88).

24. By "universalization," Matthews means Darl's persistently enlarging from the particulars of a given problem to the broadest of existentialist laments, as when he responds to Dewey Dell's inability to acquire an abortifacient in Mottston with his "How do our lives ravel out into the no-wind, no-sound, the weary gestures wearily recapitulant" soliloquy ("Machine Age" 89; p. 207 in the novel).

25. This irony resembles that which Matthews champions in *The Play of Faulkner's Language*, arguing that both Faulkner and his characters find linguistic (broadly defined) play compensatory for loss. With respect to the solace Faulkner may have found in his writing, my position is amenable to this earlier one of Matthews' (although I am obviously more concerned with the reader's experience, which in no way need be

predicated on loss, than with Faulkner's). But with respect to the characters in *As I Lay Dying* (which Matthews does not address at length in the earlier book), it is not. The most obvious potential counterexample, which I am about to return to, would be Anse's labeling of the new Mrs. Bundren. Though his linguistic feat might indeed be argued a "deferring of conclusive truth" (*Play* 31), I do not think it constitutes the ongoing and monumental "play of difference," "the pure pleasure of making marks," that Matthews, in his earlier book, sees exemplified by Quentin and Shreve's reconstruction of Sutpen's story, Lucas Beauchamp's rituals of the hunt, and Isaac McCaslin's ledger entries (31).

26. I remember being very confused by this reference the first time I read the book, but precisely because Cash is so matter-of-fact, I ended up assuming it was a previously unmentioned relative. To conclude otherwise, one must remember Anse's telling Addie that he "aint got no people" in the midst of her monologue, a hundred pages earlier (171).

CHAPTER TWO

1. *Atlantic Monthly* 151:4 (April, 1933): 2. The pitch continues: "At all events, that is what it is—and written, too, in the King's own English! Read her account of Pablo Picasso and you will not lose a word in all her four installments." Editor Ellery Sedgwick, who had been rejecting Stein's work for years, wrote to her, "During our long correspondence, I think you felt my constant hope that the time would come when the real Miss Stein would pierce the smoke-screen with which she has always so mischievously surrounded herself" (Conrad 225). The *Atlantic* did take the liberty of significantly normalizing Stein's orthography.

2. See, for example, Breslin 152, Gilmore 66–67.

3. See also, for example, 14, 251.

4. Quoted by Wagner-Martin, 201. Wagner-Martin goes on to report that Grosser was so impressed that he suspected Toklas of having written the book, but that "most others [among Toklas and Stein's intimates] were convinced that Gertrude's ear was simply so good that her replication of Alice's speech was infallible" (201).

5. John Sturrock, likewise, maintains that Stein "condescends to define her singularity rather than to demonstrate it" (228).

6. See, for example, Ashton, Berry, DeKoven, Meyer *Irresistible Dictation* (although an earlier essay on *The Autobiography* will be discussed below), Ruddick, Steiner, and Sutherland.

7. "Compromise": Bridgman 216; "popular and comprehensible": Lénárt-Cheng 124; "commodification": Conrad 223; "gossip": Sturrock 228; "anecdote": Stimpson 160; "chit-chat": Reid 186; "lie": Stimpson.

8. Exceptions to this generalized description of the criticism on the *Autobiography* include Meyer "Shipwrecked," Conrad, and Johnston, discussed more fully elsewhere in this chapter.

9. See Gilmore.

10. See "*Stanzas in Meditation*: The Other Autobiography," principally 12–18.

11. She also suggests that the "opposite of a sad life" is construed by the husband in "Possessive Case" as "'no not [a] knot again' but 'amiable stepping'" (239).

12. It is characteristic of Stein that here, as in *The Making of Americans*, she constructs her key terminology in a heady mix of nouns, verbs, and adjectives all cast so as to be legible as progressive forms: telling, listening, being, living, loving, charming, beginning, ending, and trembling.

13. I owe all these references to an unpublished manuscript by Heather O'Donnell entitled "Gertrude Stein: The Movie." The final corrective comes from an interview— "Who's Fanny? Local Girl? Gertrude Asks, as Shot in Famous Hurst-Stein Battle"— published in the *St. Paul Pioneer Press* (8 December 1934). The headlines appeared as follows: "Gerty Gerty Stein Stein Is Back Home Home Back," *New York World-Telegram* (24 October 1934); "Gertrude Stein Leaves Radcliffe in Fog, in Fog," *Boston Traveler* (20 November 1934); "A Snub, A Snub, A Snub: Gertrude Stein Gives Carmel's Highbrows the Go-By," *San Francisco Examiner* (8 April 1935). O'Donnell further quotes: "Gertrude Is Gertrude and Miss Stein Is Here," *New York American* (25 October 1934); "Gertrude Stein, Stein, Is Back, Back, and It's Still All Black, Black," *Brooklyn Daily Eagle* (24 October 1934); "On Air Is On Air Is On Air," *Springfield Sunday Union and Republican* (11 November 1934); "Stein Is Stein and Art Is Art, Alas, Alas!" *Philadelphia Inquirer* (16 November 1934); "Gertrude Stein Reaches Town! And She's Lucid, Lucid, Lucid!" *Richmond Times-Dispatch* (6 February 1935); "Oh Gertrude Oh Stein Here to Talk," *Los Angeles Times*, part one (30 March 1935):1–2; and "Stein Is Here, Is a Stein, Is in S.F.," *San Francisco Chronicle* (10 April 1935).

14. A few other critics have also proposed Toklas as the hidden key to the book's operation. Anna Linzie, for example, argues that the book is "dominated in its entirety by the story of Toklas and her indispensible role in Stein's life and work, even as the text seems to preoccupy itself with the proclamation of Stein's genius" (150). Not only is Toklas "the conduit through which Stein's text passes to become legible and publishable" (157), but also, "through the re-creation of origins as Toklas saw them, and the rehearsal of knowledge as Toklas gradually gathered it, the reader can be initiated and enlightened too" (150). This construction of Toklas as an essential "liminal figure" between Stein and the reader is entirely consistent with my thesis, but largely limits itself to reported event and, sometimes, to the significance of contradictory reports of the same event (which Linzie reads as pointing toward just this sort of double reading of the work's claims), rather than zeroing in on linguistic particulars. Thus, Linzie reads the bell's ringing within Toklas as Stein's acknowledgment of Toklas's authorizing role in her career—it is Toklas who in this way transforms Stein from an aspirant to a genius (151, 155)—while I see the nod as genuine, but also as subsumed in a series of larger literary games engineered by Stein.

Lynn Z. Bloom also sees the reader as becoming "subtly align[ed] . . . with Toklas's own pleasant and pleasured perspective," but her concern is largely with Stein's manipulation of point-of-view as a way to "leaven" her "manifest egotism" (85).

CHAPTER THREE

1. For a thorough account, see Boyd's *Vladimir Nabokov: The American Years* 265–314.

2. I owe my awareness of this pronouncement by Nabokov to Leland de la Durantaye's *Style Is Matter* (28), where it is joined by several others in a similar vein. See especially 27–30.

3. Jennifer Ingleheart makes much the same observation regarding Nabokov's "impersonation," arguing that the "unique blend of confession, autobiography, and parody" that is the literary *apologia* (109) has been strangely underaddressed by "modern critics [showing] a surprising inclination to treat the essay as a straightforward defense of *Lolita*, expressing Nabokov's views in a simple and sincere manner" (82). Her reading focuses on Nabokov's "uncompromising" use of sexually suggestive language in the afterword (84), paralleling his strategy to that of Ovid in the *Tristia* 2 and ultimately proposing Ovid, "one of the earliest and most potent examples of the writer censored for his writing" (83), as a possible model for Nabokov's performance. My own interest, as will become clear, is in other precursor texts, but I find her analysis of the ambiguity in Nabokov's language entirely apt.

4. Though, in what may be a nod to the machinations of authorship, two of the most prominent are Rigger (187) and Riggs (253).

5. Schiff quotes a letter from Véra to Andrew Field, Nabokov's future biographer, in which she writes: "But he [VN] adds that 'generally speaking' his 'memory is poor and faulty.' I disagree" (308). Schiff also notes that "[f]riends had long complained that [Nabokov] winked at his interlocutor on the rare occasion when he spoke the truth" (308) and that one interviewer concluded that "nothing—least of all the truth—could stand between [Nabokov] and a good story" (324).

6. Michael Maar's proposal that *Lolita* may ultimately owe its contours not just to previous hints and impulses in Nabokov's own writing, but to Heinz von Lichberg's earlier work of the same title, is obviously of great significance in certain contexts, but largely irrelevant to the implicit claim of literary affiliation that I am about to argue Nabokov establishes.

7. Nabokov's phraseology here echoes that employed in the opening pages of *The Real Life of Sebastian Knight* (1941). There, the narrator—exploring the life and works of his half-brother, the author Sebastian Knight—breaks away from his narration of an event in Knight's childhood to quote from a parallel situation in one of Knight's novels, only to then claim that the highly suggestive quotation is "textually in no way connected" with actual events (9). To allude, in the course of discoursing on the relations between author and novel, to a novel entirely devoted to the exploration of the relations between author and novel, and to do so by disclaiming such relations, is of course quintessentially Nabokovian. That the earlier novel is a tale of literal half-brothers seems particularly suggestive in the context of parsing the relation between Nabokov and Humbert Humbert, which will indeed turn out to be the import of the ape allusion.

8. See, for example, Appel's elucidation of this reading in his notes to the novel (420–21, 438).

9. David Andrews does note that Humbert also, especially in the early going, likens himself to a spider, and Andrews points out that both spiders and apes eat butterflies—"the insects most often identified with Lolita" (74). One might suggest that the lines of Humbert's web, which he so gleefully imagines himself spinning out in his first days in the Haze household, are converted in the course of the novel to the bars of the ape's cage.

10. As, for example, just after relating the sad tale: "I leaf again and again through these miserable memories, and keep asking myself, was it then, in the glitter of that remote summer, that the rift in my life began; or was my excessive desire for that child only the first evidence of an inherent singularity?" (13).

11. This extratextual newspaper chase echoes Humbert's recourse to the *Briceland Gazette* in an attempt to recover some trace of the first evening with Lolita at The Enchanted Hunters, and John Ray, Jr.'s invocation in the preface of newspaper accounts of Quilty's murder in the papers of September–October, 1952 (4), pointing toward the many ways in which the afterword will prove to be best read by way of tropes and figures introduced in the novel proper.

12. On the latter, see also Proffer, Appel's commentary (Nabokov, *Lolita* 330–33), and especially Peterson, who founds his analysis of the ties between the two authors as much on style as he does on subject matter, and who carefully historicizes that relation based on the vogue for Poe that attended Nabokov's youth in St. Petersburg.

13. For further discussion of parallels between Poe and *Lolita*, see DuBois, Hyde (117–18), Maddox (*Nabokov's Novels* 74), Maddox ("Necrophilia" 361–66), and Sweeney. Ingleheart notes that Henri Rousseau modeled his paintings on the flora and fauna (including apes) that he saw in the Jardin des Plantes but claimed to be drawing on memories of military experience in Mexico—said experience having since been discredited—and suggests that Nabokov might be referencing this subterfuge. Penny McCarthy calls on the same caged-ape image to establish a possible line of influence from H. G. Wells' *Apropos of Dolores* (1938), the protagonist of which also visits an orangutan in the Paris zoo, and she notes many of the same details of simian description as I (40–42). Having drawn on this material extensively to underscore the suggestiveness of her collation, however, she turns away from the orangutan in the remainder of her analysis. And while she points out a variety of ways in which Humbert Humbert "has been quietly assimilated to the ape" (41), the question of aping does not factor prominently in her account. Ultimately, the elliptical references she discerns to Wells seem, even if convincing, less central to the novel's overarching agenda than are those to Poe.

14. There is a Nabokovian resonance to "planting" an allusion in the Jardin des Plantes, as well, an observation I owe to a conversation with John Bishop.

15. Heavy exterior metal shutters swing just as far as Dupin has surmised, in order to allow in- and egress through a window; the nail apparently fastening that window shut turns out to be broken as he reasons it must be—"as if," Shawn Rosenheim writes,

"his analysis were a type of narrative thaumaturgy, able to bring about changes in the world through mere enunciation" (78).

16. Though it should be noted that Poe himself seeds the potential deconstruction of this opposition. The narrator's initial response to Dupin's elaboration of the "alien" nature of the crime and the apparent "foreignness" of the murderer is to assume that the culprit must be "[a] madman . . . some raving maniac, escaped from a neighboring *Maison de Santé*" (161), effectively doubling and inverting his earlier description of himself and Dupin as "madmen of a harmless nature" (144). Similarly, the "outré" character of the crime, its "*grotesquerie*," matches the "recherché" intellect (142), and the "freak of fancy" (144)—the "*bizarrerie*" of preferring the night to the day (144)—already attributed to Dupin. So, too, the analyst's acumen and the orangutan's destructive agility are both termed "praeternatural" (141, 159).

17. Michael Maar's proposal of an alternative intertextual lineage is apposite here. Maar champions, with great dexterity, Heinz von Eschwege-Lichberg's earlier work of the same title as a precursor that Nabokov may or may not have held consciously in mind as he wrote his novel. Beyond observing that the more sustained and pointed reworking of Poe's story seems more characteristically Nabokovian, I will not weigh in on this debate directly. I will only note that if Nabokov's intention was indeed to throw readers off the scent of von Lichberg's work, establishing this strong alternative genealogy would be a compelling strategy at the same time as it would provide another entry in the convoluted nexus of responsibility-claims. Walking away from a more obvious acknowledgment of von Lichberg's influence would appear to be a rejection of an easy basis for another assertion of mere aping—in this instance of a preexisting literary text.

18. Appel's notes to *Lolita* provide a catalogue of Nabokov's Eliot allusions both here and in subsequent novels (337–38). Nabokov recurs to the terminology of magic in the afterword's final sentence, and concludes with the Eliotic aspiration of "the native illusionist . . . to transcend the heritage in his own way" (317).

19. Humbert does give glancing, half-conscious consideration to issues of originality, condescendingly assuming that the play Lolita acts in shares a name with "an unforgettable inn" because *The Enchanted Hunters* must be based on a "banal legend" pulled from "local . . . New England lore" (200). Later he faults Quilty and Darkbloom's play in Wace for having "lifted" its "idea of children-colors" from Joyce (221).

20. *Sic* on the lack of comma before "which" [punctuated per original text].

21. *King, Queen, Knave* introduces a similar constellation also invoking "Genesis" when the female automannequin breaks down—"a rib failed to function properly. After all, I need more time than God did, Mr. Director," the Inventor explains to Dreyer—even as Martha Dreyer herself lies dying after her failed attempt to murder her husband (261).

22. As he does in relating Beardsley community events and perceptions—see, for example, his narration on 189, 194–98—or other unwanted social interactions, as the doubles tennis, 234–36. "She was," after all, "Dolly at school" (9).

23. Indeed, Humbert responds to Lolita's duplicity by hitting her ferociously—"a tremendous backhand cut that caught her smack on her hot hard little cheekbone"

(227)—the only instance in the novel where the continuous sexual violence of Humbert's relations with Lolita breaks down into plain violence.

24. In between Humbert's last words and John Ray's introduction, Humbert dies of coronary thrombosis (3), which echoes aurally, if not symptomatically, this lengthy catalog.

25. So, too, the "ecstasy ... all softness, a case of internal combustion of which she would hardly have felt the heat, even if she were wide awake" (131) that Humbert claims would have awaited him if he had had his way with the sleeping Lolita in the course of their night together at the Enchanted Hunters.

26. Vladimir Alexandrov includes in his catalog of "topics on which [Humbert and Nabokov] simply agree" their keen eye for American *poshlost*, including psychoanalysis, their appreciation of America's scenic beauty, and (with minor adjustments) their reflections on time (*Nabokov's Otherworld*, 168–70).

27. James Laughlin of New Directions, a potential publisher of the novel, cautioned Nabokov against employing a pseudonym, based on his confidence that the particulars of Nabokov's style would render such a gambit entirely unsuccessful. See *Selected Letters*, 153. Carl Proffer goes to great lengths to establish at a minute, linguistic level the commonalities between Humbert Humbert's prose and that of the rest of Nabokov's oeuvre. See especially 105–14 and 121–24.

28. Adam Phillips adumbrates the effects of Pater's work in his introduction to the Oxford University Press edition, suggesting the extent to which Pater might provide a blueprint for key elements of Humbert's philosophizing and self-justification: "The publication of *The Renaissance*, and in particular the Conclusion, was regarded as a scandal of moral negligence on Pater's part. 'Young men,' A.C. Benson wrote in one of the early books on Pater, 'with vehement impulses, with no experience of the world, no idea of the solid and impenetrable weight of social traditions and prejudices, found in the principles enunciated by Pater with so much recondite beauty, so much magical charm, a new equation of values'" (xiii).

These new, aestheticized values are also predicted by Dupin and his narrator's embrace of "that sable divinity," night: "we would counterfeit her presence. At the first dawn of the morning we closed all the massy shutters of our old building; lighted a couple of tapers which, strongly perfumed, threw out only the ghastliest and feeblest of rays. By the aide of these we then busied our souls in dreams—reading, writing, or conversing, until warned by the clock of the advent of true Darkness. Then we sallied forth into the streets, arm in arm, continuing the topics of the day, or roaming far and wide until a late hour, seeking, amid the wild lights and shadows of the populous city, that infinity of mental excitement which quiet observation can afford" (144).

29. Among the more interesting of these are, in the latter category, Kauffman's critique, mentioned above, and Trevor McNeely's accusation that aestheticism functions as a ruse to entrap unwary academics, forcing them to ignore all moral questions posed by the novel. Lucy Maddox, on the other hand (in *Nabokov's Novels*), proposes John Ray, Jr. and Clare Quilty as incarnating, each with complete self-assurance, the poles of the moralist and the aesthete between which Humbert

Humbert is torn. Julia Bader reads the novel positively, as an allegory for the creative process.

30. See, for example, Rorty and Andrews.

31. William Woodin Rowe convincingly collates in *Nabokov's Deceptive World* (99–128) numerous instances where rushing water (literally) and all manner of flames (metaphorically) accompany sexual couplings throughout the Nabokovian corpus. He also concludes, in *Nabokov and Others*, that Nabokov frequently flags "shimmers of meaning" by invoking the elements—"especially fire and water"—in close proximity to them (163). In this light, the elemental play between Humbert and Quilty I am about to discuss might read as a metafictive gloss of much more of Nabokov's oeuvre, but the point I want to stress is that, at least in *Lolita*, these elements are far from inert bystanders to the action.

32. Lolita later tells Humbert that Duk Duk Ranch, whence she repaired with Quilty, was equipped with an "indoor waterfall" (276), and Quilty first appears at Pavor Manor emerging from a bathroom, "leaving a brief waterfall behind him" (294). These consonances lead Appel to confidently identify the flushing toilet in the hotel as Quilty's; I have every reason to agree, though it is true that the text does not confirm or deny the supposition.

33. It is worth noting, too, that this first shot, the one that still feels "feeble and juvenile" to Humbert and that thereby speaks to his as yet incomplete mastery of the situation, appears to him as if it had "merely trickled in [to the rug] and might come out again" (297).

34. One might even elucidate in Darkbloom a significance beyond its anagrammatic status, reading it as a reference to the thunderheads repeatedly blossoming into the narrative with Quilty.

35. For more on authorial watermarks, see *Speak, Memory* (25) and de la Durantaye's discussion thereof (174).

36. See, for example, Julia Bader's discussion of the novel.

37. Humbert observes in the middle of the cross-country chase that "toilets . . . happen . . . to be, for reasons unfathomable, the points where [his] destiny [is] liable to catch" (211). Characteristically, though Humbert is perspicacious, he does not grasp the whole of the story.

38. By contrast, though Boyd admits that debate over *Pale Fire* may continue in the wake of his intervention, he is entirely comfortable claiming his reading as the final, bottom layer of the novel's convoluted undertaking.

CHAPTER FOUR

1. See also Zamora, whose emphasis on the employ of such techniques in the service of renewing community—particularly in the North American magical realist tradition (542)—is particularly apposite to my conclusion.

2. See also Begley, Dillon.

3. http://www.armchairnews.com/freelance/eggers.html 05/11/07

4. Kinbote of course echoes *As You Like It*'s Jacques here, his gloss on the seventh age of man as "mere oblivion / Sans teeth, sans eyes, sans taste, sans everything" (2.7.164–65). But Kinbote counters with a promise: "I shall continue to exist. I may assume other disguises, other forms, but I shall try to exist" (300). He appeals for God's aid in this project, but echoes Humbert Humbert's admonition to the reader: "Imagine me; I shall not exist if you do not imagine me" (129). Eggers follows Humbert's model on the first and last pages of his California narrative—"Please look. Can you see us? Can you see us in our little red car? Picture us.... Look at us, goddammit" (47); "Can you see this? Goddamn, look at that fucking throw did you see Toph throw that goddamn thing...?" (436)—establishing a lengthy chain of intertextual precedents for his own ontological shimmer at the book's close.

5. Eggers' run as a countercultural hero to a large segment of America's youth may by this point have passed its apogee (although his influence, through the tutoring centers he has started in San Francisco and in several other cities, continues to build), but in the years just after *AHWOSG*'s publication it was immense. Anecdotally, I can report that, in the spring of 2003, teaching his book in a course on American autobiography probably doubled my enrollments.

6. In addition to the rhetorical and thematic promises of finitude and death Eggers lards throughout the last chapter, he also lays the groundwork for the closing sentence's force through the repeated employment of "finally" in describing his parents' deaths (17, 43, 226), a fantasized version of his own (305), and that of *Might* (407).

7. Conflating Matthew 26.26–28 and Luke 22.19.

8. See VanderWilt: "The Church is made by the Eucharist" (5–6); "The Eucharist is both action and thing acted upon. At the Eucharist communicants receive a share and become communicants (*koinountes*) in Christ and in the saving acts Christ has accomplished for them" (17).

9. See VanderWilt: "Christ's presence is experienced in the Eucharist as both a present reality by the work of the Spirit and as the pledge of his absolute presence at the end of time" (19).

CHAPTER FIVE

1. Regarding the former, Fincher speaks on the DVD commentary of the screenplay's description of the character as "the most, the plainest of fellows, like you would never look twice at him on the street," and "this guy... who disappeared against the wallpaper of the city, who was like your dad with glasses that were not quite in style... [a] white-collar worker who was lost somewhere in the office building who pushed buttons on a calculator all day and then went home." On the latter, see, for example, Spacey's *See No Evil, Hear No Evil* (1989), *A Show of Force* (1990), *Consenting Adults* (1992), *Iron Will* and *The Ref* (both 1994), and *Swimming with Sharks* (1995).

2. For example, in "The Death of the Author" (53) and "From Work to Text" (60).

3. For a convincing account of the rising interpretive significance of DVD commentaries, see Parker and Parker.

4. This fact is also, as of my writing, the first-listed piece of trivia on the movie's IMDB.com page.

5. The second arc of Spacey's cinema career (films released in the latter half of the 1990s) is, in fact, filled with movies in which he plays an author-figure or narrator who dies or dissipates at the close. In addition to those discussed here, the most prominent are *L.A. Confidential* (1997), *American Beauty* (1999), and *K-PAX* (2001). However, *Seven* and *The Usual Suspects* work through the theoretical questions thus posed most substantially and provocatively, and indeed Steffen Hantke also notes *Seven*'s concern with authorship. Hantke shares some elements of my analysis, including Doe's construction as a modernist author in particular and, in passing, his literalization of the death of the author (87). Hantke's broader concern, though, is with detective fiction's general assimilability to questions of authorship, rather than with the specific ways in which *Seven* engages Barthes' essay. Hantke sees Doe's revealing himself to the police (87, 92), the cessation of his potentially endless killing spree (85), and his death (93) as necessary but unwelcome sacrifices, even signposts of victimization (93), rather than as elements central to his triumph. All these acts, in Hantke's view, compromise Doe's modernist rebellion against a postmodernized world, a rebellion Hantke ultimately reads Fincher as sympathizing with. As will become clear, I see sustained horror at Doe's agenda, methods, and larger symbolic force as central to Fincher's project.

6. For a stunning full-length discussion of Barthes' construction of the author as a representative of all that was conservative and institutional in the France of the late 1960s (and the three centuries previous), see Park.

7. Neither film plays this debate out in rigid racial or gendered terms, but some critics have been tempted by the possibilities they hint at (without theorizing Kevin Spacey's particular brand of whiteness as such). While allowing that it makes no "overt reference to racial politics, or to the specificity of African-American culture," Paul Gormley argues that, in Somerset, *Seven* presents a character endowed with "a privileged knowledge of the milieu in which [he] live[s]" (165), as well as of "the powerlessness of the individual protagonist within the postmodern urban, cinematic milieu" (163), by virtue of his blackness. Gormley ties Doe's violence to that which "the white cultural imagination associates with images of contemporary black culture" (163), and he reads the film's gritty aesthetic in the context of cinematic and televisual representations of the "'hood." Doe clearly responds to a generalized foreboding regarding urban spaces that might be coded in racial terms, but it seems a stretch to read his whiteness as an enormous displacement, given that neither the city's background violence—including the domestic crime scene at the start—nor Somerset's mode of detective work is coded as black (Gormley acknowledges the latter of these points on 165). Stanley Orr, on the other hand, offers a highly compelling analysis of the manner in which Verbal's evocations of both Kobayashi and Keyser Söze rely heavily on Orientalist conventions deeply inscribed within the noir tradition. Since his reading emphasizes white misrepresentation of the Other, it is not inconsistent with mine, but my own focus will be on the diametrical opposition between the figure Verbal conjures and the one he actually presents to the viewer. Both the macho posturing that pervades

The Usual Suspects and John Doe's sadistic misogyny (which leads him to murder a prostitute, rather than her customer, for Lust and to kill Tracy Mills on behalf of his own Envy) court feminist readings; I offer a rudimentary one in the Epilogue.

8. See *Men, Women, and Chain Saws*, especially chapter four, "The Eye of Horror."

9. The credits may be read as lineal descendents of those in *Psycho*, which are cut into horizontal strips echoing the blinds over the window in the film's first scene. But *Psycho*'s credits move individually and progress as a group in a smooth and orderly fashion at odds with Anthony Perkins' twitchy demeanor as Norman Bates, and far removed from the chaotic disarray of the shower scene. In *Seven*, on the other hand, part of the horror derives from John Doe's methodicalness and placidity, in contradistinction to the mayhem he has wrought, which at some visceral level seems to include the credits themselves.

10. Quoted in Orr 71.

11. Verbal's name ironically obscures this fact. Throughout the movie, we hear very little of his supposed loquaciousness. He frequently tends more toward the taciturn. But labeling him as "Verbal" leads the viewer to assume a transparent relation between his words and the images we see, even as a misplaced faith in the veracity of photography leads us to view the images as corroborating the truth of his words.

12. For an account of the corporate maneuvering and eventual collaboration on DVD formats, and of DVD's rise in the marketplace, see Consumer Electronics Association. For a more potted historical overview, but an exhaustive comparison of laserdisc and DVD specifications, see Taylor.

EPILOGUE

1. Closer are the fates—ranging from enforced ignorance and muteness (98) to "ag[ing] two thousand years in minutes" while being consumed by a pillar of fire (86)—of various female figures in the late-nineteenth-century male quest romances by Haggard, Kipling, and Conrad that Elaine Showalter reads in *Sexual Anarchy* as repudiating both the strictures of Victorian society and the threat to male literary privilege represented by the legacy of George Eliot and her female peers (76–81).

2. Ulrich Knoepflmacher asked the wonderful question that first drew some of these connections and that opened the path to the argument that follows.

3. I owe this last phrase to the anonymous reader of my manuscript for Stanford.

4. While I turn to Kermode and Brooks as still our most influential theorists of the idea of ending, and as critics immersed in the same cultural matrix that gave birth to my primary texts, D. A. Miller's argument for the inexhaustibility of the "narratable" in *Narrative and Its Discontents* (1981) comports loosely with the argument I am about to advance. Miller's diagnosis of twentieth-century narratology as "pivot[ing] on the priority of ending" even as "it also takes nothing so much for granted" (xii) is precisely aligned with my complaint, although his construal of the "narratable" as "instances of disequilibrium, suspense, and general insufficiency . . . opposed to the 'nonnarratable' state of quiescence assumed by a novel before the beginning and supposedly recovered by it at the end" (ix) points to a focus on narrative event that mostly

places him somewhat wide of my ultimate concerns. He does suggest at the close that Stendhal, his transition-figure for the move from nineteenth- to twentieth-century novelistic aesthetics, creates a text in which "the position of closure—that is, of an ultimate signified to which everything in the text eventually speaks—comes to be occupied by narratability itself" (280); my contention is, of course, that standing behind "narratability itself" and spoken to by it and all the attendant textual signifieds is the figure of the author. New monographs on plot have not been tremendously forthcoming in the last decades, but see MacArthur, Neupert, and Joyce Rowe. For further theorizations contemporaneous with the Kermode-to-Brooks interval, see Caserio, Mortimer, Barbara Herrenstein Smith, and Torgovnick.

5. For existing studies of female plotting in twentieth-century American writing, see DuPlessis, Eagleton, Edwards, Gilbert and Gubar, and Thickstun.

6. See Introduction, page 10.

WORKS CITED

Adams, Timothy Dow. *Telling Lies in Modern American Autobiography*. Chapel Hill: University of North Carolina Press, 1990.

Alexandrov, Vladimir E. "A Note on Nabokov's Anti-Darwinism; or, Why Apes Feed on Butterflies in *The Gift*." In *Freedom and Responsibility in Russian Literature: Essays in Honor of Robert Louis Jackson*. Ed. Elizabeth Cheresh Allen and Gary Saul Morson. Evanston, IL: Northwestern University Press, 1995.

———. *Nabokov's Otherworld*. Princeton: Princeton University Press, 1991.

Alter, Robert. *Partial Magic: The Novel as a Self-Conscious Genre*. Berkeley: University of California Press, 1975.

Andrews, David. *Aestheticism, Nabokov, and* Lolita. Lewiston, NY: Edwin Mellen Press, 1999.

Ashton, Jennifer. "Gertrude Stein for Anyone." *ELH: English Literary History* 64.1 (1997): 289–331.

———. "'Rose Is a Rose': Gertrude Stein and the Critique of Indeterminacy." *MODERNISM/modernity* 9.4 (2002): 581–604.

Atlantic Monthly Apr.–Aug. 1933.

Bader, Julia. *Crystal Land: Artifice in Nabokov's English Novels*. Berkeley: University of California Press, 1972.

Barthes, Roland. "The Death of the Author." 1967. In *The Rustle of Language*. Trans. Richard Howard. New York: Hill and Wang, 1986.

———. "From Work to Text." 1971. In *The Rustle of Language*. Trans. Richard Howard. New York: Hill and Wang, 1986.

———. *The Pleasure of the Text*. 1973. Trans. Richard Miller. New York: Hill and Wang, 1975.

———. *Sade, Fourier, Loyola*. 1976. Trans. Richard Miller. Baltimore: Johns Hopkins University Press, 1997.

Begley, Adam. "Come to the Cabaret." *The Guardian*, 15 Jul. 2000. Web. 1 May 2007. http://www.guardian.co.uk/books/2000/jul/15/biography

Benjamin, Walter. "The Storyteller: Reflections on the Works of Nikolai Leskov." In *Illuminations*. Trans. Harry Zohn. New York: Schocken, 1968.

Berry, Ellen. *Curved Thought and Textual Wandering: Gertrude Stein's Postmodernism*. Ann Arbor: University of Michigan Press, 1992.
Bleikasten, André. *Faulkner's* As I Lay Dying. 1970. Rev. and enl. ed. Trans. Roger Little. Bloomington: Indiana University Press, 1973.
———. *The Ink of Melancholy: Faulkner's Novels from* The Sound and the Fury *to* Light in August. Bloomington: Indiana University Press, 1990.
Bloom, Lynn Z. "Gertrude Is Alice Is Everybody: Innovation and Point of View in Gertrude Stein's Autobiographies." *Twentieth Century Literature* 24.1 (1978): 81–93.
Booth, Wayne. *The Rhetoric of Fiction*. 1961. 2nd ed. Chicago: University of Chicago Press, 1983.
Bourdieu, Pierre. *Distinction: A Social Critique of the Judgement of Taste*. Trans. Richard Nice. Cambridge, MA: Harvard University Press, 1984.
Boyd, Brian. *Nabokov's Pale Fire: The Magic of Artistic Discovery*. Princeton: Princeton University Press, 1999.
———. *Vladimir Nabokov: The American Years*. Princeton: Princeton University Press, 1991.
Breslin, James E. "Gertrude Stein and the Problems of Autobiography." In *Women's Autobiography: Essays in Criticism*. Ed. Estelle C. Jelinek. Bloomington: Indiana University Press, 1980.
Bridgman, Richard. *Gertrude Stein in Pieces*. New York: Oxford University Press, 1970.
Brooks, Peter. *Reading for the Plot: Design and Intention in Narrative*. 1984. New York: Vintage, 1985.
Brown, Calvin. *A Glossary of Faulkner's South*. New Haven: Yale University Press, 1976.
Burke, Carolyn. "Gertrude Stein, the Cone Sisters, and the Puzzle of Female Friendship." In *Writing and Sexual Difference*. Ed. Elizabeth Abel. Chicago: University of Chicago Press, 1982.
Burke, Seán. *The Death and Return of the Author: Criticism and Subjectivity in Barthes, Foucault and Derrida*. 1992. 3rd ed. Edinburgh: Edinburgh University Press, 2008.
Caserio, Robert L. *Plot, Story, and the Novel: From Dickens and Poe to the Modern Period*. Princeton: Princeton University Press, 1979.
Clarke, Deborah. *Robbing the Mother: Women in Faulkner*. Jackson: University Press of Mississippi, 1994.
Clover, Carol J. *Men, Women, and Chain Saws: Gender in the Modern Horror Film*. Princeton: Princeton University Press, 1992.
Conrad, Bryce. "Gertrude Stein in the American Marketplace." *Journal of Modern Literature* 19.2 (1995): 215–33.
Consumer Electronics Association. "DVD." In *Digital America 2005*. CE.org. 2005. Web. 1 Aug. 2007. http://www.ce.org/Press/CEA_Pubs/929.asp.

De la Durantaye, Leland. *Style Is Matter: The Moral Art of Vladimir Nabokov.* Ithaca: Cornell University Press, 2007.

DeKoven, Marianne. *A Different Language: Gertrude Stein's Experimental Writing.* Madison: University of Wisconsin Press, 1983.

Dettmar, Kevin. *The Illicit Joyce of Postmodernism: Reading Against the Grain.* Madison: University of Wisconsin Press, 1996.

DiBattista, Maria. *Imagining Virginia Woolf: An Experiment in Critical Biography.* Princeton: Princeton University Press, 2009.

Dillon, Brian. "A Heartbreaking Work of Staggering Genius." *The Richmond Review.* N.d. Web. 1 May 2007. http://www.richmondreview.co.uk/books/heartbreaking.html.

DuBois, Arthur E. "Poe and *Lolita*." *CEA Critic* 26.6 (1964): 1+.

DuPlessis, Rachel Blau. *Writing Beyond the Ending: Narrative Strategies of Twentieth-Century Women Writers.* Bloomington: Indiana University Press, 1985.

Dydo, Ulla. "*Stanzas in Meditation*: The Other Autobiography." *Chicago Review* 35.2 (1985): 4–20.

Dydo, Ulla, with William Rice. *Gertrude Stein: The Language That Rises 1923–34.* Evanston: Northwestern University Press, 2003.

Eagleton, Mary. *Figuring the Woman Author in Contemporary Fiction.* New York: Palgrave Macmillan, 2005.

Edwards, Lee R. *Psyche as Hero: Female Heroism and Fictional Form.* Middletown, CT: Wesleyan University Press, 1984.

Eggers, Dave. *A Heartbreaking Work of Staggering Genius.* 2000. New York: Vintage Books, 2001.

———. Interview. http://www.armchairnews.com/freelance/eggers.html. Web. 11 May 2007.

Eliot, T. S. "Tradition and the Individual Talent." In *Selected Prose of T. S. Eliot.* Ed. Frank Kermode. New York: Harcourt, 1975.

Ellmann, Richard. *James Joyce.* New and rev. ed. New York: Oxford University Press, 1982.

Faulkner, William. *As I Lay Dying.* 1930. New York: Vintage-Random, 1990.

Field, Andrew. *Nabokov: His Life in Art.* Boston: Little, Brown, 1967.

Fish, Stanley. *Is There a Text in This Class? The Authority of Interpretive Communities.* Cambridge, MA: Harvard University Press, 1980.

Foucault, Michel. "What Is an Author?" (1969) In *Textual Strategies: Perspectives in Post-Structuralist Criticism.* Ed. Josué V. Harari. Ithaca: Cornell University Press, 1979. 141–60.

Friedman, Susan Stanford. "Creativity and the Childbirth Metaphor: Gender Difference in Literary Discourse." In *Speaking of Gender.* Ed. Elaine Showalter. New York: Routledge, 1989. 73–100.

Gilbert, Sandra M., and Susan Gubar. *No Man's Land: The Place of the Woman Writer in the Twentieth Century*. 3 vols. New Haven: Yale University Press, 1988–94.

Gilmore, Leigh. "A Signature of Lesbian Autobiography: 'Gertride/Altrude.'" In *Autobiography and Questions of Gender*. Ed. Shirley Neuman. London: Frank Cass, 1991.

Glass, Loren. *Authors Inc.: Literary Celebrity in the Modern United States, 1880–1980*. New York: NYU Press, 2004.

Gormley, Paul. "Trashing Whiteness: *Pulp Fiction, Se7en, Strange Days*, and Articulating Affect." *Angelaki* 6.1 (2001): 155–71.

Gumbrecht, Hans Ulrich. *The Production of Presence: What Meaning Cannot Convey*. Stanford: Stanford University Press, 2004.

Hale, Dorothy J. "*As I Lay Dying*'s Heterogeneous Discourse." *Novel* 23.1 (1989): 5–23.

Hantke, Steffen. "Authorship in Serial Killer Narratives: David Fincher's *Se7en*." *Sun Yat-sen Journal of Humanities* 12 (2001): 75–95.

Hayes, Elizabeth. "Tension Between Darl and Jewel." *Southern Literary Journal* 24.2 (1992): 49–61.

Hirschorn, Michael. "One Story Please—Hold the Self-Consciousness." *Slate.com* 21 Feb. 2000. Web. 29 Aug. 2009. http://www.slate.com/id/2000147/entry/1004651.

———. "To Be Real." *Slate.com* 22 Feb. 2000. Web. 29 Aug. 2009. http://www.slate.com/id/2000147/entry/1004660/.

Hungerford, Amy. "Don DeLillo's Latin Mass." *Contemporary Literature* 47.3 (2006): 343–80.

Hustis, Harriet. "The Tangled Webs We Weave: Faulkner Scholarship and the Significance of Addie Bundren's Monologue." *Faulkner Journal* 12.1 (1996): 3–21.

Huyssen, Andreas. *After the Great Divide: Modernism, Mass Culture, Postmodernism*. Bloomington: Indiana University Press, 1986.

Hyde, G. M. *Vladimir Nabokov: America's Russian Novelist*. London: Marion Boyars, 1977.

Ingleheart, Jennifer. "Burning Manuscripts: The Literary Apologia in Ovid's *Tristia* 2 and Vladimir Nabokov's 'On a Book Entitled *Lolita*.'" *Classical and Modern Literature* 26.2 (2006): 79–109.

Iser, Wolfgang. *The Implied Reader: Patterns of Communication in Prose Fiction from Bunyan to Beckett*. Baltimore: Johns Hopkins University Press, 1974.

Jaffe, Aaron. *Modernism and the Culture of Celebrity*. Cambridge: Cambridge University Press, 2005.

Jameson, Fredric. *The Political Unconscious: Narrative as a Socially Symbolic Act*. Ithaca: Cornell University Press, 1981.

Johnston, Georgia. "Narratologies of Pleasure: Gertrude Stein's *The Autobiography of Alice B. Toklas*." *Modern Fiction Studies* 42.3 (1996): 590–606. Project Muse. 17 June

2003. <http://muse.jhu.edu/journals/modern_fiction_studies/v042/42.3/ johnston.html>.

Joyce, James. Ulysses: *The Corrected Text*. Ed. Hans Walter Gabler with Wolfhard Steppe and Claud Melchior. New York: Vintage, 1986.

Kakutani, Michiko. "'A Heartbreaking Work...' Clever Young Man Raises Sweet Little Brother." *New York Times* 1 Feb. 2000. Web 1 May 2007. http://partners.nytimes.com/library/books/020100eggers-book-review.html.

Kantor, Jodi. "Not All Irony Is Created Equal." *Slate.com* 22 Feb. 2000. Web. 28 Aug. 2009. http://www.slate.com/id/2000147/entry/1004658.

Kartiganer, Donald. "The Farm and the Journey: Ways of Mourning and Meaning in *As I Lay Dying*." *Mississippi Quarterly* 43.3 (1990): 281–303.

———. "Faulkner's Art of Repetition." In *Faulkner and the Craft of Fiction: Faulkner and Yoknapatawpha, 1987*. Ed. Doreen Fowler and Ann J. Abadie. Jackson: University Press of Mississippi, 1989.

———. *The Fragile Thread: The Meaning of Form in Faulkner's Novels*. Amherst: University of Massachusetts Press, 1979.

Kauffman, Linda. "Framing *Lolita*: Is There a Woman in the Text?" In *Refiguring the Father: New Feminist Readings of Patriarchy*. Ed. Patricia Yaeger and Beth Kowaleski-Wallace. Carbondale: Southern Illinois University Press, 1989.

Kermode, Frank. "The Reader's Share." *Times Literary Supplement* 11 July 1975: 751.

———. *The Sense of an Ending: Studies in the Theory of Fiction*. 1967. New ed. New York: Oxford University Press, 2000.

Kloss, Robert J. "Addie Bundren's Eyes and the Difference They Make." *South Carolina Review* 14 (1981): 85–95.

Koestenbaum, Wayne. "Stein Is Nice." *Parnassus: Poetry in Review* 20.1–2 (1995): 297–319.

Lénárt-Cheng, Helga. "Autobiography as Advertisement: Why Do Gertrude Stein's Sentences Get Under Our Skin?" *New Literary History* 34 (2003): 117–31.

Levine, Lawrence W. *Highbrow/Lowbrow: The Emergence of Cultural Hierarchy in America*. Cambridge, MA: Harvard University Press, 1988.

Lilly, Paul R., Jr. "Caddy and Addie: Speakers of Faulkner's Impeccable Language." *Journal of Narrative Technique* 3.3 (1973): 170–82.

Linzie, Anna. "'Between Two Covers with Somebody Else': Authority, Authorship, and *The Autobiography of Alice B. Toklas*." In *Authority Matters: Rethinking the Theory and Practice of Authorship*. Ed. Stephen Donovan, Danuta Fjellestad, and Rolf Lundén. Amsterdam: Rodopi, 2008. 141–62.

Luce, Dianne C. *Annotations to William Faulkner's As I Lay Dying*. New York: Garland, 1990.

Maar, Michael. *The Two Lolitas*. Trans. Perry Anderson. New York: Verso, 2005.

MacArthur, Elizabeth Jane. *Extravagant Narratives: Closure and Dynamics in the Epistolary Form*. Princeton: Princeton University Press, 1990.

Maddox, Lucy B. *Nabokov's Novels in English*. Athens: University of Georgia Press, 1983.

———. "Necrophilia in *Lolita*." *Centennial Review* 26.4 (1982): 361–74.

Marcus, Sharon. *Between Women: Friendship, Desire, and Marriage in Victorian England*. Princeton: Princeton University Press, 2007

Matthews, John T. "*As I Lay Dying* in the Machine Age." *boundary 2* 19.1 (1992): 69–94.

———. *The Play of Faulkner's Language*. Ithaca: Cornell University Press, 1982.

McCarthy, Penny. "*Lolita*: Wellsprings and Influences." *The Nabokovian* 56 (2006): 38–48.

McClure, John A. "Postmodern/Post-Secular: Contemporary Fiction and Spirituality." *Modern Fiction Studies* 41.1 (1995): 141–63.

McGurl, Mark. *The Novel Art: Elevations of American Fiction after Henry James*. Princeton: Princeton University Press, 2001.

McHale, Brian. *Postmodernist Fiction*. New York: Methuen, 1987.

McHaney, Thomas L., introd. and arr. *William Faulkner Manuscripts 7*: As I Lay Dying. New York: Garland, 1987.

McNeely, Trevor. "'Lo' and Behold: Solving the *Lolita* Riddle." *Studies in the Novel* 21.2 (1989): 182–99.

Meyer, Steven J. "Gertrude Stein Shipwrecked in Bohemia: Making Ends Meet in the *Autobiography* and After." *Southwest Review* 77.1 (1992): 12–33.

———. *Irresistible Dictation: Gertrude Stein and the Correlations of Writing and Science*. Stanford: Stanford University Press, 2001.

Miller, D. A. *Narrative and Its Discontents: Problems of Closure in the Traditional Novel*. Princeton: Princeton University Press, 1981.

Monaghan, David M. "The Single Narrator of *As I Lay Dying*." *Modern Fiction Studies* 18.2 (1972): 213–20.

Moran, Joe. *Star Authors: Literary Celebrity in America*. London: Pluto Press, 2000.

Mortimer, Armine Kotin. *La clôture narrative*. Paris: José Corti, 1985.

Mosle, Sara. "My Brother's Keeper." *New York Times*. 20 Feb. 2000. Web 1 May 2007. http://www.nytimes.com/books/00/02/20/reviews/000220.20moslet.html.

Nabokov, Vladimir. *The Annotated* Lolita. Ed. Alfred Appel, Jr. Rev. ed. New York: Vintage, 1991.

———. *The Enchanter*. New York: Putnam's, 1986.

———. *King, Queen, Knave*. 1928, 1968. New York: Vintage-Random, 1989.

———. *The Real Life of Sebastian Knight*. New York: New Directions, 1959.

———. *Selected Letters*. Ed. Dmitri Nabokov and Matthew J. Bruccoli. San Diego: Harcourt, 1989.

———. *Speak, Memory: An Autobiography Revisited*. Putnam's, 1966.

———. *Strong Opinions.* New York: McGraw-Hill, 1973.
Neupert, Richard. *The End: Narration and Closure in the Cinema.* Detroit: Wayne State University Press, 1995.
North, Michael. "Authorship and Autography." *PMLA* 116.5 (2001): 1377–85.
O'Donnell, Heather. "Gertrude Stein: The Movie." 2004. Typescript.
Orr, Stanley. "Postmodernism, *Noir,* and *The Usual Suspects.*" *Literature/Film Quarterly* 27.1 (1999): 65–73.
The Oxford English Dictionary. 2nd ed. 1989.
Park, Clara Claiborne. "Author! Author! Reconstructing Roland Barthes." *Hudson Review* 43.3 (1990): 377–98.
Parker, Deborah, and Mark Parker. "Directors and DVD Commentary: The Specifics of Intention." *Journal of Aesthetics and Art Criticism* 62.1 (2004): 13–22.
Pater, Walter. *The Renaissance: Studies in Art and Poetry.* 1873. Ed. Adam Phillips. Oxford: Oxford University Press, 1986.
Peterson, Dale E. "Nabokov and the Poe-etics of Composition." *Slavic and East European Journal* 33.1 (1989): 95–107.
Phillips, Elizabeth. "The Hocus-Pocus of *Lolita.*" *Literature and Psychology* 10.3 (1960): 97–101.
Poe, Edgar Allan. "The Murders in the Rue Morgue." In *The Complete Tales and Poems of Edgar Allan Poe.* New York: Vintage, 1978.
Proffer, Carl R. *Keys to* Lolita. Bloomington: Indiana University Press, 1968.
Psycho. Dir. Alfred Hitchcock. Paramount, 1960.
Radway, Janice A. *A Feeling for Books: The Book-of-the-Month Club, Literary Taste, and Middle-Class Desire.* Chapel Hill: University of North Carolina Press, 1997.
Rainey, Lawrence S. *Institutions of Modernism: Literary Elites and Public Culture.* New Haven: Yale University Press, 1998.
Reid, B[enjamin] L[awrence]. *Art by Subtraction: A Dissenting Opinion of Gertrude Stein.* Norman: University of Oklahoma Press, 1958.
Rocky. Dir. John G. Avildsen. United Artists, 1976.
Rorty, Richard. *Contingency, Irony, Solidarity.* New York: Cambridge University Press, 1989.
Rosenheim, Shawn. *The Cryptographic Imagination: Secret Writing from Edgar Poe to the Internet.* Baltimore: Johns Hopkins University Press, 1997.
Ross, Stephen M. "'Voice' in Narrative Texts: The Example of *As I Lay Dying.*" *PMLA* 94.2 (1979): 300–310.
Rowe, Joyce A. *Equivocal Endings in Classic American Novels.* Cambridge: Cambridge University Press, 1988.
Rowe, William Woodin. *Nabokov and Others: Patterns in Russian Literature.* Ann Arbor: Ardis, 1979.

———. *Nabokov's Deceptive World*. New York: NYU Press, 1971.
Rubin, Joan Shelley. *The Making of Middlebrow Culture*. Chapel Hill: University of North Carolina Press, 1992.
Ruddick, Lisa. *Reading Gertrude Stein: Body, Text, Gnosis*. Ithaca: Cornell University Press, 1990.
Sass, Karen R. "At a Loss for Words: Addie and Language in *As I Lay Dying*." *Faulkner Journal* 6.2 (1991): 9–23.
Savage, Dan. "Brotherly Love." *Salon.com*. 14 Mar. 2000. Web. 1 May 2007. http://www.salon.com/books/feature/2000/03/14/eggers.
Schiff, Stacy. *Véra (Mrs. Vladimir Nabokov)*. New York: Random House, 1999.
Scobie, Stephen. "'I' Is Another: Autobiography and the Appropriation of Voice." In *American Modernism Across the Arts*. Ed. Jay Bochner and Justin D. Edwards. New York: Lang, 1999. 124–36.
Sedgwick, Eve Kosofsky. *Between Men: English Literature and Male Homosocial Desire*. New York: Columbia University Press, 1985.
———. *Touching Feeling: Affect, Pedagogy, Performativity*. Durham: Duke University Press, 2003.
Shakespeare, William. *The Norton Shakespeare*. Ed. Stephen Greenblatt et al. New York: Norton, 1997.
Shelton, Jen. "'The Word Is 'Incest': Sexual and Linguistic Coercion in *Lolita*." *Textual Practice* 13.2 (1999): 273–94.
Showalter, Elaine. *Sexual Anarchy: Gender and Culture at the Fin de Siècle*. New York: Viking, 1990.
Smith, Barbara Herrenstein. *Poetic Closure: A Study of How Poems End*. Chicago: University of Chicago Press, 1968.
Smith, Sidonie. "'Stein' Is an 'Alice' Is a 'Gertrude Stein.'" In *Subjectivity, Identity, and the Body: Women's Autobiographical Practices in the Twentieth Century*. Ed. Sidonie Smith. Bloomington: Indiana University Press, 1993.
Spacey, Kevin, perf. *American Beauty*. Dir. Sam Mendes. 1999. DVD. "The Awards Edition." Dreamworks, 2000.
———. *Consenting Adults*. Dir. Alan J. Pakula. Buena Vista, 1992.
———. *Iron Will*. Dir. Charles Haid. Disney, 1994.
———. *K-PAX*. Dir. Iain Softley. Universal, 2001.
———. *L.A. Confidential*. Dir. Curtis Hanson. Warner Bros., 1997.
———. *The Ref*. Dir. Ted Demme. Buena Vista, 1994.
———. *See No Evil, Hear No Evil*. Dir. Arthur Hiller. TriStar, 1989.
———. *Seven*. Dir. David Fincher. 1995. DVD. "Platinum Series." New Line, 2000.
———. *A Show of Force*. Dir. Bruno Barreto. Paramount, 1990.
———. *Swimming with Sharks*. Dir. George Huang. Trimark, 1995.
———. *The Usual Suspects*. Dir. Bryan Singer. 1995. DVD. MGM, 1999.

Stein, Gertrude. *The Autobiography of Alice B. Toklas*. 1933. New York: Vintage-Random, 1990.
———. *Everybody's Autobiography*. 1937. New York: Vintage, 1973.
———. *Geography and Plays*. 1922. New York: Haskell House, 1967.
Steiner, Wendy. *Exact Resemblance to Exact Resemblance: The Literary Portraiture of Gertrude Stein*. New Haven: Yale University Press, 1978.
Stewart, Garrett. *Dear Reader: The Conscripted Audience in Nineteenth-Century British Fiction*. Baltimore: Johns Hopkins University Press, 1996.
Stimpson, Catherine R. "Gertrude Stein and the Lesbian Lie." In *American Women's Autobiography: Fea(s)ts of Memory*. Ed. Margo Culley. Madison: University of Wisconsin Press, 1992.
Sturrock, John. *The Language of Autobiography: Studies in the First Person Singular*. Cambridge: Cambridge University Press, 1993.
Sundquist, Eric J. *Faulkner: The House Divided*. Baltimore: Johns Hopkins University Press, 1983.
Sutherland, Donald. *Gertrude Stein: A Biography of Her Work*. New Haven: Yale University Press, 1951.
Sweeney, S. E. "Purloined Letters: Poe, Doyle, and Nabokov." *Russian Literature Triquarterly* 24 (1991): 213–37.
Taylor, Jim. "Will DVD Replace Laserdisc?" and "How Does DVD Compare to Laserdisc?" *DVD Demystified*. 2007. Web. 1 Aug. 2007. http://www.dvddemystified.com/dvdfaq.html#2.6.
Thickstun, William R. *Visionary Closure in the Modern Novel*. New York: St. Martin's, 1988.
Tischler, Alyson. "A Rose Is a Pose: Steinian Modernism and Mass Culture." *Journal of Modern Literature* 26.3–4 (2003): 12–27.
Tompkins, Jane P. *Reader-Response Criticism: From Formalism to Post-Structuralism*. Baltimore: Johns Hopkins University Press, 1980.
Torgovnick, Marianna. *Closure in the Novel*. Princeton: Princeton University Press, 1981.
Trilling, Lionel. "The Last Lover: Vladimir Nabokov's *Lolita*." *Encounter* 11.4 (1958): 9–19.
Turner, Catherine. *Marketing Modernism Between the Two World Wars*. Amherst: University of Massachusetts Press, 2003.
VanderWilt, Jeffrey Thomas. *A Church Without Borders: The Eucharist and the Church in Ecumenical Perspective*. Collegeville, MN: Liturgical Press, 1998.
Vickery, Olga W. *The Novels of William Faulkner*. Louisiana State University Press, 1964.
Wagner-Martin, Linda. *"Favored Strangers": Gertrude Stein and Her Family*. New Brunswick: Rutgers University Press, 1995.

Wicke. *Advertising Fictions: Literature, Advertisement, and Social Reading.* New York: Columbia University Press, 1988.

Wimsatt, W. K., Jr., and M. C. Beardsley. "The Intentional Fallacy." *Sewanee Review* 54 (1946): 468–88.

Winnicott, D. W. *Playing and Reality.* 1971. New York: Routledge, 1989.

Zamora, Lois Parkinson. "Magical Romance/Magical Realism: Ghosts in U.S. and Latin American Fiction." In *Magical Realism: Theory, History, Community.* Ed. Lois Parkinson Zamora and Wendy B. Faris. Durham: Duke University Press, 1995.

Zimmer, Dieter, ed. *Vladimir Nabokov: Gesammelte Werke.* 23 vols. Reinbek bei Hamburg: Rowohlt, 1989 .

INDEX

Absalom, Absalom! (Faulkner), 48, 173, 182n25
Adam and Eve story, 91–92
Adams, Timothy Dow, 67
advertisements, 20, 22, 178n9
aesthetics, 10, 49–50, 59, 97, 98, 187nn28–29; anti-representational, 8; avant-garde, 5, 27, 110, 159; and education, 27, 63–64, 71–73; and elitism, 2, 23, 68; and mimesis, 31, 113, 123, 170. *See also* linguistic play
AHWOSG. See Heartbreaking Work of Staggering Genius
allegory, 14, 60
Alter, Robert, 177n1
Amélie (film), 138
anagrams, 80, 155, 180n10, 188n34. *See also* linguistic play
Anchor Review (journal), 78
Andrews, David, 185n9, 188n30
"Annabel Lee" (Poe), 84, 85, 104
Appel, Alfred, Jr., 84–85, 103, 186n18, 188n32
Aquinas, Thomas, 139
Aristotle, 131
As I Lay Dying (Faulkner), 4–5, 26, 28, 31–52, 79, 132, 161, 163, 165
author(s), 18–19; as character, 26–27, 90–91, 97–98, 103–6, 136–37, 163; "dearth" of, 5, 6; death of, 5, 7, 29, 110–11, 127–28, 135, 163–65, 173–74; "figure" of, 173; imprimatur of, 21; self-effacement of, 5, 25–26, 54, 135–37, 149; stand-ins for, 29; "watermark" of, 103, 188n35. *See also* self-depiction

authorial absence/presence, 6; in Eggers, 117; in Faulkner, 4–5, 26, 34, 51–52; in Nabokov, 76, 107; in *Seven* and *Usual Suspects*, 136–37; in Stein, 4–5, 54, 70, 74
The Autobiography of Alice B. Toklas (Stein), 4–5, 26–27, 53–75, 156, 182n1

Bader, Julia, 188n29
Baldwin, Stephen, 155
Barthes, Roland, 3–12, 28, 138, 173; on authority, 156–57; and deconstruction, 6; and Eggers, 110–11, 127–28, 131, 132; on fetishization, 10–11; and Foucault, 6–8; on reading, 8–11, 149–50, 159, 170; and "reality effect," 153; and *Seven*, 135–38, 149–50; and *Usual Suspects*, 137, 150, 156–57. Works: "Death of the Author," 5–11, 29, 110–11, 135–38, 168, 177n5; *Pleasure of the Text*, 9–11; *Sade, Fourier, Loyola*, 12; *S/Z*, 177n3
Bataille, Georges, 8
Baudelaire, Charles, 11, 138
Beardsley, Monroe, 3
beginnings. *See* openings
Begley, Adam, 113
Benjamin, Walter, 174
Benson, A. C., 187n28
Bishop, John, 185n14
Bleikasten, André, 46, 178n5, 180n15
Bloom, Lynn Z., 183n14
Bonaparte, Marie, 84
Booth, Wayne, 18
Bourdieu, Pierre, 23
Boyd, Brian, 105, 106, 186n38
Braque, Georges, 64

Brecht, Bertolt, 137
Breslin, James E., 55, 57, 61, 62
Brontë, Emily, 178n1
Brooks, Peter, 170, 172–74, 191n4
Burke, Carolyn, 65
Burke, Seán, 8, 177n3
Burroughs, William S., 177n2
Byrne, Gabriel, 151

Cage, John, 177n2
Canby, Henry, 24–25
Capote, Truman, 139
Catholicism. *See* Eucharist
celebrity, 20–22; of Eggers, 28, 109–10, 126, 131–32, 162, 189n5; of Stein, 54, 55, 57, 66, 68–69, 162
Cervantes, Miguel de, 177n1
Cézanne, Paul, 64
Chaucer, Geoffrey, 139
Christie, Agatha, 153
Clarke, Deborah, 165
class, 2, 77, 178n10; and mass appeal, 20–25, 110, 117, 122–23, 162; and race, 49, 135, 138, 190n7
Clover, Carol, 145
commodification, 21, 28, 48–49, 57, 117, 162
Communion. *See* Eucharist
conclusions. *See* endings
Cone, Etta, 65
Conrad, Joseph, 191n1
cross-referentiality, in Faulkner, 33, 35
culture wars, 135, 138. *See also* gender roles

Dangerous Minds (film), 125
Dante Alighieri, 17, 139
"Death of the Author" (Barthes), 5–11, 29, 110–11, 135–38, 168, 177n5
deconstruction, 3, 6, 27, 33, 48, 143
Defoe, Daniel, 53, 58
de la Durantaye, Leland, 105, 106, 184n2
DeLillo, Don, 111
Derain, André, 64
Dettmar, Kevin J. H., 177n4
DiBattista, Maria, 12, 178n7
Diderot, Denis, 177n1
doppelgangers, 81, 84. *See also* repetition
Dostoevsky, Fyodor, 84

Duchamp, Marcel, 177n2
Dupee, F. W., 78
DVD technology, 136, 149, 158–59, 161, 191n12
Dydo, Ulla, 56, 58–59, 61, 70

Eggers, Dave, 109–33, 164–65; and Barthes, 110–11, 127–28, 131, 132; and celebrity, 28, 109–10, 126, 162, 189n5; and Faulkner, 28, 119, 132, 161; *A Heartbreaking Work of Staggering Genius*, 5, 25, 28, 29, 109–33, 168–71; and Magritte, 115–16; and Nabokov, 114–16, 163, 189n4; and Stein, 162
Eliot, T. S., 21, 140, 141; and Nabokov, 88–89, 186n18
endings: of *AHWOSG*, 113, 125–29, 131, 132, 169–70, 189n4; of *Autobiography of Alice B. Toklas*, 4–5, 26–27, 53–56, 58, 60–61, 70, 74, 156; of *As I Lay Dying*, 4–5, 31, 32, 50–52; of *Lolita*, 189n4; of *Pale Fire*, 114; of *Seven*, 146–49, 191n9; of *Ulysses*, 132; of *Usual Suspects*, 155–58. *See also* openings
Eschwege-Lichberg, Heinz von, 184n6, 186n17
Eucharist, 2, 28, 111, 128–31, 189nn7–9

faith, 111, 112, 120, 131–33
Faulkner, William, 31–52, 77; as absent author, 4–5, 26, 34, 51–52; cross-referentiality in, 33, 35; and Eggers, 28, 119, 132, 161; and Joyce, 23; monologues of, 26; and Nabokov, 79; phonograph in, 44, 50, 181n18, 181n21; and Stein, 25–26, 53, 56, 74; use of repetition by, 32, 37–40; women in, 165. Works: *Absalom, Absalom!*, 48, 173, 182n25; *As I Lay Dying*, 4–5, 26, 28, 31–52, 79, 132, 161, 163, 165; *Go Down, Moses*, 182n25; *Light in August*, 48; *Sanctuary*, 181n19; *Sound and the Fury*, 16, 18, 23–24, 178n1, 182n25
Feldman, Morton, 177n2
feminism, 23, 191n7. *See also* gender roles
fetish, text as, 10–11
Field, Andrew, 82, 184n5
Fielding, Henry, 177n1
Fincher, David, 5, 134, 189n1. *See also Seven*

Finnegans Wake (Joyce), 18
Fish, Stanley, 19–20
Flaubert, Gustave, 173
Formalism, Russian, 8
Foucault, Michel, 3, 6–8
Frazer, James George, 140
Freeman, Morgan, 134
Freud, Sigmund, 84, 85
Friday the 13th (film), 145
Friedman, Susan Stanford, 164

gender roles, 23, 164–66; in *AHWOSG*, 168–71; in *Autobiography of Alice B. Toklas*, 165, 166; in *Lolita*, 166; in *Seven*, 163–64, 167–68, 171; in *Usual Suspects*, 164, 167, 168, 190n7. *See also* marriage
Gentlemen Prefer Blondes (Loos), 24
Geography and Plays (Stein), 64–67, 69
Gilmore, Leigh, 57
Glass, Loren, 22–23
Gormley, Paul, 190n7
Gris, Juan, 73
Grosser, Maurice, 55, 182n4
Gumbrecht, Hans Ulrich, 129–31

Haggard, H. Rider, 191n1
Hale, Dorothy J., 46
Hantke, Steffen, 190n5
Hayes, Elizabeth, 180n13
A Heartbreaking Work of Staggering Genius (Eggers), 5, 25, 28, 29, 109–33, 168–71
Hedaya, Dan, 151
Hemingway, Ernest, 147
hermeneutics, 4, 129–31
Hirschorn, Michael, 113
Hitchcock, Alfred, 136–37, 191n9
Huelsenbeck, Richard, 177n2
Hungerford, Amy, 111
Hustis, Harriet, 179n6
Huyssen, Andreas, 23

identification: in Eggers, 116, 169; in Faulkner, 26, 34–35, 47, 51, 163; in Nabokov, 27, 78, 79; reader, 2–3, 18, 24, 174; in *Seven*, 147–49; in Stein, 27, 64, 74; in *Usual Suspects*, 156, 159
Ingleheart, Jennifer, 184n3, 185n13

intentional fallacy, 3
Internet, films and, 158–59, 161
intimacy: with Eggers, 116–17, 127; with Faulkner, 51; with Stein, 27, 58, 65, 68, 69, 74
Iser, Wolfgang, 15–17

Jacob, Max, 73
Jaffe, Aaron, 20–22
James, Henry, 59, 63
Jameson, Fredric, 13–14
Jeon, Joseph, 178n4
Jeunet, Jean-Pierre, 138
Johnston, Georgia, 69–71
Jonson, Ben, 16
Joyce, James, 18, 23–25, 110; *Ulysses*, 16, 21, 132, 140, 141, 172, 178n9

Kakutani, Michiko, 113
Kantor, Jodi, 113
Kartiganer, Donald, 40–41, 181n21
Kauffman, Linda, 90
Kermode, Frank, 18, 170, 172, 174, 191n4
Kipling, Rudyard, 191n1
Kloss, Robert J., 180n13
Knoepflmacher, Ulrich, 191n2
Koestenbaum, Wayne, 61–62
Kopelson, Arnold, 147

language: Barthes' view of, 5–6, 8; private versus public, 46–47; and "verbal reality," 55
Laughlin, James, 187n27
Levertov, Denise, 164
Lichberg, Heinz von. *See* Eschwege-Lichberg, Heinz von
linguistic play, 2, 18–19; anagrams, 80, 155, 180n10, 188n34; in Barthes, 6, 9–10; in Faulkner, 26, 31–33, 35, 49–50; in Joyce, 18, 172; in Nabokov, 90–91, 103, 105, 184n7; neologisms, 42; palindromes, 64–68; in *Seven*, 149; in *Usual Suspects*, 152–53, 191n11. *See also* puns
Linzie, Anna, 183n14
Lolita (Nabokov), 5, 76–108, 114, 162–64, 166, 189n4
Loos, Anita, 24

Maar, Michael, 184n6, 186n17
Macbeth (Shakespeare), 139, 171, 172
Maddox, Lucy, 187n29
magical realism, 111–12, 188n1
Magritte, René, 115–16
The Making of Americans (Stein), 61, 68, 73
Mallarmé, Stéphane, 7, 8, 9
Mandelstam, Nadezhda, 90
Marcus, Sharon, 13–15
marriage, 170; in Faulkner, 51; in Stein, 58, 65, 74. *See also* gender roles
masks. *See* self-depiction
mass appeal, 20–23, 110, 117, 122–23, 162. *See also* class
Matisse, Henri, 63, 64, 68, 72
Matthews, John T., 47–50, 179n7, 181nn24–25
McBride, Henry, 66
McCarthy, Penny, 185n13
McClure, John A., 111–12
McGurl, Mark, 22–24
McHale, Brian, 114, 117–18
McNeely, Trevor, 187n29
McQuarrie, Christopher, 152, 154, 156. *See also Usual Suspects*
metafiction, 48, 117–18; Eggers' use of, 110, 114; Nabokov's use of, 114, 188n31
Meyer, Steven J., 60
Miller, D. A., 191n4
Milton, John, 91, 139
mimesis, 2–3, 9, 25; and aesthetic play, 31, 113, 123, 170; extralinguistic elements of, 33; in Faulkner, 35, 52; in Stein, 65
modernism, 15–24, 170, 172–73; Booth on, 18; of Faulkner, 49–50; and impersonality, 13; Iser on, 15–17; Jaffe on, 20–22; and mimesis, 2–3, 25, 35; and Nabokov, 107, 114; versus postmodernism, 23; in *Seven*, 140–42, 150; of Stein, 63; Stewart on, 17–18, 20; Tompkins on, 16, 17
Moran, Joe, 22
Morrison, Toni, 111–12
Morris, Robert, 177n2
Mosle, Sara, 113

"The Murders in the Rue Morgue" (Poe), 84–92, 96, 107–8, 186n16, 187n28

Nabokov, Véra, 82, 90
Nabokov, Vladimir, 76–108, 157; as author-character, 90–91; and Eggers, 114–16, 163, 189n4; and Freud, 84, 85; memory of, 184n5; metafiction of, 114, 188n31; and middlebrow culture, 25; and Poe, 84–92, 96, 107–8, 185n12, 185n13; and Stein, 56, 79. Works: *The Enchanter*, 83–84; *The Gift*, 83; *King, Queen, Knave*, 186n21; *Lolita*, 5, 76–108, 114, 162–64, 166, 189n4; "On a Book Entitled *Lolita*", 27, 78, 82, 90–91, 104, 107, 162; *Pale Fire*, 98, 105, 114–16, 186n38, 189n4; *Pnin*, 98; *The Real Life of Sebastian Knight*, 184n7; *Speak, Memory*, 98, 188n35; *Strong Opinions*, 91, 116
New Criticism, 8, 13
Nightmare on Elm Street (film), 145
North, Michael, 177n2

O'Donnell, Heather, 183n13
Odyssey (Homer), 140
ontological playfulness, 28; in Eggers, 111–12, 114, 116, 129; in Nabokov, 92, 105–7; in *Seven*, 135; in *Usual Suspects*, 157
openings: of *AHWOSG*, 116–17, 130; of *As I Lay Dying*, 38; of *The Autobiography of Alice B. Toklas*, 59, 72–73; of *Everybody's Autobiography*, 67; of *The Real Life of Sebastian Knight*, 184n7; of *Seven*, 134, 136, 140, 148; of *Usual Suspects*, 154–55. *See also* endings
Orr, Stanley, 153, 155, 190n7
Ovid, 184n3

Pale Fire (Nabokov), 98, 105, 114–16, 186n38, 189n4
palindromes, 64–68. *See also* linguistic play
Palminteri, Chazz, 151
Paltrow, Gwyneth, 144
Park, Clara Claiborne, 177n2, 190n6
Pater, Walter, 98, 187n28

Perkins, Anthony, 191n9
personae. *See* self-depiction
Peterson, Dale E., 185n12
Phillips, Adam, 187n28
Phillips, Elizabeth, 84, 85
Picasso, Pablo, 64, 68, 73
Pitt, Brad, 134–35
The Pleasure of the Text (Barthes), 9–11
Poe, Edgar Allan, 84–92, 96, 107–8, 185nn12–13, 186n16, 187n28
pornography, 77–78
postmodernism, 15, 136–37; and Eggers, 28, 111–13, 133, 163; and mimesis, 2–3, 35; versus modernism, 23; post-, 2, 30; self-depiction in, 3–4
poststructuralism, 4, 8, 136–37, 156, 163
Proffer, Carl, 82–83, 90, 187n27
Proust, Marcel, 9
Psycho (film), 191n9
psychoanalysis, 84, 85
puns, 18; in Faulkner, 33; in Nabokov, 103; in *Seven*, 142, 149; in Stein, 56, 62, 67, 74. *See also* linguistic play
Pynchon, Thomas, 111–12

race, 49, 135, 138, 190n7. *See also* class
Radway, Janice, 22–25
Rainey, Lawrence, 20–22
Rauschenberg, Robert, 177n2
reader-response theory, 11, 15–19
reading, 2–4, 17–25, 158; and authorship, 7, 9, 137; Barthes on, 8–11, 149–50, 159, 170; Eggers on, 28, 29, 117, 127, 128; Faulkner on, 34–35; Fish on, 19–20; Iser on, 15–17; Marcus on, 13–15; Rainey on, 21–22; Sedgwick on, 13, 14; Tompkins on, 16–17
Real World (TV series), 113, 122–23, 131, 132
Reed, Ishmael, 111–12
reflexivity: in Eggers, 110, 112–13, 122, 130; in Faulkner, 48–52; in Nabokov, 77, 81, 96–97; in *Seven*, 140, 145–49; in Stein, 55, 70–73; in *Usual Suspects*, 155–59
repetition: Eggers' use of, 125, 127; Faulkner's use of, 32, 37–40; Nabokov's use of, 79, 81, 84, 87, 91–96; *Seven*'s use

of, 149; Stein's use of, 55, 59, 64–68; *Usual Suspects*' use of, 155, 157–58
Robbe-Grillet, Alain, 8, 177n2
Rocky (film), 157
Rorty, Richard, 97, 188n30
Rosenheim, Shawn, 185n15
Rousseau, Henri, 72, 73, 185n13
Rowe, William Woodin, 188n30
Russian Formalism, 8

Sade, Marquis de, 139
Savage, Dan, 113, 131
Schiff, Stacy, 82, 90
Scobie, Stephen, 165
Sedgwick, Ellery, 168, 182n1
Sedgwick, Eve Kosofsky, 13, 14, 168
self-depiction, 3–5, 12–13, 27, 82, 136, 163; by Eggers, 29, 116–17, 122, 163; by Nabokov, 82–83, 106, 184n3; by Stein, 53–55, 62–63, 66; by Woolf, 12. *See also* author, as character
Seven (film), 5, 25, 28–29, 110, 134–51, 158, 162; depictions of women in, 163–64, 167–68, 171
Shakespeare, William, 80, 99, 139, 171, 172, 189n4
Shelton, Jen, 90
Showalter, Elaine, 191n1
Sidney, Philip, 164
Silence of the Lambs (film), 145
Silko, Leslie Marmon, 111–12
Singer, Bryan, 5, 153, 155–56. *See also The Usual Suspects*
Smith, Sidonie, 57–58
Sollers, Philippe, 8
The Sound and the Fury (Faulkner), 16, 18, 23–24, 178n1, 182n25
Spacey, Kevin, 5, 25, 134–59, 162, 189n1, 190n5
Stein, Gertrude, 77, 161–63, 172; as absent author, 4–5, 70, 74; celebrity of, 54, 55, 57, 66, 68–69, 162; and Eggers, 162; and Faulkner, 25–26, 53, 56, 74; and gender roles, 164–66, 171; and intimacy, 27, 58, 65, 68, 69, 74; and middlebrow culture, 25; and Nabokov, 56, 79; notebooks of, 59, 69–71; parodies of, 26, 66; use of

Stein, Gertrude (*continued*)
repetition by, 55t, 59, 64–68. Works: *Autobiography of Alice B. Toklas*, 4–5, 25–27, 53–75, 79, 156, 172, 182n1; *Everybody's Autobiography*, 67; *Geographical History of America*, 67; *Geography and Plays*, 64–67, 69; *Making of Americans*, 61, 68, 73; "Stanzas in Meditation," 56; *Three Lives*, 61, 62
Stein, Leo, 63, 67
Stendhal, 192n4
Sterne, Laurence, 177n1
Stevenson, Robert Louis, 84
Stevens, Wallace, 172
Stewart, Garrett, 17–18, 20, 129
Sturrock, John, 182n5
Sundquist, Eric, 34, 51, 179n8, 180n9

Tautou, Audrey, 138
Taylor, Jim, 191n12
Tchaikovsky, Pyotr Ilich, 11, 138
Three Lives (Stein), 61, 62
Toklas, Alice, 26–27, 56–59, 63–64, 67–75, 162; appreciation of art by, 27, 63–64, 71–73; and gender roles, 164–66, 171; as Stein's editor, 70–71, 74, 165, 183n14
Tompkins, Jane P., 16–17
transitional objects, 40–41, 51–52, 132
Turner, Catherine, 20–22

Ulysses (Joyce), 16, 21, 132, 140, 141, 172, 178n9
universalization, 49, 181n24
The Usual Suspects (film), 5, 28–30, 110, 150–59; and Barthes, 137; depiction of women in, 164, 167, 168, 190n7; and middlebrow culture, 25, 162; and Stein, 156

VanderWilt, Jeffrey Thomas, 189nn8–9
Van Gogh, Vincent, 11, 138
"verbal reality," 55
Vickery, Olga, 179n8, 180n15

Wagner-Martin, Linda, 182n4
Walker, Andrew Kevin, 136, 145, 149. *See also Seven*
Wells, H. G., 185n13
"What Is an Author?" (Foucault), 6–7
Whitehead, Alfred North, 68
Wicke, Jennifer, 178n9
Wimsatt, W. K., 3
Winnicott, D. W., 40–41, 52
women. *See* gender roles
Woolf, Virginia, 12
Wuthering Heights (Brontë), 178n1

Zamora, Lois Parkinson, 188n1
Zimmer, Dieter, 82

The authorized representative in the EU for product safety and compliance is:
Mare Nostrum Group
B.V Doelen 72
4831 GR Breda
The Netherlands

www.ingramcontent.com/pod-product-compliance
Lightning Source LLC
Chambersburg PA
CBHW020756160426
43192CB00006B/345